Basic
baking

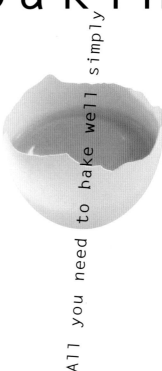

All you need to bake well simply

Sebastian Dickhaut Jennifer Newens Cornelia Schinharl

Basic baking
Contents

Think
Basic
That's all you need to know

Jodie thinks a really good chocolate cake is to die for—or at least worth ruining her diet for when she wants to feel like she's in love. Alex is rumored to bake like a god, but he's only really perfected blueberry muffins; the rest tastes like @#$%^. Susanna has an oven that's three years older than she is and makes a streusel cake that's three times better than her mother's. No matter what Nancy bakes, it never turns out the way she wants.

Do these people sound familiar? Just like friends of yours? This book is for Jodie so that she can bake herself a chocolate treat anytime the mood strikes. And it's for Alex so that he can expand his baking repertoire, and impress even more of the ladies. For Susanna, we've provided dozens more recipes to test in her work-horse oven. For Nancy, there are some foolproof recipes so that she can finally be satisfied with her creations.

But most of all, this book is for you. Perhaps you're comfy with your cooking, but a little shaky in the baking department. Inside there's a recipe for all baking moods and occasions, from quick-as-a-flash cookies to sit-overnight sourdough bread to easy-but-elegant tortes. And remember, when the frustrations start to come to the surface again, think Basic. That's all you need to know.

Know How

Joe: "Could you please whip us up a marble cake—ASAP?"
Jane: "Sorry, can't do it. But if you can be a little patient…"

Cooking can go fast, but baking can't. On the other hand, baking is simpler than cooking. If you've got butter, sugar, eggs, and flour, you're halfway to having a cake. And if you have nuts, vanilla, and some air, it will be a pretty special cake. Chocolate, whipped cream, and sprinkles? Cool—it's a torte.

"Mix it!
Beat it!
Finish it off!
And then
make it
beautiful."

Sounds dangerous—but baking is not difficult. Still, a baker's knowledge is a bit different than a cook's—e.g., a baker must know how to cream the butter and when to beat the eggs. And a baker's job can be more relaxing than a cook's. Since nothing more can be done once the batter goes in the pan and into the oven, a baker can sit back and relax. And that's neither dangerous nor difficult.

Seven Baking staples

Flour

French: farine; Italian: farina; Spanish: harina

To bake means to have flour on hand. That's because flour gives baked goods their proper consistency. Even at the dough or batter stage, the other baking ingredients cling securely to flour. And later on, in the oven, flour makes sure everything sticks together. Flour is something like the mortar in a brick wall: It doesn't start to work until it's wet. Once it dries out again, everything is in the right position.

Flour works so well because of its clumping action. Or to put it more intelligently, because the starch in flour binds to anything moist, from eggs to cream cheese and everything in between. But even when combined only with water, flour doesn't turn hard as a rock. That's because it contains another special protein—gluten. Gluten allows the flour to swell and turn sticky when it's kneaded, forming a stable network in the dough in which tiny little bubbles can hang. That's when it happens: In the oven, the water in the dough starts to boil, its steam blows up the bubbles, and the flour network simultaneously gets more solid. The end result is a delicious piece of bread or pastry.

Wheat flour contains a large amount of gluten and makes great baked goods. You can find many types of wheat flour on the grocery store shelves, but in Basic baking, when we say "flour," we mean all-purpose flour. If we want you to use another type of flour, we'll say so, such as the semolina flour in the Orange Cake on page 35. Avoid substituting alternative flours that you find in the health food store that are not made of wheat. These flours do not contain enough gluten for our recipes.

A cousin of flour, cornstarch, can be combined with all-purpose flour to make cake textures finer, while on its own it thickens pastry creams to be used for fillings. Bread crumbs or ground nuts can pinch hit for flour in certain types of recipes.

Sugar

French: sucre; Italian: zucchero; Spanish: azucar

Sugar, another cousin of flour, helps to transform bread into cake. It, too, can stand in for flour for some jobs. For example, when eggs are beaten, sugar gives them enough substance to get moving and turn into foam, and enough stability to hold that foam. Unlike flour, nothing binds to sugar. However, sugar is even greedier for moisture than flour. Due to that excessive thirst, moist, sugary batters must go quickly into the oven or they will disintegrate. Granulated sugar is used most often for baking. Powdered sugar—AKA confectioners' sugar—is second runner up, especially in frostings. Coarse sugar is used for garnishing. If you can't find coarse sugar in the baking supply section at the supermarket, grab some sugar cubes instead. Put them in a locking plastic bag, seal the bag, and then beat the cubes with a rolling pin until they are broken up into coarse bits.

Brown sugar is regular sugar mixed with molasses, which gives it, and the recipes it's used for, a deep, caramely flavor and color. Brown sugar comes in light, golden, and dark forms. We like golden for its versatility.

Butter

French: beurre; Italian: burro; Spanish: mantequilla

Butter makes a dough or batter tender. That's because of the compounds that it creates. If butter is stirred for a long time until it becomes creamy, it divides up into many, many little fat bubbles that make a particularly fine flour network in the batter. The result is a tender, moist cake—e.g., the Drunken Apple Cake on page 64. If the butter hits the batter in coarse pieces, the flour keeps to itself. That makes crispy, flaky pasty—e.g., the Double-Crust Apple Pie on page 64. The lovely, rich butter flavor of both the cake and the pastry doesn't develop properly until each is in the oven. That's where the butter melts in the oven's heat and creates the steam necessary to create the desired texture. Baked goods containing butter are still very soft when they come out of the oven and don't solidify completely until they're cooled.

Butter is churned from cream that has been skimmed from fresh milk. Interesting factoid: It takes 6 quarts of milk to make 8 ounces of butter. Shortening can also be used for baking, but most of our recipes use pure butter. Avoid using margarine for baking, as most brands contain large amounts of water that can adversely affect the outcome of the recipe. Besides—we think that if you're going to have dessert, you should go ahead and SPLURGE!

Egg

French: oeuf; Italian: uovo; Spanish: huevo

Perhaps the chicken did come first. But the egg really made it famous! Depending on what you do with the egg, it can make baked goods airy, moist, or crisp. Or all three at once.

Here's how it works: The egg inflates when it is vigorously beaten. With every stroke of the whisk, the protein in the egg forms more small bubbles that take in air until they are full, which makes them grow. The end result is a light-colored foam that expands the flour network in the dough or batter and swells up when baked, causing baked goods to rise. That's how the egg makes baked goods moist and light. At the same time, the fat in the yolk helps bind ingredients together, while the protein in the egg white imparts a crispy texture. Perhaps the most impressive action of the egg is when the white is beaten solo into a thick, firm foam called a meringue. This solid network of protein bubbles makes baked goods airy and crispy, depending on how it is used.

Eggs work best when they are fresh. Check the expiration date printed on the carton and use them before it arrives. In Basic baking, when we say eggs, we mean large eggs. It doesn't matter if they're white or brown, caged or free range—it's your preference. Just make sure they are the correct size. Using medium or extra-large eggs could cause subtle differences in the recipe.

Cream

French: crème; Italian: panna; Spanish: crema

Luxurious baked goods often contain cream, which comes into its own once the oven has cooled. Then the cream is beaten until stiff and spread over baked goods or even injected inside them. Or at the very end, whipped cream is given the place of honor next to the strawberry shortcake. We think that eating whipped cream is really a basic need, rather than a luxury, so that's why we include it among the baking staples.

Whipped cream can give baked goods a special finishing touch. Airy and heavy at the same time, it gives a fruit tart just the right base, and lends a pleasant contrast to a rich chocolate torte. Whipped cream transmits almost every flavor well—thanks to its high percentage of fat and air. Like egg whites, cream, when beaten, transforms to a foamy network of small bubbles, expanding as more air is beaten into them.

The recipes in this book call for "whipping cream," which contains at least 30% butterfat. If you can find it, buy heavy whipping cream, which has a higher butterfat content—up to 40%—and will have a richer, thicker consistency and yummier flavor.

Sour cream and crème fraîche have about the same amount of fat as whipping cream, and have beneficial bacterial cultures, giving them their distinctive tangy flavor. Sour cream or crème fraîche, when included in a pastry cream or in batter or dough, make it particularly moist. The same applies to yogurt, cream cheese, or ricotta cheese, which, in addition to providing moisture, also help baked goods to rise.

Air

French: air; Italian: aria; Spanish: aire

All baked goods need air in some way, shape, or form. To get air into baked goods we employ a leavening agent—something that can hold the air or cause the air to be created during baking. Common leaveners—air creators—are baking powder, baking soda, yeast, and eggs. Butter, even, can be considered a leavener—especially in the case of a flaky pastry.

Light and airy baked goods are particularly dependent on one part of the air—carbon dioxide (you know, the stuff that makes the bubbles in Champagne or mineral water). Carbon dioxide is produced when certain substances are combined, for example, baking powder or baking soda and liquid. At first nothing much happens. But in a hot oven the carbon dioxide bubbles really go crazy, causing the cake to expand.

Yeast also produces carbon dioxide when mixed with liquid, but it requires a source of food—like flour or sugar—to do its trick. Cozy, warm, and well nourished by the flour and sugar, the yeast excretes carbon dioxide gases, causing the dough to rise like crazy. In Basic baking we use rapid-rise yeast, which is a recently developed hybrid of active dry yeast. In the old days, your mom probably made a stinky mixture of yeast, sugar, and water that had to stand for a while before it could be mixed into the dough. Now, with rapid-rise yeast, you can skip this "proofing" step. The yeast can be mixed right into the flour, and then the other ingredients added and kneaded to make the dough. The liquid used is a little warmer than your mom might have used—110° to 120°F to her 105° to 110°F. An instant-read thermometer will help you get it just right.

Salt and spice

French: sel et poivre; Italian: sale e ezpecie; Spanish: sal y especia

Just a small pinch of salt can make even your sweetest baked goods taste better. Salt works by balancing the flavors in a recipe as well as enhancing each individual ingredient's qualities. When baking bread, salt's role is to help tighten the gluten, the protein in wheat, in order to help the dough rise to its maximum capacity.

Spices add interest to many baked goods. Cinnamon is perhaps the most common spice used, but ginger, nutmeg, cloves, and allspice are all close runners up. If you're a perfectionist, you can grind your spices fresh before using them with a mortar and pestle or in an electric coffee mill. For the rest of us: Purchase ground spices in small quantities and use them up fast. If you fear your spices are more than 6 months old, or have been stored improperly (i.e., not in a cool and dark place), better discard them and start again.

Mixing

Mixing is fundamental to making baked goods. Two common types of baked goods in this book—batter cakes and choux paste—illustrate the concept of mixing and its role in baking.

Batter Cakes

Batter cakes have in common the fact that butter plays a strong role in the recipe and that the texture of the batter is thick and foamy. A chemical leavener is seldom used. Instead, batter cakes get their air via mechanical means (i.e., mixing the heck out of the ingredients!!).

Equipment

The equipment for making batter cakes consists of three general items: A mixing implement (or two or three), a bowl, and a pan. For mixing, you'll need an electric mixer and a manual mixer (wooden spoon and/or rubber spatula). You can mix batter cakes by hand all the way, but you'll risk polluting the environment with sweat and curses. As for the bowl, make sure it is stable on the countertop before mixing. You can stabilize a bowl by shaping a dishtowel into a ring, placing it on the counter like a nest, and setting the bowl in the middle. The best batter cake pans have tall sides—we especially like springform pans (see page 32)—so that the batter won't spill over the top while baking. Bundt pans also work well, but make sure there is enough batter in the recipe to adequately fill up the pan.

The Ingredients

Butter, sugar, eggs, and flour are essential ingredients for making batter cakes. If you have time, leave the ingredients at room temperature for two hours before mixing the batter so they can warm up and bind together as well as possible. Put the butter and sugar in a bowl and mix them with an electric mixer until the mixture is light and creamy (1). This method will only work properly when the butter is soft. Then, add the eggs one at a time and keep mixing until there are no more eggs outside the bowl and the bowl is full of a lemon yellow-colored foam.

Now comes the flour. In rich batter cakes (containing about the same quantities of butter, eggs, and flour),

it's time to switch to the wooden spoon—with or without a hole in it (2). The spoon is used to stir in the flour until it disappears. For this type of cake, using the electric mixer the whole time will cause the cake to be tough and dry. In less rich batter cakes (with about half as much butter as flour, and which include baking powder), half of the flour can be stirred in using the mixer, but the second half should be stirred in with the wooden spoon.

Batter cakes can be made lighter when stiffly beaten egg whites are added in at the end. In that case, the best thing to do is to stir a third of the egg whites into the batter to lighten its texture, then carefully fold in the remainder.

Oh—that reminds us: Folding is a special type of mixing. Folding is used to combine a light and airy mixture into a heavier, denser mixture while retaining as much of the air as possible. To fold, pour the light mixture on top of the heavy mixture. Using a large rubber spatula, draw the spatula down through the mixture until it reaches the bottom of the bowl, then run it along the bottom of the bowl, then up the other side. After each motion, turn the bowl 1/4 turn and repeat until the two mixtures are incorporated.

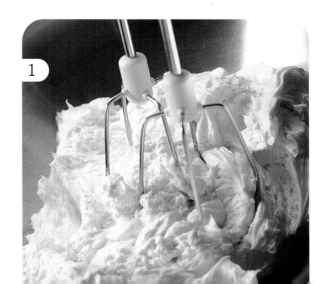

The Oven

Batter cakes need to be baked right after mixing, or the energy of the leavening will dissipate. Butter the pan, pour in the batter, give it a smart slap on the bottom to remove large air bubbles, and pop it into the preheated oven, usually 350° to 400°F. After baking, leave the cake in the pan for another 10 minutes. It will shrink from the sides a little, making it easy to turn out onto the cooling rack. That's where it will cool completely. Batter cakes usually stay fresh for about a week when properly wrapped.

Choux Paste

Choux paste, also called pâte à choux, is easy to make once you understand the rules, and it makes the most elegant of desserts—think cream puffs, éclairs, and profiteroles. This pastry is cooked in a saucepan until it clumps and scorches, after which it's baked on a baking sheet.

The Equipment

Because choux paste is made on the stove, it needs a saucepan. The pan should hold 3 quarts, have a thick bottom (to prevent burning), and have a handle that can be held securely. You won't need fancy power tools for choux paste—it's stirred with a wooden spoon. To shape the pastry, a spoon or a pastry bag is used to form the choux paste mounds on a baking sheet.

The Ingredients

Choux paste can be made using water (easier to stir, browns less when baked) or milk (scorches easily, bakes to a golden brown). The liquid is brought to a boil with butter and taken off the heat so that nothing evaporates—the quantities must be very accurate to make this type of pastry. Then, all of the flour is added at once. It may not seem like a good idea, but trust us—it's the only way to achieve the proper texture. Return the pan to the burner and keep stirring with the spoon until you have a nice smooth lump of dough. Note: A crust may form on the bottom of the pan (3) as you are making it. Remove the pan from the heat.

The eggs are added next. To keep them from curdling, the hot choux paste is first put in a bowl and cooled for 15 minutes. Then, one egg is stirred in until it disappears. This step is repeated until all the eggs are incorporated. Choux paste is just right when it hangs shiny and thick from the spoon and doesn't lose its shape when piped through a pastry bag.

The Oven

Whether it's piped or spooned onto a baking sheet, choux paste must go right onto the middle rack of a preheated oven at a minimum of 400°F—otherwise it turns gray and dries out. Because the flour has already swollen a lot in the heat of the saucepan, it binds the dough securely during baking. The egg and liquid in the dough produce steam, causing the pastry to swell like a balloon. Careful: Don't open the oven during the first two-thirds of the baking time or you'll ruin everything! The finished pastries go right onto a cooling rack. If you're making cream puffs, cut them open right away to keep them from getting clammy inside. Cream puffs and éclairs taste their very best when fresh, but can be frozen after cooling and thawed quickly and easily.

Beating

Also known as whipping or whisking, beating is another key technique in the realm of baking. Egg foam cakes, such as sponge cakes and meringues, are baking staples that illustrate the beating-whipping concept to a T. Eggs are the essential ingredient here.

Egg-Foams

Egg-foam cakes can be made traditionally (with separate mixtures of beaten egg yolks and whites), in Viennese style (with warm beaten egg yolks and melted butter), or using the Basic method. Though it defies all of the traditional rules, we're going to show you the Basic method for making sponge cake, which seems a little backward—the egg yolks are mixed into the meringue instead of being beaten separately before the two are combined. Don't worry—it's easy, and produces pretty darn good cakes. Meringues, another example of egg foams, can be made into cakes and even cookies.

Whisks and Beaters

The most important tool for beating egg-foam batters is a whisk—preferably with a plug and cord on one end of it! Today's electric mixers have a whisk attachment in addition to the dual beaters. You can use a hand whisk to make egg-foam batters, but be prepared to remain at it for 45 minutes! A stand mixer is a great, efficient tool, but you won't find these in many Basic kitchens due to their bulk and expense. The hand whisk is handy for folding in the flour.

Egg Parts

For a successful egg foam cake, the egg yolks and whites must be separated. Do this carefully because a single drop of yolk will keep the egg white from behaving properly. Once you get through your first dozen, you'll be an egg separating pro!

For best results, you'll need three bowls: One can be small, since it is just used as a transportation bowl.

That way if you have a mishap—get some egg yolk into your egg white—it will cost only one egg. If you work without the transportation bowl, one thing is sure: If things go wrong, it will always be with the last egg, after the stores have closed and right after the neighbors have made scrambled eggs out of their emergency supply.

Start with a firm strike of the egg shell on the edge of a bowl or counter. Crack the egg right in the middle. After striking the egg, put your thumbs onto the edges of crack, place your other fingers behind the egg, and turn the whole thing so that one of the pointed ends is facing straight up toward the ceiling. Holding it over the transportation bowl, lift off the top half of the egg shell, taking care that the yolk stays inside the cavity of the lower shell half. Part of the egg white will flow into the bowl, while the yolk and the rest of the white should stay in the lower half of the shell. Carefully pour the yolk into the other shell half, letting the egg white spill over the edges into the bowl. Repeat this back and forth motion until all of the egg white is in the transportation bowl. Put the yolk in its designated bowl and discard the shell. Dump the egg white out of the transport-bowl and into its designated bowl. When in doubt, it's better to leave a bit of egg white on the yolk than to risk getting yolk in the egg white.

Making Meringue

The transformation from egg white to meringue may seem to you like a small miracle. Here's the scientific view: When egg white is vigorously beaten, its components separate and recombine as air-filled protein bubbles that get stronger, more numerous, and larger with every stroke, until the whole thing has become a mass of foam. You can help along this process and make the resulting mixture more stable by using room temperature egg whites (though cold egg

whites will still work) and adding 1/8 teaspoon of cream of tartar per egg white. Cream of tartar is an acidic powder derived from wine grapes. Look for it on the spice shelf at the supermarket. Remember: Make sure that your mixing bowl and beaters are completely clean and free of any oily residue before you begin whipping. One drop of oil or speck of food in the bowl will ruin the entire batch. To allow the air to get in everywhere when beating with the hand mixer, keep the mixer moving and make sure the bowl isn't too narrow or tall. The egg whites will go through three distinct transformations: First, they'll turn foamy. Next they'll form soft peaks—the mixture will stand up in the bowl when the beater is lifted and drop over at the top like a chocolate kiss. Finally, the egg whites will form stiff peaks, when the chocolate kiss-shaped piles stand straight up, and you can turn the bowl over without losing any of the egg white mixture. Caution: Stop beating now, or risk overbeating the egg whites.

The other ingredients in an egg-foam batter are added at different stages of the meringue's development. Cream of tartar is added at the beginning, while the egg whites are still liquid, to keep the mixture stable. The sugar is usually beaten in slowly during the soft peak stage. The result is a solid, glossy foam in which a knife leaves a smooth cut (1). Depending on the strength of the machine, making meringue takes about 10 to 15 minutes. Careful—if you beat the egg whites too slowly the air will all dissipate again.

Baking Meringue

If you're baking the meringue batter, you'll probably add a large amount of sugar to the mixture. Remember the cream of tartar for stability! The meringue is barely baked—rather it's dried—for a long time at 200° to 250°F. More heat would cause the meringue to brown (taboo) before it thoroughly dries (a must). For it to stay that way, the best thing is for it to spend the night on a rack in a turned-off oven. When the meringue comes out, it should be stored in an airtight canister or locking plastic bag.

Basic-Style Sponge Cake

If you are making sponge cake, the work continues with the reunification of egg white and egg yolk—here's where we break the traditional baking rules. One yolk after the other is mixed into the meringue using a hand whisk until it disappears and the whole thing is finally a foamy batter (2). We know—it seems weird, but it makes a delicious cake!

Of course, the batter still lacks flour. The flour is sifted to maintain the batter's lightness, and then it's carefully folded in. Here's how it goes: Through a wire-mesh sieve, sift the flour onto the egg mixture, stick in the hand whisk, and slowly rotate it toward the top, using a light touch to coax the batter back into the bowl. Repeat. And repeat again. Keep going until the flour has barely disappeared into the egg mixture. Keep it short so that most of the air stays in the batter.

The Oven

To keep the air from dissipating, the batter must go straight into the oven. Pour the batter into the pan and make sure the surface of the batter is nice and smooth. After baking, usually at 350°F (springform) to 400°F (baking sheet), let the sponge cake stand briefly before turning it out onto a cooling rack and pulling off any parchment paper. If it's to be cut into layers, a night's rest will do the cake good.

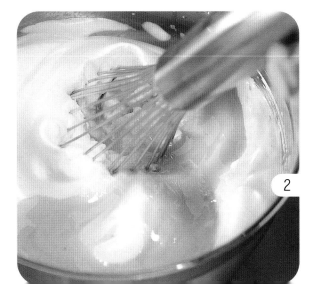

Kneading

When a lot of flour gets together with a little liquid, stirring and beating will do no good. Now's when you need to knead. Kneading can be a good workout if you're so inclined, but a food processor or mixer can do the job easily. Kneading the flour strengthens its protein, gluten, to provide structure for the dough. You need a lot of gluten for yeast breads so kneading is encouraged. You don't need gluten for flaky pastry, so kneading is discouraged. Yeast dough and flaky pastry dough stand at opposite ends of the kneading spectrum.

Yeast Dough

Yeast dough is probably the most feared of the Basic doughs and batters. Yet the yeast cells are such grateful little creatures. If we give them just a bit of food, air, and heat, they do the nicest things for us, like eating drinking and multiplying. The byproduct? Lots and lots of gas. Carbon dioxide, that is.

Yeast—The Most Important Element

Yeast can be confusing these days because there are lots of types on the market. Which to choose? Think Basic. We use rapid-rise (also called quick-rise) yeast. Rapid-rise yeast is a tough customer, able to take more abuse than its cousins, fresh yeast (the yeast of choice in professional bakeries), and active dry yeast (the stuff your Mom used back in the old days). RR yeast doesn't need to be "proofed" before mixing it with the rest of the ingredients; rather, it can be mixed directly with the flour. Be careful with the salt—it's not a good idea to let the salt come directly in contact with the yeast or it could damage it. Better to mix the yeast into the flour first so that there is a buffer when the salt is added. The liquid—warmed to 120°F—and other ingredients are then added to the yeast mixture and the whole thing is stirred and kneaded to make a smooth dough. There are lots of advanced bread recipes out there, but for Basic baking we'll stick with the Basics (pun intended)—single rise, no sponge breads that can be put together and baked in a single evening.

The Need to Knead

Kneading can be done with a food processor or stand mixer, but sometimes it's fun to get your hands dirty and become one with your food. First, mix the ingredients in a large, heavy bowl. When the mixture can no longer be manipulated with a wooden spoon, use your hands: Pull the ingredients together and squeeze with your fingers until everything comes together in a mass. Then, push the dough down with the heels of your hands. Fold the far end of the dough over the near end of the dough and give it a quarter turn. Repeat the pushing, folding and turning process for about ten minutes until the dough is nice and smooth and elastic. Form the dough into a ball and let it rest in the center of the bowl. (If you're using a food processor, let the machine run for about 60 seconds after the ingredients come together in a ball.)

Cover the bowl with a dishtowel and put it in a warm draft-free spot—try the top of a kitchen cabinet, far from open doors and windows (1). Blissed out on starch, the yeast in the dough begins to reproduce, forming carbon dioxide bubbles that inflate the solid dough network like a balloon. (Refrigerator trick: Put yeast dough that has been kneaded but has not yet risen into a covered bowl in the fridge. Let it rise overnight and it will be ready for baking in the morning).

The Oven

Once the dough has approximately doubled in size, it is "punched down" to remove the air and briefly kneaded again. Then it is shaped—Rolled into a loaf, twisted into a braid, or rolled out into pizza crust. Depending on the recipe, the dough may rise again or go straight into the oven. Once in the oven, the yeast dies. If the gluten network that was formed during kneading is strong, the dough will become a warm, crusty loaf of bread with a crisp crust.

Flaky Pastry

Flaky pastry wants nothing to do with its rough-and-tumble brother, yeast dough. The less flaky pastry is touched, the happier it is. The leavening in flaky pastry is steam, created when the butter inside melts and the steam evaporates leaving pockets of air. If flaky pastry dough is kneaded too much, the result is tough, dry crust instead of delicate, tender crust.

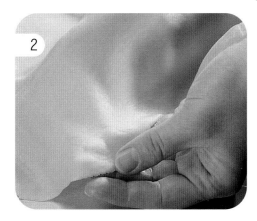

Keep Things Cold

The secret of tender flaky pastry is that the flour binds directly with the butter. Very little liquid is used, which would cause the flour to swell. The butter should be very cold—right out of the freezer or refrigerator is ideal. If the butter is too warm and soft, it turns the flaky pastry into brittle pastry. The water or liquid should be ice cold. If you're a real pastry nut, chill all the ingredients—flour, butter, sugar (if called for), and egg (if called for)—the night before you plan to make the pastry.

Though you can make it by hand, making pastry with a food processor is easy and painless—and you may even end up working it less than if you did it by hand. Put the flour and salt in the food processor's work bowl that has been fitted with the metal blade. Cut the cold butter into small cubes and throw the cubes on top of the flour mixture. Pulse the machine (turn it on and off) 25 to 40 times until the butter and flour mixture looks like cornmeal. Careful: From now on each time you turn on the machine it will cause the pastry to toughen. Add the minimum amount of water or liquid to the work bowl and pulse a few times until the ingredients ALMOST come together. You may need to add more of the liquid and pulse a few more times. Dump the mixture onto a work surface and gently push the pastry crumbs together with your hands. Chilling

the pastry before rolling it out makes the texture more uniform than if you rolled it out just after mixing. Some recipes say to chill the pastry in the pan before baking—usually when the pastry is to be blind-baked. This is done to enhance the dough's flakiness and minimize shrinkage while it's baking.

Rolling out the Pastry

There are two ways to line a pan with pastry, the pushing method and the rolling method. For the pushing method, distribute small pieces of the dough over the surface of the pan. With your fingertips, flatten the pastry pieces and push them together until they form a layer of dough about 1/8 inch thick over the surface of the pan. Trim the excess dough around the edges, keeping enough of it to make a raised dough surface around the edge of the pan.

For the rolling method, first form the dough into a disk, then place it on a work surface between two large sheets of plastic wrap. With a rolling pin, roll the dough starting at the center and pushing to the outside edges, turning the rolling pin frequently to keep the dough even (2). Roll the dough into a circle that is one inch wider than the diameter of the pan. Transfer the dough to the pan: Gently roll it around the rolling pin halfway, and move it over the pan. Or, fold the dough into quarters and carefully lift it to the pan. Placing the center of the dough in the center of the pan, lay the dough in the pan. Smooth the dough in the pan and make a raised edge for the crust.

Blind Baking

Sometimes flaky pastry needs to be baked in the pan before the filling is put into it—AKA Blind Baking. To blind bake a pastry crust, first prick the bottom in several places with a fork and line the whole thing with parchment paper or aluminum foil. Don't press it down, or the pastry will stick to the paper later. Fill the lined pastry with a 3/4-inch-high layer of dried beans or pie weights so that the bottom will stay nice and flat and the edge will stay up while baking. Bake the crust according to the recipe, usually in a 400° to 425°F oven.

seeds

extracts

vanilla

lemons

nuts

coconut

fresh fruit

chocolate

jam

powdered
sugar

raisins

the
sweet 14

Everything that
makes baking better

cocoa

sprinkles

readymade
supplies

Seeds

French: graines; Italian: semi; Spanish: semillas
Poppy seeds, sesame seeds, caraway seeds and sunflower kernels—all popular additions to baked goods both savory and sweet. What would Sunday morning be without a poppy seed bagel? Like spices, seeds should be bought in small quantities and used up fast. Some seeds, like nuts, can go rancid, so you may want to store them in the refrigerator or freezer. Always buy seeds in small quantities to ensure that they are fresh.

Extracts

French: arôme; Italian: aroma; Spanish: sacars
Baking extracts, such as almond and vanilla, are essential components of many baked goods. Unlike liqueurs, extracts retain their flavors even when heated at high temperatures. Look for the words "pure" or "natural" on the bottle's label. Imitation extracts, though less expensive, will, in our opinion, ruin the flavor of your cake or pastry or frosting. Besides, as we've said before, if you're going to splurge on dessert, why skimp on the ingredients?

Vanilla

French: vanille; Italian: vaniglia; Spanish: vainil
Though vanilla can be found in extract form, vanilla beans give desserts the best and truest vanilla flavor. Vanilla beans are the fruit of a rare orchid. The fact that the flower blooms only onc a year and that the pods must be harvested by hand explains why they are so expensive. Also, these pods don't gain their familiar aroma and flavor until after they have gone through a lengthy process of fermenting and curing. At home, vanilla beans should be slit along their length to expose the tiny black seeds inside and scraped out with the back of a small knife. The pods themselves can be simmered in pastry creams or custards, but should be strained out before serving.

Lemons

French: citron; Italian: limone; Spanish: limón
Lemon is sour, which goes well with everything sweet. And lemon's zest—the colored part of the peel—has enough flavor for 10 cakes. When the juice and zest are combined they can work miracles, as lovers of lemon cake know. Fans of orange and lime report the same. Ideally, choose organic lemons and be sure to wash them in hot water before grating the zest. Watch out: The juice can cause egg and/or butter to curdle when it's stirred in—a bit of flour or cornstarch will prevent that problem. Lemon juice has another use for Basic bakers: It keeps apples and pears from turning brown.

Nuts

French: fruit à coque; Italian: noci; Spanish: tuercas
Almonds are the number one nut used in baking. They are available with and without skin, sliced or slivered, chopped or ground, and as almond paste or marzipan. Almonds should be stored in a cool, dark, dry place for up to 6 months. Almonds' competition: Hazelnuts (whole, chopped, or ground; keep for 6 months); walnuts (whole, halves, or pieces—watch out, they soon turn rancid out of the shell; refrigerate for 3 months); peanuts (the cheapest; keep 9 months); pine nuts (exotic, expensive; keep 3 months): pistachios (cute, aromatic, expensive; keep 6 months). Roasting makes all nuts taste better—toss them in a dry skillet over medium heat until they smell aromatic.

Coconut

French: noix de coco; Italian: noche di cocco; Spanish: coco
Coconut factoids: The flesh of the fruit is actually the fiber (good for doormats) and the shell is used to make charcoal. Basic bakers are more interested in what is underneath—the seed with its delicious milk and white meat. The coconut that we usually see is grated and dried before reaching the shelves of the baking section. The oil pressed out of it is sold commercially for frying and is also found in the chocolate section as a cocoa butter substitute. Coconut milk is available thick (better) and thin, and unsweetened (better) or sweetened. Coconut milk lends an exotic taste to puddings and custards.

Fresh fruit

French: fruit; Italian: frutta; Spanish: fruita
Fresh fruit is a must in the Basic kitchen—so much so that we devoted an entire chapter to fresh fruit desserts. Raspberries, strawberries, apples, cherries, apricots, peaches...need we go on? Whenever possible, we recommend choosing organic fruits to use in baked goods—or any dishes, for that matter. Remember to wash fruit before using it. Berries need just a brief rinse, while other fruits can stand a longer shower. Apples can be peeled or unpeeled, depending on the recipe or your mood. Ditto for peaches. See page 57 for a super-easy way to get the peach skins off.

Chocolate

French: chocolat; Italian: cioccolata; Spanish: chocolate
Chocolate comes in many forms and in many levels of sweetness. Buy the highest quality chocolate you can find—you won't be sorry. In Basic baking, we don't mess with the unsweetened stuff. Bittersweet, semisweet, milk and white chocolates are our choices here. Note: You may have heard that white chocolate isn't really chocolate. True, because it doesn't contain any chocolate "liqueur." To find the best quality white chocolate, make sure the label lists cocoa butter as a major ingredient. Couverture is a wor used to describe professional-quality chocolate. If you find it, buy it! It will give terrific results.

Jam

French: confiture; Italian: confettura; Spanish: confitura

Jams are versatile supplies in the Basic kitchen, serving as a coating, filling, or glaze, depending on the recipe. Apricot and raspberry jams are good choices because they complement many different flavors. Jams are ideal for covering fruit tart bases (heated and strained first) before filling and for coating cakes before frosting them. They're also a good substitute for fruit in cookies. Of course, it's essential for morning pastries or fresh baked bread, or, melted, it can stand in for syrup. If the jam has pieces of fruit, it's a good idea to strain it through a fine-meshed sieve before using it as a coating or glaze.

Powdered sugar

French: sucre en poudre; Italian: polvere zucchero; Spanish: azúcar a en polvo

Baking snobs call it confectioners' sugar, but we don't really know what that means. We prefer to call it powdered sugar because that's really what it is—regular sugar that has been pulverized until it becomes a fine powder. Powdered sugar is used to sweeten light and fluffy things, like whipped cream or frosting, because it dissolves so easily. But the very best thing about powdered sugar is its decorative use. You can use powdered sugar to garnish many different types of cookies, cakes, and pastries. And if you mess up when getting the cake out of the pan, powdered sugar will hide even the most hideous of flaws.

Raisins

French: raisin; Italian: uva passa; Spanish: pasa
Traditionally grapes were dried in the sun to make raisins, but nowadays they're often dried by machine. The longer the grapes are dried, the darker their color will be. One pound of grapes produces 4 ounces of raisins full of concentrated sugar. Cakes that contain raisins need less sugar and stay moist longer than those without raisins. Raisins can be an optional ingredient in many baked goods, but what would oatmeal cookies be without them? If you're in the mood for a change, try substituting other dried fruits—dried cranberries, dried cherries, or chopped dried apricots—for raisins.

the sweet 14

Everything that makes baking better

Cocoa

French: cacao; Italian: cacao; Spanish: cacao
Cocoa powder comes from cocoa beans that are fermented, roasted, ground, and dried twice. The cocoa butter that exists naturally in the cocoa beans is extracted, leaving the dark brown powder. Cocoa can be stirred into pastry cream to make it chocolateier. If cocoa is to be blended into a whole cake, it is first mixed with the flour to achieve a smooth texture. A bonus: Just like powdered sugar, cocoa can be used to decorate baked goods and hide their flaws. Use a fine-meshed sieve to remove any lumps from the cocoa.

Sprinkles

We use this term liberally, applying to all manner of dragées and other tiny adornments. These are pure luxury, because nobody really needs this culinarily incorrect combination of sugar, and food coloring. But sprinkles change regular cakes into birthday cakes, and transform wedding cakes into works of art. If you think they look too cheap, use sugared flowers from a baking supply store. Or if you're into the natural look, use candied violets or marzipan fruits. Use your imagination—there's a lot of cool stuff out there. Try tiny chocolate candies, licorice bits, or candied citrus peels.

Readymade Supplies

Why make everything yourself when other people can also make some pretty good stuff? For example, if you don't feel like baking your own ladyfingers for Tipsy Charlotte on page 70, buy some from the local bakery. Or vanilla wafers for the Chocolate Bars, page 91, or Petit Beurre cookies for the Chocolate Cookie Cake, page 71. Not to mention rolls, croissants, or bread for bread puddings or French toast. And of course, the graham crackers for the crust of the Cheesecake, page 52. Who would make those themselves? Of course, the bigger the role played by the readymade bakery product, the better the quality you must use.

Finishing Touches

Everything's already baked? Great! But you still have a bit more to do, if you want to hear the oohs and aahs when you present the strawberry shortcake, or buttercream torte. Now you have to cut, fill, and frost. The empty shell will become a masterpiece—but only after it is decorated.

Constructing a Torte

You might be wondering...What's the difference between a cake and a torte? Let's not worry about the technical terms. For our Basic purposes, a cake is just a cake—one layer. It may or may not have a simple frosting or topping. A torte, however, is composed of multiple elements—usually a cake, a filling, and a frosting or glaze. Often a torte has many layers. Got it?

When putting together a torte, the goal is to make sure the insides are nicely plastered together. After it's decorated, the torte may look like a work of art, but if it hasn't been put together well on the inside, it will become obvious as soon as you cut into it. Here's some Basic torte-making advice: Stay solid and stay simple. The best tortes are constructed on a stable base. The components should be uncomplicated. It is when they are put together that the torte's elements transform it from a Plain Jane to a Ravishing Rita.

Even Layers

A torte usually starts with sponge cake, from which two or three layers are to be made. Cutting the cake into layers works well one day after baking, because the cake is less crumbly than just after it's baked. There are two ways of doing this—with a strong piece of string or with a long knife. If you choose the string route, thin unwaxed, unflavored dental floss is the perfect tool. Make sure the piece of dental floss is long enough so that it can be drawn around the diameter of the cake with lots of room to spare. Cross the ends together and pull them together (1) to cut an even layer out of the cake. If you prefer to use a knife, choose one that is at least as long as the cake is wide—even better if it's serrated. Put one hand on top of the cake, and with the knife use a sawing motion to cut into the cake towards the center. Turn the cake every so often so that the cut can go all the way around the diameter of the cake. Keep going until the middle is reached and the cake has been cut through.

Well Filled

Torte fillings are usually whipped cream, pastry cream, jam, or something chocolatey. Often the cake layers are soaked with a flavorful liquid to keep them moist. The more smoothly the filling is spread, the less wobbly the whole thing will be later. The pros use a metal spatula or bench scraper to spread the filling, but a large knife or rubber spatula also works well. It's a good idea to put the bottom torte layer on something solid, such as a serving platter, before you start to assemble it. That way you won't have to try and move it—and potentially harm it—after it's decorated.

Now it's time to put on the finishing touches. To do this, you'll need a bit of dexterity. Hold the cake on its platter in one hand, and spread roughly half of the filling or frosting around the sides. Turn the platter in your hand as you spread the frosting over the sides to give it an even coating. If you're having trouble turning the cake, you can set the cake down to make an adjustment. Or, ask a trusted helper to turn it with both hands. It doesn't matter if a bit of the filling oozes out. Put the cake down and put the rest of the filling or frosting on top. Smooth the filling all over the top of the cake until it looks pretty. Try using a circular motion rotating around the center of the cake (2).

Homemade Whipped Cream

Whipped cream is the simplest cake filling and accompaniment to baked goods. Yet some people think it's too difficult to make and opt for the stuff that comes from a can. But even if the can's label says it's the real thing, it is full of additives. Wouldn't you rather go for the fresh stuff? Whipped cream is actually very easy to make. One caveat: Unless you're a masochist, don't try to make it by hand—by the time you're done it'll feel like your arm is going to fall off. Make sure

Fancy Fillings

Sometimes you need a bit more than pure whipped cream in and around your cake. The quickest variation: To make chocolate whipped cream, add sifted cocoa into sweetened whipped cream. Richer: Melt 5 ounces of high-quality semisweet chocolate and stir it into 1 cup of warmed whipping cream. Cool the mixture overnight, and whip it up in the morning. Liquids like liqueur or flavored syrup can be folded into whipped cream right at the end.

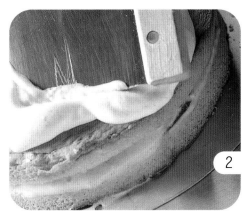

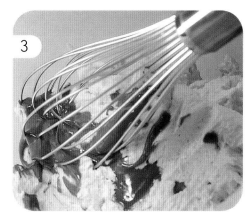

your whipping cream is very cold. For that matter, try to use a bowl and beaters that are cold, too—just stick them in the fridge for a few minutes. Choose a wide bowl. A stainless steel one is ideal, but not essential. Beat the cream with an electric mixer on medium speed until it almost looks ready, and then test it. The whipped cream is done as soon it gets thick and can stand up in solid peaks from the whisk. If it gets more solid, yellowish, and clumpy, it's butter. And you'll have to throw it away and start over. If you are one of those who is likely to overwhip the cream, change to a hand whisk when it's almost done and continue beating until it's ready. For you adventurous souls, keep beating with the mixer on low. If you're adding sugar to the whipped cream, sprinkle it in while whipping when the peaks—the chocolate kiss-shaped mounds that form in the cream as it's whipped—are small to medium in size.

Pastry creams are even more luxurious than flavored whipped cream. Pastry cream is a versatile staple in the Basic kitchen. To it, you can add whipped cream, softened butter, or melted chocolate (3), depending on the desired outcome (see the chapter Elegant But Easy for more details). Important: Everything should be at room temperature when the pastry cream is mixed so that nothing curdles or fails to distribute evenly.

Making Things Beautiful

After the baked goods are baked and filled they're not necessarily ready to go to the table. With just a little extra effort you can add a little extra something to impress your guests (and yourself!).

Decorating 101

The simplest way to make baked goods look nice is to shake a sifter of powdered sugar over them. But please don't be too generous unless there's something to hide, because most things are sweet enough. Also nice: Put a stencil on a cake before sprinkling the powdered sugar, providing a pattern with nice contrast. The next easiest thing is to make icing by adding liquid to the powdered sugar—juice, syrup, liqueur, or coloring, if desired. Stir a good 3 tablespoons of liquid into 1 ⅓ cups of powdered sugar to make icing that will flow well. Using 2-2 ½ tablespoons makes it thicker and good for decorating cookies. With 4 tablespoons of liquid you'll get a transparent film that can be quickly poured or spread over cakes for a nice sheen.

Even better is a chocolate glaze (see page 110) or cream frosting (melt 6 ounces chocolate, plus 2 ounces of butter in 1/2 cup whipping cream). Both the coating and frosting are poured over the cake while they are lukewarm. If the coating is spread on, you'll need less of it but it won't turn glossy. It's perfect when poured on all at once while turning and tilting the cake so that the coating runs everywhere—like when you're swirling crêpe batter in a skillet. Set the coated cake on a rack with a baking sheet underneath to collect the drips.

Beautiful Around the Edges

A cake decorated on the edges has many good sides: More flavor, nice appearance, and a visual screen to cover any minor defects. Usually only small odds and ends are applied to whipped cream or wet frosting: Grated chocolate, sliced almonds, chopped nuts, grated coconut, and sprinkles are some examples. To apply these, hold the cake with one hand by its base at an angle. Fill the other hand with your decorating tidbits, then cup it and move it along adjacent strips of the side of the cake, one after the other from top to the bottom. This way, things tend to slide down rather than fall. If necessary, everything can be pressed in a bit more at the end.

Pastry Bags

For more serious cake decorations you'll need a pastry bag and tip or two. To keep everything neat and clean, fold down the edge of the pastry bag about 2 inches, like the cuff on high boots, before filling it. Place the tip into the bag and secure it so that it protrudes evenly from the hole. Then spread the thumb of your left hand (lefties use the right hand) loosely in one direction and the other fingers in the other direction, as if holding a glass between them.

Hang the bag and tip between them so the thumb and index finger keep the bag's opening open. Use a rubber spatula to shovel in the frosting or topping,

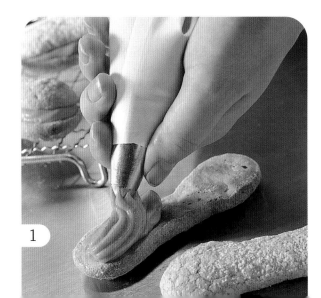

1

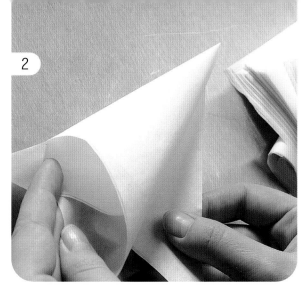

pressing down a couple of times to remove any air bubbles. Once the bag is 3/4 full, scrape the rubber spatula over the index finger to clean any filling off of the spatula and set it aside. Unfold the bag's "cuffs," pull the bag upward, and twist it several times to close the opening. Hold the bag like a clamp between the thumb and index finger, while at the same time press down with the other fingers to evacuate all of the air.

What about the other hand? Use it only for guidance, pressing just a little bit. Grip the bottom of the bag, like you're about to flip a frying pan, while holding the bag—thumb in front, other fingers behind. Now you can start: Using a slight rotation by the lower hand at the point, pull the vertical bag slightly upward while squeezing briefly with the upper hand. At the end, dip the tip lightly into the decoration before removing it to avoid leaving behind a little tail (1). Done. Again? OK: A single rotation at the point by the lower hand, additional pressure by the upper hand, both pull the bag straight up, dip—and you're done. And now again. And again. Again. With a bit of practice this will become a single movement. If you want to do a dry run, pipe the frosting or filling onto a parchment-lined baking sheet, throw it in the freezer, and then position the successful frozen designs on the cake.

Personalized Cakes

You can give your cakes a personal touch by writing messages on them, whether it's just "happy birthday" or a brief love letter. There are many ways to inscribe messages, such as with little candies, sprinkles, or colorful icing. If you're using the candies or sprinkles, it's helpful to sketch your design with the icing first and then fill it with the garnishes. The icing will help them adhere.

You can write longer messages on the cake using an icing tube. You can find one at the grocery store next to the baking supplies, or you can make your own miniature pastry bag out of a piece of parchment paper. For the homemade version, cut out a 6-inch-square piece of parchment and fold it half diagonally into a triangle. Roll the triangle into a stiff bag in which the center point of the long side is the point of rotation. It will also become the end of the bag where the icing oozes out. The two protruding parchment corners can be folded to help the bag stay in place: Fold the outside corner toward the inside and the inside corner toward the outside. If you're insecure, apply a piece of Scotch tape on the outside to secure the bag (2). Now fill the bag no more than halfway with icing or melted chocolate, fold it closed, cut a small opening at the point, and start writing—your writing hand leads, while the other one uses the thumb and index finger pressure to squeeze. Tip: Use a toothpick to outline your message in advance.

Nice Additions

Remember Play Dough? Here's an edible version that you can use to decorate cakes. Marzipan (look for it in the baking supply section of the supermarket) kneaded with powdered sugar can be colored, rolled out, and cut out to form flowers, leaves, or letters. It can also be used to make little figures, such as baby carrots. Mix a little red and yellow food coloring into the marzipan base, and make little pointed orange rolls out or it. Notch them with the dull side of a knife, and top them off with some green marzipan tops. You can see a couple of them on page 41.

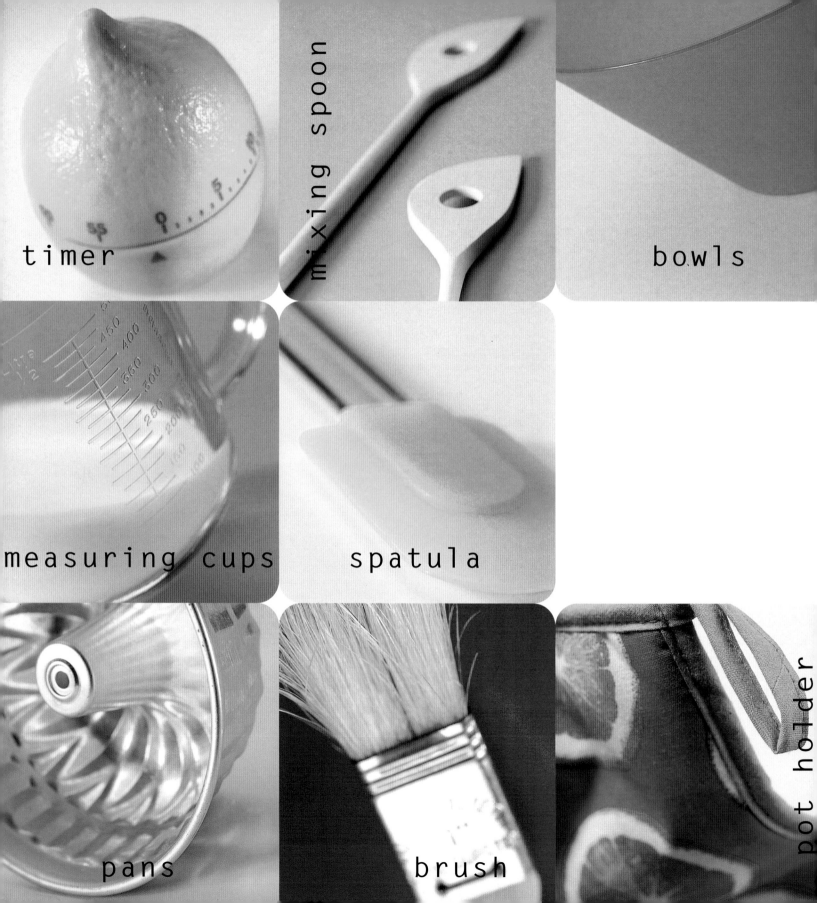

timer

mixing spoon

bowls

measuring cups

spatula

pans

brush

pot holder

sifter

measuring spoons

cooling rack

grater

the smart

16

baking won't work without them

parchment

rolling pin

whisk

pastry bag

Timer

Timers built right into the stove have the disadvantage that you can't take them with you into the living room and they are never repaired once they break. Instead, purchase a wind-up model that you can take with you wherever you go. To be sure the timer rings loudly, wind it past the desired time and then set it back to a time that is a bit shorter than you think you need. That way you can check the cake's progress before the designated time to make sure it's done. Baking a cake a bit more is, after all, better than scraping the burnt cake out of the pan.

Mixing spoon

A spoon is a fundamental tool in the Basic kitchen. A large one is ideal, preferably wooden or plastic, though a metal spoon works just as well. We've discovered that the spoon with a hole in it (it doesn't have a proper name) is a cool variation on the spoon theme, especially when making baked goods, because it passes easily through batter, dough, or pastry cream. If the spoon has a pointed edge, it can get into the most hidden nooks and crannies, (and a mixing bowl has more of them than you might think).

Bowls

Anyone who bakes can't have enough bowls. One must is the "mother bowl" for whipping cream, kneading dough, and the like. If 3 quarts fit into it, it will fit well in the Basic kitchen. If it's heavy, round, stable, and slip-resistant (best done by a rubber ring on the bottom, although a damp towel will help out in an emergency), then it is a good mother. Made of metal? Fine. Made of solid plastic? Also fine. The rest of the family: One or two smaller chips off of old mother's block for related work like whipping egg whites. A high bowl with a spout works well for mixing batters. Cheap little bowls are good to have around for small jobs, but coffee cups also work.

Measuring cups

You'll probably want two types of measuring cups—dry measuring cups and liquid measuring cups. Dry measuring cups, usually come in nesting sets ranging from 1/4 cup up to 1 cup. You'll recognize the liquid cup by its clear glass or plastic construction, and lines on the side indicating the amounts. Measure liquids in dry measuring cups, but you have to be careful to avoid spilling. We don't recommend measuring dry substances in the liquid model because it is extremely hard to be accurate. Transfer dry ingredients to the measuring cup with a large spoon, and level them off using a knife or other straight edge. For liquids, place the measuring cup on a counter and crouch down so that you can view the level of liquid straight on.

Spatula

If it's just a rigid scraper, it's worthless. The traditional rubber spatula is preferred. Its handle looks like a Popsicle stick with a somewhat rectangular rubber-like plastic piece (or is it a plastic-like rubber piece?) on it, which is pliable enough at the edges to really get everything out of the bowl. Today's high-tech models are made of heat-resistant material so they won't melt when stirring hot stuff. A spatula works best if three of the edges are rounded and the top one is rectangular. The next best alternative: The semicircular professional spatula (also called a bench scraper) made of solid plastic, which is also great for scraping odds and ends from your countertop, and for spreading buttercream on your cake.

Pans

Almost every pastry in the world can be baked using one of the quartet of Basic baking pans: Loaf pan, Bundt pan, springform pan, and baking sheet. Depending on your dedication to baking, a muffin tin, pie pan, tart pan (with removable bottom), and ring-shaped cake pan can also squeeze in. We love the springform pan—its two-part construction with detachable sides is nearly idiot-proof. You can find springform pans sold cheaply in nesting sets at any kitchenware store. Pans with dull surfaces cause baked goods to bake slightly faster than those with shiny surfaces. Pans with a nonstick surface are easier when it comes to cleaning up, but make sure you follow the manufacturer's instructions for maintaining them.

Brush

A brush is essential in the Basic kitchen, whether for greasing baking pans, coating pastry with egg before baking, or covering it with glaze before serving. A traditional pastry brush—flat, made of wood, with a good inch of natural bristles—is the best tool for the job. Pastry brushes are sold in housewares and kitchenware stores. Even a 1-inch paintbrush will do the trick—just don't ever use it for paint! Since odors tend to stick to the natural substances of the brush, keep it away from the glazed pork roast, and thoroughly wash it with hot water and let it air dry after each use.

Pot holder

When the oven is on, the potholder shouldn't be far away, because baking just won't work without it. Don't worry what it looks like—you won't care about the designer potholder's stylish colors if you get a blister the first time you use it! What's most important is that a pot holder is large and thick enough to hold onto a baking sheet for a few seconds, but not so large and thick that the sheet slips onto the floor when you're trying to pull it out of the oven. If you're really in a bind, or just don't have a well-equipped kitchen, grab a thick dishtowel and fold it over a few times (that's what the pros do!).

Sifter

Sifting flour adds a special something to light and airy baked goods—specifically, the air in the pastry. Flour that has been sifted several times makes sponge cake even lighter. Forget about those old-fashioned sifters that look like a metal coffee cup with a fan blade in the bottom. A mesh sieve is sufficient if the holes are fine enough that it takes a little tapping to get all the flour to go through. And don't forget: This all-purpose kitchen tool is also good for washing strawberries and straining jam, for draining cherries, (think Black Forest Torte!) and for sprinkling powdered sugar over baked goods. Just make sure you wash and dry the sifter well between uses, or have a couple of them on hand.

Measuring spoons

Like their big brothers the measuring cups, measuring spoons are indispensable in the Basic kitchen. Our favorites are the sturdy stainless-steel kind, which will hold their shape over time and continue to provide accurate measurements. It's good to have a range of measuring spoons beginning at 1/4 teaspoon and ranging up to 1 tablespoon. Here are some other helpful measuring tips: A pinch is the amount you can hold between your thumb and index finger; a dash is like a few quick shakes of the salt shaker. To taste means that it really doesn't matter how much you use, just as long as it tastes right to you.

Cooling rack

Most baked goods need to cool, or at least rest, before going to the next step—be it decorating, or slicing and serving. But where are you going to put them? Leaving the baked goods on top of the stove is not an option, because the heat from the oven will prevent them from cooling off properly. That's where a cooling rack comes in. It elevates the baking pan off of the counter so that air can circulate all around and the baked items will cool rapidly. Don't have a cooling rack? You can easily find one at a kitchenware store or supermarket. Or try this trick: Use one of your oven shelves, elevated with small cups or ramekins, as a stand-in.

Grater

You'll need a grater for many different jobs, such as grating lemon zest and shredding cheese. If you choose a box grater, you'll have surfaces for your entire grating needs, from fine to coarse. But sometimes it's good to specialize. A lemon zester, a grater created specifically to remove lemon and other citrus zests, expertly removes just the yellow layer of lemon peel without the bitter white pith underneath. There are many types of lemon zesters on the market today. We like the long, skinny one better than the short foot-shaped one, because you don't have to chop the zest after you remove it.

the smart 16
baking won't work without them

Parchment

Does a baker absolutely need parchment paper? Technically no, because a brush and melted butter will also do its job, allowing the cake or cookies to be easily removed from the pan or baking sheet. But parchment does seem to add an extra layer of protection against burning and it makes clean-up a breeze. Parchment paper can be found in most grocery stores these days, but if you can't find it there go to your nearest kitchenware store. Don't worry if it seems expensive—the cost is well worth it to save your frayed nerves!

Rolling pin

The rolling pin can seem intimidating to inexperienced bakers, but using it is really easy. Wooden rolling pins are by far the best choice. Plastic ones are cheap and unreliable, and the marble ones are just too heavy and expensive for our purposes. Two main types of rolling pins are available—the French rolling pin, a long cylinder about 2 inches thick, and the American rolling pin with two handles joined by an axis. The handles are particularly handy when they can be securely gripped and don't wobble. A rolling pin should roll properly (test it!), be at least 12 inches long (measure it!), and be heavy for its size (feel it!).

Whisk

Even hand kneaders and equipment freaks can't do without a whisk. People who love to work by hand use the whisk to make whipped cream or beat eggs until they are foamy, which is why the balloon-type whisk with lots of flexible wires is the best one for the Basic kitchen. The fat model will incorporate more air into your mixture than the skinny model and it will require less work of your arm. If the handle doesn't have any hooks or edges, it will fit well into your hand while beating. A whisk is utilized in the Basic-style sponge cake method for folding in the dry ingredients at the end of mixing (see page 13).

Pastry bag

Its turn comes after everything is baked. The pastry bag pipes creams and fillings onto cakes and tortes with its pointed star tip. The tip shouldn't be too narrow or the piping will look stingy. Perfect: Two sizes of star tips. You'll also want a plain tip to make rosettes and logs, and to inject fillings. The bag itself should be made of a stable but flexible material and shouldn't be too small. If it extends from the hand to the middle of the forearm, it will be easy to fill and it will last a while. Cleaning is simple: Fill the bag with warm water, squeeze out any excess filling, wash the bag well, and invert it over a bottle to dry.

the recipes

Plain &

What could be better than cake? ...A second piece!

Simple

No whipped cream for you? No sauce, either? You must be one who likes pure flavors and top-quality ingredients. Just the cake, please.

Many people's favorite cakes are of the plain and simple variety—think buttery pound cake or creamy cheesecake. And a pumpkin pie from your own oven turns even the tiniest city apartment into your childhood home where the Thanksgiving feast lasted for hours.

Cake is comfort food, evoking memories of mom's love and childhood bliss. It's easy: Butter, eggs, sugar, and flour are mixed together, thrown into the oven, and POOF! These simple ingredients are magically turned into cake. What could be better? Nothing, except maybe the second piece.

Dear Aunt Betty:
I love to bake and I love to eat cakes, but what happens in between is horrible: Getting the thing out of the pan is like pulling teeth—torture! My cakes hardly ever come out voluntarily, and when they do they're in several pieces. What am I doing wrong?

Tortured in Tacoma

Dear Tortured:
First, answer this: How does your pan look? Old, rusted, and misshapen? Throw it out. Clean, smooth, and in its original shape? Keep going. You should coat the pan well with butter, particularly in the grooves around the bottom edges. A paper towel wrapped around your finger(s) will help you spread the butter smoothly. Or, save the butter wrappers and use them to coat the pan. Some recipes call for coating the pan with flour, too. Put a few tablespoons into the pan, shake it all around until everything's coated (it helps to do this over the sink), and shake out the excess flour.

When using parchment paper, remember that every wrinkle will show on the surface of the cake after it is baked. Here are some tricks: For regular cake pans, cut out parchment into a circle (use the bottom of the pan to trace a stencil) and a strip (cut it so that it lies flat against the sides of the pan. Use a smear of butter to hold the parchment down securely. For springform pans, cover only the bottom with paper, clamp the paper in using the edge of the pan, and tear off any bits of paper that stick out—a perfect fit!

Pan Speak

When baking cakes, it's typical for the outside of the cake to bake faster than the inside—especially when the cake is more than 4 inches in width and height. Over the centuries, cake pan designers have come up with some pretty clever gizmos to help combat this problem. Following are some examples:

The Loaf Pan
This is the simplest solution, because it takes the 4-inch zone to the limit in height and width. The loaf cake gets the heat from all sides, which is able to get to the middle fast enough to bake it evenly. The length of the loaf pan ensures that there is plenty of cake for everyone to eat. Loaf pans are good for heavy doughs and batters that don't need to rise too high.

The Bundt Pan

This refined cake pan seems to conquer the 4-inch rule, ignoring it for both height and width. The trick: The hole in the center allows the heat to come from the middle of the cake, as well as the outside, producing more even baking. Bundt pans are good for doughs and batters that rise a lot, like batter cakes with a lot of eggs and baking powder, or yeast doughs. Heavier doughs may need to be baked in a savarin or ring pan, which have smaller sides than a Bundt pan.

The Springform Pan
The plain and simple baker may not use this pan much, though he or she admires its clever design (a removable bottom and a clamp-secured baking ring). Springform pans are more often utilized for elaborate baking that consists of many elements, for example, sponge cake layers for fruit tarts or buttercream tortes. Exceptions: Cakes that are deliberately flat, like Orange Cake, page 35, or desserts that incorporate pastry, such as the Linzertorte on page 42.

The Jellyroll Pan

This pan is a special solution, because it's almost irresponsibly wide and doesn't go far in height. But there is method in its madness, because ultimately the huge width and lack of height compensate for each other and produce delicious, evenly baked cakes. The jellyroll pan is good for batters that rise substantially. It's also a good place for oddly shaped items, like yeast breads or choux paste, for baking.

It is also important to leave the cake in the pan after baking for about 10 minutes before trying to release it. Don't let it get too cold or it will start to stick. Run a small knife around the edge of the pan, invert a cooling rack onto the pan (the round ones are good for this), turn the whole thing over, and wait. Is it coming out? If so, congratulate yourself and pull the parchment paper off the bottom (if necessary). Nothing coming? Hold the pan and the rack together in both hands and jerk them quickly downwards—don't throw them down, even if you really want to. Nothing yet? Place a cold, damp cloth around the pan before turning it out. Still nothing? Then you'll have to pry the cake out with a knife or spatula. That's still better than throwing it out the window—and I've tried both.

Cakes at their Best

Some cakes should be eaten right after baking, while others need a bit of time to rest in order to taste their best. This table shows, in general terms, when baked goods taste best and for how long.

Type	On Baking Day	The Next Day	After a Couple of Days	Long Term
Butter cake	OK, but not yet all that flavorful	Moist and flavorful	Still good; heavy cakes or those with fruit are even better	Store in a cool place in an airtight container for 1-4 weeks
Choux Paste	At its best	Rather tough and dry	Don't bother	Freeze while very fresh in an airtight container for up to 1 month
Sponge cake	Best for a topping or garnish	Good if properly wrapped; ideal for cutting into layers for tortes	Tough and dry	Dry and grind for crumbs or use stale for "bread" pudding
Flaky pastry, baked before filling	OK, if fully cooled	Better because it's flakier	OK, if wrapped airtight in a dry place	Best to freeze the dough, wrapped tightly for up to 3 months
Flaky pastry, baked with filling	Best	OK, but it may soften	Too soft, tastes old	Best to freeze the dough, wrapped tightly for up to 3 months
Yeast cake	Very best	Probably still good	Stale, hard	Freeze while very fresh wrapped tightly for up to 1 month

Marble Cake
Simple, delicious

Don't forget: The butter, eggs, cream cheese, and milk should be at room temperature.

Makes 20 to 24 slices:

4 ounces bittersweet chocolate

1/2 cup almonds

1 cup (2 sticks) unsalted butter, softened

1 tablespoon cream cheese, optional

3/4 cup sugar

5 eggs

3 ⅓ cups flour

2 teaspoons baking powder

1/2 teaspoon salt

Scant 1/2 cup milk

2 tablespoons rum

Powdered sugar

1 First butter a Bundt pan. Then sprinkle a handful of flour into it and turn the pan back and forth until the flour is evenly distributed. Shake out the rest.

2 Now grate the chocolate. It's simplest in the food processor (grating disk), but it takes a bit more elbow grease using a manual grater. Remember that chocolate melts between warm fingers. Transfer the chocolate to a bowl. Add the almonds to the processor (metal blade) and process until they are finely ground.

3 Preheat the oven to 350°F. Put the butter into a mixing bowl along with the cream cheese and the sugar. Mix them with an electric mixer until everything looks light and creamy. Add the eggs one at a time, mixing until no trace of the egg is left before adding the next egg.

4 In another bowl, mix the flour with the baking powder and salt. Add the flour mixture and milk alternately into the butter mixture, mixing between additions. Put half of the batter in another bowl. Stir the grated chocolate, the almonds, and the rum into one half of the batter.

5 Using a large spoon, add a big glob of light-colored batter to the pan. Then add some dark batter, followed by light batter, and so on. Now comes the marbleizing: Use a fork to draw spirals through the batter to slightly mix the dark and light batters so that they make stripes and swirls.

6 Bake the cake on the middle oven rack for 1 ¼ hours. After 1 hour, check with a toothpick to see whether the cake is done (see Tip on page 38). Leave the cake in the pan for 5 to 10 minutes, turn it out onto a rack, and let it cool completely. Dust the cake with powdered sugar before eating.

Time needed: Almost 2 hours, but only about 30 minutes involves work.

Variation:

Marble Cake with Peanut Butter

Mix 3/4 cup (1 ½ sticks) of softened, unsalted butter and 3/4 cup of peanut butter with 1 ½ cups sugar until light and creamy, then gradually beat in 5 eggs one after the other. In another bowl, mix 1 ½ cups flour with 2 teaspoons baking powder and 1/2 teaspoon salt and add it to the butter mixture alternately with 1/2 cup milk, mixing between additions. Divide the batter in half, mixing 4 ounces melted bittersweet chocolate into one of the halves and 2 ounces chopped bittersweet chocolate into the other. Add both batters alternately to a buttered Bundt pan, draw a fork through it as described above, and bake on the middle oven rack at 350°F for 50 to 60 minutes.

Orange Cake
Nice and quick

Makes 8 to 12 slices:

For the batter:

1 orange

4 eggs

1/3 cup sugar

6 tablespoons semolina (health food or specialty food store)

1/2 cup fresh-squeezed orange juice (from about 3 oranges)

1/4 teaspoon cream of tartar

2/3 cup flour

1 ½ teaspoons salt

For soaking:

1/2 cup fresh-squeezed orange juice

1/3 cup sugar

1 Make the batter: Wash the orange in hot water, dry it, and finely grate 1 to 2 teaspoons of the zest. Separate the eggs. Beat the egg yolks with the sugar and the orange zest until they become thick, foamy, and have expanded somewhat in volume. Stir the semolina and the orange juice into the yolk mixture and set it aside for 10 minutes. In a clean, grease-free bowl, beat the egg whites until stiff, adding the cream of tartar when the eggs are foamy.

2 Preheat the oven to 375°F. Butter the sides of the pan; cover the bottom of the pan with parchment paper.

3 Mix the flour with the salt. Heap the egg whites on the egg yolk mixture, sift the flour mixture onto it, and carefully fold everything together using a hand whisk. Pour the batter into the pan, smooth out the top, and bake it on the middle oven rack for about 20 to 25 minutes.

4 While the cake is baking, make the soaking liquid: Boil the orange juice and sugar together until they make a thick syrup, about 5 minutes. Set the pan aside.

5 After baking, let the cake stand in the pan for 5 to 10 minutes, then release the side of the springform pan and transfer the cake to a plate. Brush the cake with the warm syrup until the cake absorbs all of the syrup.

Time needed: 1 hour, including 30 minutes doing something

Chocolate-Nut Cake
Stays tasty for a few days

Makes 24 slices:

8 ounces top-quality milk chocolate

8 ounces hazelnuts

6 eggs

3/4 cup flour

1 teaspoon baking powder

1 teaspoon ground cinnamon

1/2 teaspoon salt

1 cup (2 sticks) unsalted butter, softened

1 cup sugar

3/4 teaspoon cream of tartar

8 ounces semisweet chocolate (optional)

1 Break the milk chocolate into pieces and process them in a food processor (metal blade) until they are finely ground; transfer the chocolate to a bowl. Add the hazelnuts to the food processor and process them until finely ground; mix them with the chocolate. Separate the eggs. In a bowl, mix the flour with the baking powder, cinnamon, and salt.

2 Preheat the oven to 400°F. With a mixer, beat the butter and sugar until they are light and creamy, then gradually mix in the egg yolks one at a time. Slowly mix the nut-chocolate mixture into the butter mixture, and then gently mix in the flour mixture. In a clean, grease-free bowl and with clean beaters, beat the egg whites until stiff, adding the cream of tartar when they turn foamy. Fold the egg whites into the batter until everything is incorporated.

3 Coat an 11-inch loaf pan generously with butter and pour in the batter. Bake the cake on the middle oven rack for 45 to 55 minutes. Toothpick test for safety's sake (see Tip on page 38). Let the cake stand for 5 to 10 minutes in the pan, then turn it out onto a rack. Let it cool, wrap it well with plastic wrap or foil, and let it sit overnight before eating (if you can control yourself).

4 If desired, finely chop the semisweet chocolate and melt it in a saucepan over medium-low heat; let it cool slightly. Pour or spread the chocolate over the cake, then stick it in the fridge for 15 minutes before slicing.

Time needed: 1 ½ hours, including 50 minutes doing something

Chocolate-Almond Cake
Sweet and satisfying

Makes 8 to 12 slices:

4 ounces bittersweet chocolate

1 cup flour

1/2 cup chopped almonds

1 teaspoon baking powder

1/2 teaspoon salt

6 eggs

3/4 teaspoon cream of tartar

One 7-ounce tube of marzipan (baking section or specialty foods store)

2/3 cup sugar

1 teaspoon vanilla extract

8 ounces semisweet chocolate

2 tablespoons chopped pistachios

1 Chop the bittersweet chocolate into pieces that are not too fine. Mix the chocolate with the flour, almonds, baking powder, and salt.

2 Preheat the oven to 350°F. Butter a 10- or 11-inch springform pan.

3 Separate the eggs. In a clean, grease-free bowl, beat the egg whites, adding the cream

of tartar when they're foamy, until they form stiff peaks. Cut the marzipan into cubes, then process them in a food processor (metal blade) with the sugar until finely ground. Add the egg yolks to the machine one after the other and process until smooth. Transfer the mixture to a bowl and stir in the vanilla extract. Stir in the chocolate-flour mixture. And now add the egg whites: Stir in 1/3 of them, fold in another 1/3 of them, then fold in the last third.

4 Smooth the batter into the pan. Bake on the middle oven rack for about 45 minutes. Leave the cake in the pan for 10 minutes, then transfer it to a rack to cool.

5 Chop the semisweet chocolate and melt it in a saucepan over low heat. With a thin spatula or wide knife, spread the chocolate over the top and sides of the cake and scatter the pistachios on top. When the chocolate's dry you can cut the cake into slices and eat it!

Time needed: 1 ½ hours, about half of that time active

Chocolate Chunk Spice Cake
Your friends will never guess the secret ingredient

Makes 24 slices:

4 ounces bittersweet chocolate

4 eggs

1/2 teaspoon cream of tartar

1 cup (2 sticks) unsalted butter, softened

1 cup sugar

1 ⅔ cups flour

1/2 teaspoon salt

1 teaspoon baking powder

1 teaspoon ground cinnamon

2 teaspoons cocoa powder

1/2 cup dry red wine (that's the secret; really!)

1 Finely chop the chocolate using a large, heavy knife. Separate the eggs. In a clean, grease-free bowl, beat the egg whites, adding the cream of tartar when they are foamy, until stiff, and put them in the fridge so that they stay firm.

2 Beat the butter and sugar with an electric mixer until the whole thing is nice and creamy and light.

3 Preheat the oven to 350°F. Butter and flour an 11-inch loaf pan.

4 Now, add the egg yolks to the butter mixture one after the other, mixing them until there's no longer a trace of yellow before adding the next one. In a separate bowl, mix the flour with the salt, baking powder, cinnamon, cocoa, and chopped chocolate. Mix the flour mixture into the butter mixture alternately with the red wine. Stir in one-third of the egg whites; fold in the rest.

5 Pour the batter into the pan, smooth the top, and bake on the middle oven rack for almost 1 hour. Leave the cake briefly in the pan (5 to 10 minutes), then remove it and let it cool on a rack.

Time needed: 30 minutes active, almost 1 hour relaxed

Pound Cake
About as plain and simple as you can get

Makes 24 slices:

1 cup (2 sticks) unsalted butter

5 eggs

1 cup sugar

1 teaspoon vanilla extract

1 ¾ cups flour

1 teaspoon baking powder

1/2 teaspoon salt

Powdered sugar

1 Melt the butter in a saucepan over low heat so that it doesn't brown or scorch. Cool until lukewarm.

2 Preheat the oven to 350°F. Butter an 11-inch loaf pan and coat the pan with flour.

3 Break the eggs into a bowl, add the sugar and vanilla extract, and beat everything with a mixer until it's light, foamy and has increased in volume (about 2 to 3 minutes on medium speed).

4 Mix the flour with the baking powder and salt. Add a bit of the flour mixture into the egg mixture and mix until smooth. Then, mix in the remaining flour mixture alternately with the melted butter, mixing until smooth between additions.

5 Pour the batter into the pan and smooth out the top. Bake the cake on the middle oven rack for about 1 hour. For safety's sake, do the toothpick test (see Tip below) and if necessary bake the cake a little longer.

6 Leave the cake in the pan for 5 to 10 minutes, then turn it out, turn it back over, and let it cool completely on a rack. Before serving, sift a thin layer of powdered sugar over the cake.

Time needed: 1 ½ hours, of which only 30 minutes involves doing something

Variations:

Sweet Lemon Bread
With a mixer, mix 1/2 cup (1 stick) of softened, unsalted butter with 2/3 cup sugar until light and creamy. Then mix in 4 eggs and the grated zest of 2 large lemons. In another bowl, stir together 1 ⅔ cups flour, 3/4 cup cornstarch, 1/2 teaspoon salt, and 1 teaspoon baking powder. Gradually mix the flour mixture into the butter mixture alternately with 2/3 cup milk. Bake in a buttered and floured 11-inch loaf pan at 350°F for about 1 hour. After cooling, combine 1 ⅓ cups powdered sugar and 2 to 3 tablespoons lemon juice until smooth and glossy. Spread it onto the cake and let it dry.

Chocolate Bread
Finely grate or grind 10 ounces of bittersweet chocolate in a food processor (grating disk or metal blade), and mix it with 2 tablespoons cocoa powder. Beat 1 cup (2 sticks) of softened, unsalted butter with 2/3 cup sugar until light and creamy. Then stir in 4 eggs one after the other. In another bowl, stir together 3 ⅓ cups flour, the chocolate mixture, 2 teaspoons baking powder, and 1/2 teaspoon salt. Stir the chocolate-flour mixture into the butter mixture alternately with approximately 1 cup of room-temperature milk. Pour the batter into a buttered and floured 11-inch loaf pan and bake at 350°F for about 1 hour. Optional: After cooling spread the bread with about 8 ounces of melted semisweet chocolate and let it dry before slicing.

Basic Tip

The Toothpick Test

To test most cakes for doneness, insert a toothpick or thin skewer into the cake. If the cake is done, the toothpick should be clean when you pull it out. When you are inserting the toothpick, make sure you stick it into the cake itself, rather than, say, a chocolate chunk, which will not yield a clean result. Also, make sure you insert the toothpick into the middle of the cake—the spot that gets done last. Be careful: For a Bundt cake or similar item, the middle of the cake is not in the middle of the pan. This test doesn't work for some cakes, especially when you are using heavy, dense ingredients.

Zucchini Bread
Eat your vegetables

Makes 20 to 24 slices:

8 ounces zucchini

1 cup blanched almonds

1 orange or lemon

4 eggs

1/2 teaspoon cream of tartar

1 cup brown sugar

Pinch of ground cloves

Pinch of ground allspice

1 teaspoon ground cinnamon

2/3 cup flour

1 teaspoon baking powder

1/2 teaspoon salt

Powdered sugar

1 Wash the zucchini and finely grate it. Finely chop the almonds. Wash the orange or lemon in hot water, dry it, and grate the zest.

2 Preheat the oven to 350°F. Line an 11-inch loaf pan with parchment paper, cutting and/or folding the edges to make it fit.

3 Separate the eggs. In a clean, grease-free bowl, beat the egg whites until they are very stiff, adding the cream of tartar when they are foamy. In another bowl, beat the egg

yolks and the brown sugar until they are nice and foamy and are a light yellow color. In another bowl, stir together the cloves, allspice, cinnamon, flour, baking powder and salt until well blended. With a wooden spoon, stir the flour mixture into the egg yolk mixture along with the zucchini and the almonds. The egg whites come last: Stir in one half, then fold in the other.

4 Pour the batter into the pan and smooth the surface. Bake it for about 50 minutes on the middle oven rack; it should feel firm, but still be moist when it's done. Leave the bread in the pan for 5 to 10 minutes, then invert it onto a cooling rack. Just before serving, dust the cooled bread with powdered sugar.

Time needed: 1 1/4 hours, including 50 minutes of waiting

Pumpkin Pie
Not just good at Thanksgiving

Makes 12 slices:

For the pastry:

1 1/3 cups flour

1 tablespoon sugar

Pinch of salt

1/2 cup (1 stick) cold unsalted butter

1 to 2 tablespoons cold water

For the filling:

2 cans pumpkin (15 ounces)

4 eggs

1 cup sour cream

1 cup sugar

2 teaspoons grated lemon zest

1 teaspoon ground cinnamon

1/2 teaspoon ground nutmeg

Pinch of ground cloves

1/2 teaspoon salt

Whipped cream

1 For the pastry: Put the flour, sugar, and salt in a food processor and pulse to mix the ingredients. Cut the butter into small pieces, add it to the machine, and pulse 25 to 40 times until the mixture is the texture of cornmeal. Add the cold water and turn the machine on and off several times until it almost comes together in a ball. Remove the dough and press it into a disk. With a rolling pin, roll the pastry between 2 layers of plastic wrap into a circle that's 1 inch bigger than the diameter of the pan. Carefully transfer the pastry to a 10- or 11-inch pie pan, forming an edge approximately 3/4-inch high. Trim the edges with a small knife and patch up any holes in the pastry. Chill the pastry in the pan for about 1 hour.

2 Make the filling: Mix the pumpkin with the eggs, sour cream, sugar, lemon zest, cinnamon, nutmeg, cloves, and salt. Everything should be nice and smooth.

3 Preheat the oven to 400°F. Pour the pumpkin mixture into the pastry, smooth the top, and bake the pie on the lowest rack of the oven for about 1 hour, until the filling has set and browned. Let the pie cool, but serve it while it is very fresh accompanied by whipped cream.

Time needed: 3 hours, but only 40 minutes is active

Carrot Cake Squares
Irresistible

Makes 20 to 24 squares:

For the batter:

1 pound carrots

2 cups pecan (or walnut) halves or pieces

1 2/3 cups whole-wheat flour

2 teaspoons baking soda

2 teaspoons ground cinnamon

1 cup raisins

1 1/3 cups brown sugar

4 eggs

1 cup vegetable oil

Cream Cheese Frosting (see Tip below)

1 Peel and grate the carrots. Finely chop the nuts. Mix the flour with the baking soda, cinnamon, raisins, and sugar, then stir in the carrots and nuts.

2 Preheat the oven to 350°F. Butter the baking pan.

3 In a bowl, beat the eggs until foamy, then gradually beat in the oil. Mix the egg mixture with the carrot mixture and pour it into the baking pan, smoothing the surface. Place the pan on the middle oven rack and bake for 40 to 50 minutes, until the cake is firm but still moist. Let the cake cool in the pan.

4 Make the Cream Cheese Frosting and spread it on the cake. Cut the cake into squares.

Time needed: 1 hour 20 minutes, 50 minutes of which is active

Swiss-Style Carrot Cake
Jazzed up with a little kirsch

Makes 16 slices:

2 cups almonds

8 ounces small carrots

Grated zest of 1 large lemon

1 teaspoon lemon juice

2 tablespoons kirsch (cherry brandy, optional)

1/3 cup flour

2 teaspoons baking powder

1/4 teaspoon salt

6 eggs

3/4 teaspoon cream of tartar

2/3 cup sugar

Cream Cheese Frosting (see Tip below)

Marzipan carrots (optional, see page 23)

1 In a food processor (metal blade), process the almonds until they are finely ground. Transfer them to a bowl. Fit the food processor with the fine grating disk, if desired. Peel, trim, and very finely grate the carrots (you can grate the carrots in the food processor or with a manual grater). Mix the grated carrots with the lemon zest, lemon juice, and kirsch, if using.

2 Preheat the oven to 350°F. Butter and flour a 10- or 11-inch springform pan.

3 In a bowl, mix the ground almonds, flour, baking powder, and salt. Separate the eggs. In a clean, grease-free bowl, beat the egg whites until stiff, adding the cream of tartar when the egg whites are foamy, and

gradually sprinkling in the sugar when the egg whites have reached soft peaks. Fold the egg yolks into the egg white mixture one after the other. Heap the carrots and flour mixture on top of the batter and carefully mix everything using a hand whisk.

4 Pour the batter into the pan and bake it on the middle oven rack for about 40 minutes. Don't forget to test for doneness with a toothpick (see Tip, page 38) Leave the cake in the pan for 5 to 10 minutes, then remove the pan sides and let the cake cool completely on a rack.

5 Make the frosting and spread it onto the cooled cake. Garnish with marzipan carrots, if you like.

Time needed: 1 1/4 hours, including 35 minutes active

Basic Tip:

Cream Cheese Frosting

With a mixer, beat the 8 ounces of softened cream cheese, 1/2 cup powdered sugar, 6 tablespoons (3/4 stick) softened, unsalted butter, and 1/2 teaspoon vanilla extract until smooth.

Chocolate-Pine Nut Cake
Almost like candy

Makes 12 slices:

1 cup (2 sticks) unsalted butter

6 ounces bittersweet chocolate

6 eggs

3/4 teaspoon cream of tartar

1/2 cup sugar

Grated zest of 1 lemon

1/2 cup pine nuts

2 tablespoons cornstarch

1/4 teaspoon salt

Powdered sugar and cocoa

1 Cut the butter and chocolate into small pieces and melt them it in a saucepan over low heat. Cool.

2 Separate the eggs. In a clean, grease-free bowl, beat the egg whites until they are nice and stiff, adding the cream of tartar when the egg whites are foamy. Refrigerate the whites.

3 Put the egg yolks in another bowl. Add the sugar and lemon zest and beat the mixture until it is it is foamy and light yellow in color (about 2 minutes on medium speed). Gradually stir in the butter-chocolate mixture and the pine nuts.

4 Preheat the oven to 350°F. Butter and flour a 10- or 11-inch springform pan. Mix together the cornstarch and salt. Put the egg white mixture on top of the chocolate mixture, and sift the cornstarch mixture over the top. Gently mix everything together with a hand whisk.

5 Pour the batter into the pan and bake it on the middle oven rack for about 45 minutes, until slightly firm to the touch. Leave the cake in the pan for 5 to 10 minutes, transfer it to a rack. Cool completely. Garnish the cake with powdered sugar and cocoa, sifting them over the cake in a decorative pattern.

Time needed: 35 minutes active, 45 minutes of lazy time

Linzertorte
Good all week

Makes 10 to 12 slices:

3 cups sliced almonds

1 ⅓ cups flour

2/3 cup sugar

1/2 teaspoon salt

1 heaping teaspoon ground cinnamon

Pinch of ground cloves

Grated zest of 1/2 lemon

1 cup (2 sticks) cold unsalted butter

4 egg yolks

3/4 cup raspberry jam

1 Put 2 ½ cups of the almonds in a food processor (metal blade) and run the machine until the almonds are finely ground. Add the flour, sugar, salt, cinnamon, cloves, and lemon zest and run the machine briefly to blend the ingredients. Cut the butter into cubes and add it to the food processor. Pulse the mixture about 30 times, until the ingredients look evenly crumbly. Add 3 of the egg yolks and pulse the machine until the ingredients just start to come together. You may have to add just a bit of ice water to make everything stick. Form the dough into a disk, wrap it in plastic wrap, and chill it for at least 30 minutes.

2 Preheat the oven to 350°F. Cut off two-thirds of the dough, put it in a 10- or 11-inch springform pan, and push it out in all directions using your fingers into an even layer. You can make it a bit thicker at the edge, but not much.

3 Stir the jam until smooth and spread it over the dough. Roll out the remaining dough on a lightly floured work surface until it is about 1/8 inch thick. Use a knife to cut it into strips about 1/2 inch wide. Count the number of strips that you have, then arrange half of them on top of the jam, evenly spaced and parallel to each other. Lay the remaining strips perpendicular to the first ones to create a lattice.

4 Lightly beat the remaining egg yolk with a little water and brush it onto the pastry lattice. Bake the Linzertorte on the middle oven rack for about 45 minutes. After half that time has passed, sprinkle the remaining 1/2 cup almonds on top. Cool.

Time needed: 1 ¾ hours, including 35 minutes doing something

Honey Cake
Super simple

Makes 24 slices:

4 lemons

6 tablespoons olive oil

1/4 cup (1/2 stick) unsalted butter

3/4 cup honey

2 ⅓ cups flour

3 teaspoons baking powder

1 ⅔ cups semolina (health foods store)

1/2 teaspoon ground nutmeg

1/2 teaspoon salt

2 cups milk

6 egg whites

1/2 teaspoon cream of tartar

1/4 cup sesame seeds

1 Wash the lemons in hot water, dry them, and finely grate the zest of 2 of the lemons. Squeeze the juice from all 4 of them. In a saucepan, combine the oil, butter, and 1/2 of the honey and heat over medium-low heat, stirring, until the mixture is smooth; transfer to a bowl. In another bowl, mix the flour, baking powder, semolina, nutmeg, and salt.

2 Preheat the oven to 400°F. Line a jellyroll pan with parchment paper.

3 Set aside 1/2 cup of the lemon juice, then stir the rest into the warm honey mixture along with the lemon zest and the milk. Stir in the flour mixture. In a clean, grease-free bowl, beat the egg whites until stiff, adding the cream of tartar when the egg whites are foamy. Fold the beaten egg whites into the batter with a hand whisk.

4 Smooth the batter in the pan, sprinkle it with the sesame seeds, and bake it on the middle oven rack for 25 to 30 minutes. Do the toothpick test to check for doneness (see Tip on page 38). Mix together the remaining honey and lemon juice and spread the mixture over the cake while it is still hot, then cool it completely. Let the cake stand overnight, lightly covered, before eating.

Walnut Tart
With 2 crusts

Makes 16 slices:

For the pastry:

2 ⅓ cups flour

6 tablespoons powdered sugar

Pinch of salt

3/4 cup (1 ¼ sticks) cold unsalted butter

1 egg

For the filling:

3 cups walnut halves or pieces

1 cup sugar

1 ¼ cups whipping cream

2 tablespoons honey

Grated zest of 1 lemon

1 tablespoon lemon juice

1 egg yolk

1 tablespoon milk

1 For the pastry: Put the flour, sugar, and salt in a food processor (metal blade) and pulse to mix the ingredients. Cut the butter into small pieces, add it to the machine, and pulse 25 to 40 times until the mixture is the texture of cornmeal. Add the egg and turn the machine on and off several times until it almost comes together in a ball—you may

need to add a teaspoon or two of ice water to help things along. Remove the dough and press it into a disk. Wrap the disk in plastic wrap and chill it for at least 1 hour.

2 For the filling: Chop the walnuts. Pour the sugar into a saucepan and turn on the heat to high. Wait until the sugar starts to turn liquid around the edge, then reduce the heat a bit and stir well with a wooden spoon until the sugar is melted and light brown in color. Pour in the cream, honey, and lemon juice and keep stirring until the sugar melts and the mixture becomes thick. Stir in the nuts, and lemon zest and let the mixture cool.

3 Preheat the oven to 350°F. Cut off two-thirds of the pastry and roll it out between two layers of plastic wrap into a circle that is 1 inch bigger than the diameter of a 10-inch or 11-inch tart or springform pan. Carefully transfer the pastry to the pan. Roll out the rest of the pastry to a thin circle that is about the diameter of the pan.

4 Spoon the nut mixture into the pastry-lined pan. Carefully transfer the top crust onto the filling. Fold the bottom crust over the top crust, trimming off the excess pastry, and press the pastry edges together. Lightly beat the egg yolk with the milk and brush it onto the top crust. Bake on the middle oven rack for about 45 minutes, until the crust is golden brown. Cool and wrap in aluminum foil. It's best served the next day at room temperature.

Yeast Braid
A hit at breakfast

Makes 20 slices:

3 ⅓ cups flour

1/2 teaspoon salt

1/3 cup sugar

1 tablespoon rapid-rise yeast

1/2 cup milk

1/2 cup slivered almonds (optional)

1/2 cup (1 stick) unsalted butter, softened

1 egg (room temp)

3 egg yolks (room temp)

Grated zest of 1 lemon

1 tablespoon melted butter

1-2 tablespoons coarse sugar

1 Put the flour, salt, and sugar in the bowl of a food processor (metal blade or dough blade) and pulse the machine to combine them. Add the yeast and pulse again. Heat the milk to about 120°F (check it with an instant-read thermometer). Roughly chop the almonds, if using.

2 Add the butter, egg, egg yolks, lemon zest, and milk to the machine and process until the ingredients come together in a ball. Set the timer for 60 seconds and run the machine for the duration—this will knead the dough. Dump the dough onto a floured work surface and, with your hands, knead in the almonds. Transfer the dough to a lightly oiled bowl, put it in a warm place, cover it with a dishtowel, and let it rest in peace for about 1 to 1 ½ hours. It should approximately double in size during that time.

3 Line a baking sheet with parchment paper and sprinkle a work surface with flour. Put the dough on the work surface, lightly knead it with your hands, and divide it into 3 equal pieces. Roll each dough piece into a long cylinder that is about 1 ½ inches thick.

4 Lay the 3 pieces of dough next to each other on the baking sheet and press the ends together on one side. Now—think back to when you were a kid and you (or your sister) used to braid your (or her) hair. Move the left

dough piece over the middle one, then the right one, then the left one again. Remember? When the braid is finished, press the other ends together, too. Cover the braid with a dishtowel and let it rise for another 30 minutes.

5 Preheat the oven to 350°F. Brush the braid with melted butter, sprinkle it with coarse sugar, and bake it on the middle rack of the oven for about 45 minutes until it has risen beautifully and browned. Let it cool. Eat the bread while very fresh!

Time needed: 2 ¼ hours, including only 35 minutes with something to do

Variation:

Filled Yeast Braid

Grind 2 ½ cups of nuts in a food processor (or use about 3 ounces of poppy seeds). Add 3 tablespoons of sugar, 1/4 cup of whipping cream, a pinch of ground cinnamon, and 1 egg, and process until the mixture is smooth. After making the dough rolls above, press each one flat and spoon 1/3 of the filling down the length of each dough piece. Pull the dough over the filling to enclose it and roll the strand again until it is round in shape. Braid and bake the bread as described above.

Cinnamon-Pecan Rolls
Morning nirvana

Makes 16 rolls:

For the dough:

1/2 cup (1 stick) unsalted butter

2/3 cup milk

2 ⅔ cups flour

1/4 cup sugar

1/2 teaspoon salt

1 tablespoon rapid-rise yeast

1 teaspoon vanilla extract

For the filling:

2/3 cup brown sugar

2 teaspoons ground cinnamon

Grated zest of 1/2 lemon

1 cup pecans or walnuts

1/2 cup chopped raisins or dried currants (optional)

Pinch of salt

1/4 cup (1/2 stick) unsalted butter

2 tablespoons apple jelly or 1 recipe Cream Cheese Frosting, (see Tip on page 41)

1 Make the dough: In a saucepan, heat the butter and the milk over low heat until the butter is melted. Remove from the heat and cool until it is about 120°F (check it with an instant-read thermometer).

2 In a food processor (metal blade or dough blade), combine the flour, sugar, and salt and pulse to combine the ingredients. Add the yeast and pulse to combine. Add the vanilla extract to the butter-milk mixture, then, while the machine is running, pour it into the flour mixture. Process the ingredients until they just come together. Set your timer for 45 seconds and let the machine run for the duration to knead the dough.

3 Transfer the dough to an oiled bowl, cover the bowl with a dishtowel, and let it rise in a warm, draft-free place for about 1 to 1 ½ hours, until the dough expands to about twice its size.

4 Make the filling: Mix together the brown sugar, cinnamon, lemon zest, pecans or walnuts, raisins or currants (if you want), and salt. Melt the butter in a saucepan and remove it from the heat.

5 Butter a 10- or 11-inch pie or springform pan. Punch down the dough and roll it out with a rolling pin on a floured work surface into a rectangle about 1/4 inch thick. Brush the dough with the melted butter. Sprinkle the nut mixture on top of the butter, leaving a small border around the edges. Starting at the long side, roll up the dough around the filling and pinch together the seams. Cut the roll into slices about 1 inch thick. Press the slices next to each other into the pan with the cut surfaces facing up. Let the rolls rise for another 30 to 40 minutes. Preheat the oven to 350°F.

6 Bake the rolls on the middle oven rack for 45 minutes, until they have risen, browned, and smell so good you can hardly wait to bite into one. If desired, carefully warm the jelly in a saucepan until melted. Brush the melted jelly onto the rolls while still warm and let them cool slightly before eating. This will give the rolls a glossy finish. Or, cool the rolls and then spread with cream cheese frosting.

 45

Time needed: 3 hours, including approximately 45 minutes active

Lemon Bars
A two-tiered tangy treat

Makes 9 to 12 bars:

For the bottom layer:

1 cup flour

1/4 teaspoon salt

1/4 cup powdered sugar

1 tablespoon dark brown sugar

Grated zest of 1 lemon

1/2 cup (1 stick) cold unsalted butter

For the top layer:

3 eggs

1 1/2 cups sugar

Pinch of salt

1/2 cup fresh lemon juice

1 tablespoon flour

Powdered sugar

1 Preheat the oven to 350°F. Make the bottom layer: Place the flour, salt, and both kinds of sugar in the bowl of a food processor (metal blade). Pulse the machine to blend the ingredients. Cut the butter into pieces. Spread the butter pieces around on top of the flour mixture and pulse several times until the butter is reduced to pea-sized pieces. Press this mixture into an 8-inch square pan with your fingers, trying to get everything even,

and bake on the middle oven rack for 10 minutes. Remove the pan from the oven.

2 Make the top layer: Wipe out the bowl of the food processor, then add the eggs. Pulse the machine to break up the yolks. Add the sugar, salt, and lemon juice, and process for 10 seconds. Sprinkle the flour over the egg mixture and process for 4 seconds.

3 Pour the lemon-egg mixture into the pan over the bottom layer and return it to the oven. Bake for approximately 45 to 50 minutes. The top should be a dark, golden brown and the middle of the dish should be fairly firm when you jiggle the pan.

4 Remove the pan from the oven and cool on a rack for 15 minutes. Sprinkle powdered sugar through a sieve or sifter over the top of the lemon bars. Let everything cool completely before cutting into bars.

Almond-Butter Yeast Cake
Nicely old fashioned

Makes 20 slices:

For the batter:

1/2 cup milk

2 2/3 cups flour

3 tablespoons sugar

1/2 teaspoon salt

1 tablespoon rapid-rise yeast

1/4 cup (1/2 stick) unsalted butter, softened

2 eggs (room temperature)

Grated zest of 1 lemon

For the topping:

5 tablespoons coarse sugar (see Tip, page 62)

1-2 teaspoons ground cinnamon

1/2 cup (1 stick) unsalted butter

1 cup chopped almonds

1 Make the batter: Heat the milk in a saucepan to 120°F (check it with an instant-read thermometer). In a food processor (metal blade or dough blade), combine the flour, sugar, and salt, then pulse the machine

to combine the ingredients. Add the yeast and pulse to combine. Add the butter, eggs, milk, and lemon zest, and process until the dough comes together in a ball. Let the machine run for 60 more seconds to knead the dough.

2 Transfer the dough to a lightly oiled bowl and let it stand, covered with a dishtowel, in a warm place for about 1 to 1 1/2 hours until it has approximately doubled in size.

3 Butter a baking sheet, put the dough on it, and evenly roll the dough out with a floured rolling pin to the edges of the pan. Preheat the oven to 400°F.

4 Make the topping: Mix together the sugar and cinnamon. Cut the butter into small cubes. Use your fingers to press little dents into the rolled-out dough. Put a cube of butter into each dent. Sprinkle the almonds and cinnamon-sugar over the surface of the dough.

5 Bake the butter cake on the middle oven rack for approximately 25 minutes, until it's nice and brown. Let it cool and eat it immediately!

Time needed: 2 1/2 hours, but only about 30 minutes in action

Kugelhopf
Perfect for tea time

Makes 25 slices:

1/2 cup raisins

2 tablespoons rum or apple juice

1 cup blanched almonds or walnuts

1/2 cup milk

1/2 cup (1 stick) unsalted butter

3 ⅓ cups flour

2/3 cup sugar

1/2 teaspoon salt

1 tablespoon rapid-rise yeast

1 egg (room temperature)

4 egg yolks (room temperature)

1 teaspoon vanilla extract

2 teaspoons grated lemon zest

Powdered sugar

1 Mix the raisins with the rum and set aside. Chop the almonds into moderately fine pieces. Heat the milk with the butter in a saucepan until the butter melts. Let the mixture cool until it is about 120°F. In a large bowl, mix the flour with the sugar and salt. Add the yeast and stir well. Make a well in the middle of the bowl.

2 Put the egg and egg yolks, vanilla, lemon zest, raisins, and almonds into the well, then pour in the milk-butter mixture. With a

wooden spoon, mix everything together. The dough should be soft but still pull away from the sides of the bowl. Dump the dough onto a floured work surface and knead it with your hands for 5 to 10 more minutes.

3 Grease a Bundt pan with butter, being sure to get the butter into all of the pan's grooves. Put the dough in the pan, spreading it out evenly. Cover the pan with a dishtowel, put it in a warm place, and leave it alone for 2 to 3 hours. The dough will rise just a little, but will rise more while it bakes.

4 Preheat the oven to 350°F. Bake on the middle oven rack for about 1 hour, until it has risen and browned. If the cake starts to get too brown, cover it with aluminum foil. After baking, let the cake stand briefly, turn it out of the pan and cool it on a rack. Dust with powdered sugar.

Time needed: 1 ½ hours not including standing time

Poppy Seed Squares
Last awhile

Makes 20 squares:

For the dough:

6 ounces cream cheese, softened

6 tablespoons vegetable oil

1 egg

2 tablespoons sugar

Grated zest of 1 lemon

2 cups flour

3 teaspoons baking powder

1/2 teaspoon salt

For the topping:

6 eggs

3/4 teaspoon cream of tartar

1 cup (2 sticks) unsalted butter, softened

1 teaspoon vanilla extract

1 ⅔ cups honey

Pinch of ground cinnamon

1 ½ cups almonds, ground

3 ounces poppy seeds

1 For the dough, mix the cream cheese, oil, egg, sugar, and lemon zest with an electric mixer until smooth. In another bowl, mix together the flour, baking powder, and salt. Add the flour mixture to the cream cheese mixture and stir it with a wooden spoon. You'll probably need to use your hands, coated with flour, to knead the dough into a uniform texture. Also: If the dough is too dry, you can knead in 1 to 2 tablespoons of water.

2 Preheat the oven to 350°F. Butter an 11-x-7-x 2-inch baking pan, place the dough in it, and push it out evenly with your fingers. Slide the pan onto the middle rack of the oven and bake for 10 minutes.

3 Make the topping: Separate the eggs. In a clean, grease-free bowl, and with clean beaters, beat the egg whites until they are very stiff, adding the cream of tartar when the egg whites are foamy. In another bowl, mix the butter until very creamy. Add the egg yolks one by one, mixing between additions. Stir in the vanilla, honey, cinnamon, almonds, and poppy seeds. Fold in the egg white mixture.

4 Reduce the oven temperature to 325°F. Take the baking pan out of the oven and spread the poppy seed mixture on the dough. Bake the whole thing for 30 to 40 minutes, until the topping feels firm. Cool before cutting into squares.

47

Banana Nut Bread
Jennifer's grandmother's recipe

Makes 16 slices:

1/2 cup unsalted butter, softened

1 cup sugar

3 ripe bananas

2 eggs, beaten well

2 cups flour

1 teaspoon baking soda

1/2 teaspoon salt

1 cup chopped walnuts

Butter or cream cheese

1 Butter a 9-inch loaf pan and coat it with flour. Preheat the oven to 300°F.

2 With a mixer, beat the butter with the sugar. Peel the bananas, mash them well, add them to the butter mixture with the eggs, and blend everything well.

3 In another bowl, mix together the flour, baking soda, salt, and nuts, and add them to the banana mixture. Mix everything well.

4 Pour the batter into the pan and bake for 1 hour, until it starts to pull away from the edges. Let the bread stand in the pan for 5 to 10 minutes, then turn it out onto a rack to cool. To eat, slice the bread thinly and spread with butter or cream cheese.

Time needed: 1 hour, 15 minutes

Honey-Nut Loaf
Good for Breakfast

Makes 24 to 28 slices:

1 cup hazelnuts or almonds

3/4 cup honey

5 tablespoons brown sugar

3 ⅓ cups flour (or more if necessary)

2 teaspoons baking powder

1 teaspoon ground cinnamon

1/8 teaspoon ground cloves

Grated zest of 1 large lemon

1 egg

About 1 cup buttermilk

1 tablespoons brandy or other spirits

(whatever you have in the pantry, but it's also fine without)

1 Put the nuts in a food processor (metal blade) and process until they are finely ground. Warm the honey and the sugar in a saucepan, but don't make it too hot or the honey will burn. Stir until the sugar is melted. Remove the pan from the heat, transfer it to a bowl, and let the mixture cool.

2 In another bowl, stir together the flour, baking powder, cinnamon, cloves, ground almonds, and lemon zest. Preheat the oven to 350°F. Line an 11-inch loaf pan with parchment paper. To do so, cut into the sides of the paper using scissors so the paper will lie smoothly in the pan.

3 Add the egg, buttermilk, and brandy to the honey mixture and stir with a wooden spoon until smooth. Stir in the flour mixture. The result will be a thick dough that will tear roughly from the spoon. If it's too thick, add more buttermilk. Too thin? Add a bit of flour.

4 Put the dough in the pan, smooth the surface, and bake it on the middle oven rack for about 1 hour. Do the toothpick test (see Tip on page 38). Leave the cake in the pan briefly, then turn it out and cool it on a rack.

Time needed: 1 ½ hours, including 30 minutes active

Mabel's Streusel Coffee Cake
A favorite from one of Jen's distant relative

Makes 12 slices:

For the batter:

3/4 cup sugar

1 ½ cups flour

1 tablespoon baking powder

1/4 teaspoon salt

3/4 cup (1 ½ sticks) cold unsalted butter

1 egg

1/2 cup milk

1/2 teaspoon vanilla extract

For the topping:

2 tablespoons unsalted butter

1/2 cup brown sugar

1 tablespoon flour

2 teaspoons ground cinnamon

1/2 cup chopped pecans (only if you want)

1 Preheat the oven to 375°F. Suspend a mesh sieve over a bowl, then pour in the sugar, flour, baking powder, and salt. Sift the ingredients into the bowl and mix well.

2 Cut the butter into small pieces. With a fork or your fingers, blend the butter into the flour mixture until it looks like cornmeal.

3 In a small bowl, beat the egg slightly. Add the milk and vanilla, and mix well. Add the egg mixture to the flour mixture and mix well with a wooden spoon—the batter will be stiff.

4 Next, make the topping: Melt the butter in a small saucepan and remove it from the heat. Mix the remaining topping ingredients together in a bowl. Pour in the butter and mix until the ingredients are well blended.

5 Butter an 8-inch square pan. Spread half of the batter in the pan, and sprinkle with half of the topping. Carefully spread the remaining batter on top, then sprinkle the remaining topping on the very top. Bake for about 30 minutes until it is done—do the toothpick test (see Tip on page 38).

Tip

Tip: If you can't find coarse sugar in your supermarket's baking section, buy some sugar cubes instead. Crush a few sugar cubes with a food processor to make your own coarse sugar. Or, put the cubes in a locking plastic bag and pound on them with a rolling pin until they are the right texture.

Birthday Cake
Impress your friends

This is the cake that we all dreamed of but never got. Make it, and you'll really make someone's day.

Makes 16 slices:

For the batter:

1/3 cup cornstarch

2/3 cup flour

2 teaspoons baking powder

1/4 teaspoon salt

6 egg whites

3/4 teaspoon cream of tartar

1 cup sugar

3 egg yolks

1 teaspoon vanilla extract

For the frosting:

1/4 cup (1/2 stick) unsalted butter, softened

1 ⅔ cups powdered sugar

2 to 3 tablespoons milk or cream (Or, make lemon frosting using fresh lemon juice)

Colored sprinkles or other birthday cake decorations, colored birthday candles

1 Preheat the oven to 325°F. Line the bottom of a 10- or 11-inch springform pan with parchment paper (see Aunt Betty's Baking Bits, page 32). Stir together the cornstarch, flour, baking powder, and salt. Sift the mixture three times (we know, sifting's a pain, but it really helps to make the cake nice and light).

2 In a clean, grease-free bowl, beat the egg whites until they stand in stiff peaks and the mixture becomes glossy. While beating, add the cream of tartar when the egg whites become foamy. Then, gradually add the sugar when the egg whites reach soft peaks.

3 With a hand whisk, mix the egg yolks into the egg white mixture one after the other, adding the vanilla extract with the last one. Sift the flour mixture over the egg mixture and carefully fold it in using a hand whisk. Pour the batter into the pan and bake the cake on the middle oven rack for 40 to 50 minutes (remember to do the toothpick test—see Tip on page 38).

4 Turn off the oven, leave the oven door ajar, and let the cake stand for 15 minutes. With the tip of a small knife, loosen the cake edges from the pan. Release the springform edge, turn the cake out onto a rack, remove the bottom of the pan, and pull off the parchment paper. Let the cake cool completely before frosting.

5 Make the frosting: Mix the butter with an electric mixer until creamy, then gradually sprinkle in the powdered sugar while continuing to beat. Beat in the milk or cream until the frosting is a spreadable consistency, about 5 minutes on medium speed should do it.

6 Generously spread the frosting onto the cooled cake. Decorate the cake as desired, and let the frosting set for up to 2 hours. Don't forget the candles!

Time needed: 1 ½ hours, including about 35 minutes active, plus 2 hours drying time.

Variations:

Spring or Summer Birthday Cake

Omit the frosting. Thickly cover the cake with whipped cream and decorate it with fresh berries and fresh mint leaves.

Fall or Winter Birthday Cake

Omit the frosting. Melt 6 ounces of milk chocolate and 1 tablespoon of butter in 1 cup of whipping cream. Cool the mixture until it starts to thicken. Pour the mixture over the cake, spreading it over the top and letting it trickle down the sides. Decorate the cake with shaved chocolate to resemble tree leaves and bark. In winter, dust the cake with powdered sugar (sprinkled through a mesh sieve) to resemble snow.

Cheesecake
Always in style

Makes 12 slices:

For the crust:

1 ½ cups flour

1/4 teaspoon baking powder

1/2 teaspoon salt

1/4 cup sugar

1/2 cup (1 stick) cold unsalted butter

1 egg yolk

1-2 tablespoons sour cream or plain yogurt

For the filling:

1/2 cup (1 stick) unsalted butter

5 eggs

16 ounces cream cheese, softened

5 tablespoons sugar

1 cup milk

Grated zest and juice of 1 large lemon

2/3 cup flour

1/2 teaspoon baking powder

1 tablespoon kirsch or other liqueur, optional

1/2 teaspoon cream of tartar

1 First make the crust: Put the flour, baking powder, salt, and sugar in a food processor (metal blade) and pulse to combine. Cut the butter into pieces, add it to the machine, and pulse it 25 to 30 times until the mixture is crumbly. Add the egg yolk and sour cream and pulse until the dough is smooth (you may need to add a touch of ice water in order to coax the ingredients together). Shape the dough into a disk, wrap it in plastic wrap, and chill it for about 1 hour.

2 Preheat the oven to 350°F. Roll out the dough between two sheets of plastic wrap until it is a circle about 1 ½ inches larger than the diameter of the pan. Carefully transfer the dough to a 10- or 11-inch springform pan, leaving about a 1-inch-high edge all around. Use a paring knife to trim the edge of the dough so that it is even.

3 Line the dough with a piece of parchment paper and a layer of pie weights or dried beans and bake it on the middle oven rack for 15 minutes.

4 Make the filling: Melt the butter in a saucepan over low heat and let it cool. Separate the eggs. With a mixer, mix the cream cheese until smooth. Add the melted butter, sugar, milk, and egg yolks, and mix well. Mix in the lemon zest, lemon juice, flour, and baking powder. Add the liqueur now, if you're using it.

5 In a clean, grease-free bowl with clean beaters, beat the egg whites until they stand in stiff peaks, adding the cream of tartar when the whites get foamy. Stir 1/3 of the egg white mixture into the cream cheese mixture to lighten it, then fold in the rest. Pour the filling into the prebaked crust and smooth the top. Bake the cheesecake for 45 to 60 minutes until the filling is set and slightly browned.

6 Leave the cake briefly in the pan, then release the edge of the springform and let the cake cool completely. After cooling, refrigerate the cheesecake for a couple of hours before eating it.

Time needed: 1 ¾ hours, including 45 minutes active

New York Cheesecake
Rich and dense

Makes 12 slices:

For the crust:

1/2 cup (1 stick) unsalted butter

8 ounces graham crackers

Pinch of ground cinnamon

1 tablespoon sugar

1/2 teaspoon vanilla extract

For the filling:

28 ounces cream cheese, softened

1 cup sugar

4 eggs

2 tablespoons lemon juice

1 cup sour cream

1 tablespoon sugar

1/2 teaspoon vanilla extract

1 Make the crust: Melt the butter and let it cool. Coarsely break the graham crackers and process them in a food processor (metal blade) until finely ground.

2 Mix the butter with the graham cracker crumbs, cinnamon, sugar, and vanilla, and press the mixture into an ungreased 10- or 11-inch springform pan to make an even bottom crust.

3 teaspoons grated lemon zest

6 tablespoons lemon juice

1/4 teaspoon cream of tartar

Powdered sugar

1 With a mixer, mix the butter with the sugar and ricotta until light and creamy. Separate the eggs and mix the egg yolks into the ricotta mixture one after the other. In another bowl, stir together the flour, baking powder, and salt. Mix the flour mixture into the ricotta mixture; then mix in the lemon zest and juice.

2 Preheat the oven to 350°F. Coat a 10- or 11-inch springform pan with butter.

3 In a clean, grease-free bowl and with clean beaters, beat the egg whites until stiff, sprinkling in the cream of tartar when the egg whites get foamy. Carefully fold the egg whites into the ricotta mixture. Pour the batter into the pan, then place on the middle oven rack and bake for about 45 minutes. Let the cake remain in the pan for 10 minutes. Release the sides of the pan and let the cake cool completely on a cooling rack. Dust the cake with powdered sugar before serving.

Time needed: 1 hour 10 minutes, including 25 minutes doing something

Crustless Cheesecake
Studded with raisins

Makes 12 slices:

1/2 cup raisins

1 tablespoon rum

4 eggs

1/2 teaspoon cream of tartar

2 pounds cream cheese, softened

1 cup sugar

1/2 teaspoon vanilla extract

Grated zest and juice of 1 large lemon

1 cup flour

2 teaspoons baking powder

Plain bread crumbs

Powdered sugar

3 Preheat the oven to 300°F. Make the filling: With a mixer, mix the cream cheese with the sugar until blended. Add the eggs one at a time, mixing until incorporated. Mix in the lemon juice. Pour the mixture over the crust and smooth the top. Bake the cheesecake on the middle oven rack for about 1 hour.

4 Mix the sour cream with the sugar and vanilla and spread it onto the cheesecake filling. Bake for another 10 minutes. Pull the cheesecake out of the oven and let it stand for 5 to 10 minutes. Let the cake cool completely on a rack, then chill it for at least 2 hours before serving.

Time needed: 1 ¾ hours, including 30 minutes active

Lemon Ricotta Cake
Bottomless

Makes 12 slices:

1/2 cup (1 stick) unsalted butter, softened

2/3 cup sugar

8 ounces ricotta cheese

3 eggs

1 ⅔ cups flour

1 ½ teaspoons baking powder

1/2 teaspoon salt

1 Soak the raisins in the rum. Separate the eggs. In a clean, grease-free bowl, beat the egg whites until stiff, adding the cream of tartar when the egg whites turn foamy, and put them in the fridge. Thoroughly butter a 10- or 11-inch springform pan and sprinkle it with bread crumbs. Preheat the oven to 350°F.

2 Beat the cream cheese with the sugar until smooth. Mix in the egg yolks one at a time, adding the vanilla extract with the last one. Mix in the lemon zest and juice. Mix in the raisins.

3 Pour the egg whites onto the cream cheese mixture; sprinkle the flour mixed with the baking powder over that. Gently fold everything together using a hand whisk. Pour the batter into the pan.

4 Bake the cake on the middle oven rack for at least 1 hour until the filling just barely moves when you jiggle the pan. Let the cake cool in the pan, release the edge of the springform, and chill it for at least 2 hours. Dust it with powdered sugar before eating.

Time needed: 1 hour 20 minutes, including only 20 minutes doing something

Fresh& fruit

Want a masterpiece in minutes? Just add fruit.

y

Do you like your cakes with a little more juice? Would you like some vitamins with your pie? You must be the type that likes fruity desserts. With apples, pears, and pineapples. With cherries, strawberries, and raspberries. With apricots, peaches, plums, and nectarines. With lemons, mangos, and bananas. Need we go on? If you're not salivating by now, you should open to a different chapter.

Fresh fruits in season are a great addition to desserts. But these days there are some great canned and frozen fruits on the market, too. Add a piecrust that you made last week and froze, or a sheet of frozen puff pastry, and you can make a masterpiece in minutes!

Making Hot Chocolate

We are grateful to you wonderful modern café owners. Thank you for taking the trouble to make a good cup of cappuccino and a smooth, full-bodied cup of drip. Unfortunately, your hot chocolate often comes from a readymade powder, and is topped off with whipped cream from a can. It doesn't have to be that way. Look at what we make when we crave a smooth, creamy mouthful of happiness:

1 For one cup of hot chocolate, finely chop 2 to 3 ounces of bittersweet chocolate and stir it with 2 tablespoons hot milk in a warmed cup.

2 Then, bring about 1 cup of milk to a boil with a tiny pinch of salt (yes salt—it really brings out the flavor of the chocolate and you'll never notice it's there) and beat it vigorously with a whisk until foamy.

3 Pour the foamy milk into the cup and gently stir it with the chocolate until smooth. Sugar and whipped cream? Only if you need it.

Aunt Betty's Baking Bits

Dear Aunt Betty:
I always serve whipped cream with my fruity desserts, but it's getting a little tiresome. Are there other garnishes that I could use to add interest to my desserts?

Bored in Boulder

Dear Bored:
Whipped cream and strawberries do go together like Snow White and the Seven Dwarfs. But there are some sweet princes who can make fruit tortes taste even more like a fairy tale. For example: A spoonful of mascarpone cheese or crème fraîche sweetened with a bit of sugar and vanilla extract are a new twist on the old whipped cream routine. Add a couple of almonds on top for interest. Or try this: Mix a fruit puree into the whipped cream to give it a little extra color and flavor.

And don't forget vanilla ice cream! It's great when served next to a warm dessert. Or melt it down and serve it as a quick vanilla sauce (AKA crème anglaise to gourmets). But don't stop there—other flavors of ice cream make great garnishes and sauces. Try nut, chocolate, or coffee flavors. Just make sure the flavors are compatible with the dessert you're serving.

Looking for something that's not in the creamy category? Try chopped candied citrus peels or ginger, or fruit compotes, or purees. Again: Be sure that the flavors complement each other. If you're unsure, just try a bite of each and wait to see what your mouth does.

Four Quick Shortcakes

Everyone loves strawberry shortcake. And you can even buy the bases for them already made in the supermarket (look for them in the produce section). Below is a speedy version of strawberry shortcake plus three variations on the theme, using different types of fruit and garnishes. Sliced pound cake or angel food cake can stand in for the shortcake bases.

Quick Strawberry Shortcake
Wash and clean 10 ounces of fresh strawberries and cut them in half. Arrange them on a shortcake base. Cover the strawberries with a layer of fruit glaze (also available in the produce section). Serve with whipped cream.

Quick Raspberry Shortcake
Mix 1/2 of an 8-ounce container of vanilla yogurt and 1/2 cup of mascarpone cheese with 2 tablespoons sugar and spread it onto a shortcake base. Top it with 6 ounces of fresh raspberries (cleaned first!) and sprinkle with powdered sugar.

Quick Exotic Fruit Shortcake
Cut 4 bananas into slices and mix them with 2 tablespoons lemon juice. Beat 1 cup of whipping cream with 2 tablespoons powdered sugar until stiff and mix it with about 1/2 cup diced mango or papaya (you can find prepared mango or papaya spears in jars in the produce section). Arrange the banana slices on a shortcake base and spread the mango whipped cream on top.

Quick Nectarine Shortcake
Beat 1 cup whipping cream with 2 tablespoons powdered sugar and 1 tablespoon grated lemon zest until stiff. Spread the whipped cream over the base. Wash and slice 4 to 6 fresh nectarines and arrange them on top of the whipped cream. Sprinkle with a tablespoon or two of chopped candied ginger.

Eating in Season

The right fruits for seasonal cakes

Fruits for spring cakes:
Strawberries, possibly nectarines and mangoes; some winter or summer fruits may be good too

Fruits for summer cakes:
All berries, cherries, plums, peaches, nectarines, apricots, melons, rhubarb, kiwi

Fruits for fall cakes:
Apples, pears, grapes, figs

Fruits for winter cakes:
Oranges, tangerines, limes, pineapple, passion fruit, and other exotic fruits

Fruits for all cakes:
Apples, lemons, bananas

14 Fruits & their Functions

Fruits have personalities of their own it seems, behaving alternately like a shy child or rebellious teenager. Following is a table showing some of the most commonly used fruits and revealing some of their quirks.

	Bake or not?	Watch out!	What do I make with them?
Apples, pears	Must always be baked	Quickly turn brown; lemon juice and working fast are helpful	Butter cakes, strudels, pies, and turnovers
Apricots, nectarines, peaches	Can be baked	Peel them for fillings (see Tip above)	Tarts, pies, cobblers
Blackberries, strawberries, raspberries	Best not to bake them	When sugared they release a lot of juice. Draining and blotting help, or use fruit that's already ripe and sweet	Shortcakes, tarts, charlottes, roulades, cobblers, use for garnishes
Blueberries	Both	Use only firm fruits for baking	Baked: Muffins, butter cakes, cobblers Raw: Sponge cake, tortes, roulades, tarts
Cherries	Can be baked	Use only firm fruits for baking	Strudel, streusel cakes, pies, sheetcakes
Oranges, lemons	Zests: Bake, use raw; Juices: Both	Wash them well to remove pesticide residue and wax	Butter cakes, sponge cakes, tarts, muffins
Pineapple, kiwis	Better on a cake than in it	Make whipped cream bitter; simmering in syrup first helps reduce bitterness	Upside-down cake (p), fruit tarts (k), choux paste tarts (p & k)

Apple Strudel
A crispy, comforting treat

Plan ahead! The phyllo dough needs to thaw for several hours or overnight before it is ready to use. Raisin fans can scatter 1/2 to 1 cup of raisins over the apples once they're lying on the pastry.

Makes 2 strudels (each with about 10 slices):

For the pastry:

1 package (1 pound) frozen phyllo pastry

About 1/2 cup almonds or hazelnuts

1/2 cup (1 stick) unsalted butter

For the filling:

3 ⅓ pounds tart apples (Granny Smiths are good!)

2-3 teaspoons grated lemon zest

1 tablespoon fresh lemon juice

1/4 cup (1/2 stick) unsalted butter

3-5 tablespoons sugar (depending on how tart the apples are)

1 teaspoon ground cinnamon

1 cup sour cream or crème fraîche

1 Follow the instructions on the package for thawing the pastry. Do not remove it from the box until just before you're ready to use it!

2 In a food processor (metal blade), process the nuts until they're finely ground and set them aside. When you're ready, melt the butter in a small saucepan and set it aside. Line a jellyroll pan (a large, rimmed baking sheet) with parchment paper.

3 Peel, quarter, and core the apples. Cut the apples into thin slices. Toss them in a bowl with the lemon zest and juice. If the apples turn a bit brown while standing, that doesn't matter, because they'll be brown after baking.

4 Now let's talk about the pastry. Phyllo is very delicate, so you'll want to treat it with care. Remove the pastry from the package, unroll it, and lay it flat on a clean countertop. Cover the entire surface of the pastry with plastic wrap—you may have to use a couple of sheets. Now, cover the plastic wrap with a slightly damp dishtowel. This is how the phyllo should remain at all times, unless you are lifting it over to your work surface.

5 Place another clean dishtowel on the work surface and smooth it with your hands. Lift off the towel-plastic wrap cover from the pastry and move just one sheet of it over to the towel-lined work surface. Remember to cover the pastry again! Lightly brush the whisper-thin pastry with melted butter. Now do it again: Uncover the pastry protector, peel off 1 sheet of the pastry, and place it on top of the buttered pastry sheet (line up the edges). After you cover the unused pastry, lightly brush the next pastry layer with melted butter. Repeat this layering and buttering procedure until you have used half of the package of phyllo—you'll use about 8 to 10 sheets.

6 Spread half of the apples on top of the buttered pastry layers, but leave about a 1-inch border all the way around. Sprinkle the apples with half of the ground nuts, sugar, cinnamon, and sour cream (spoon this in dollops over the surface of the apples).

7 Flip all of the pastry edges toward the inside and brush them with butter. Then, lift the towel on the side closest to you. Lift it a little bit more, and the dough will start to roll by itself, lifted by the towel. It should end up on the other side of the towel. You may have to squeeze it a little with your hands in order to encourage it into a tight roll. Using the towel, lift the strudel to the pan and let it roll in. Arrange the roll so that it is seam-side down and brush it with melted butter.

8 Preheat the oven to 375°F. Using the rest of the pastry and filling ingredients, fill and roll the remaining strudel (in other words, repeat steps 5, 6, and 7). Pop the strudels in the oven. They will need about 30 minutes' time on the middle oven rack to become crispy, golden brown, and great smelling. Eat the strudels hot (perhaps with vanilla ice cream!), lukewarm, or cold. In other words, you can enjoy them more than once.

Time needed: 1 ½ hours

Variation:

Cream Cheese-Cherry Strudel

For the filling, beat together 2 tablespoons softened, unsalted butter, 6 tablespoons sugar, 1/2 teaspoon vanilla extract, the grated zest of 1 lemon, and 3 egg yolks (save the whites!) until the mixture is foamy. Stir in 2 pounds of softened cream cheese, which has been mixed with 4 tablespoons of sour cream. In a separate, clean and grease-free bowl, beat 3 egg whites with 3/4 teaspoons of cream of tartar until stiff and fold them into the cream cheese mixture. Drain 2 pounds of frozen cherries (you can also use fresh cherries, washing them and removing the stems and pits). Prepare the phyllo in exactly the same way as for apple strudel (steps 4 and 5 above). Sprinkle the strudels with 2 to 3 tablespoons each of ground almonds, and spread the cream cheese mixture onto them. Scatter the cherries over the top of the cream cheese mixture. Roll up the strudel, transfer it to the pan, and brush it with melted butter. Bake at 375°F for 30 to 45 minutes until it is nice and brown. Sprinkle the strudel with powdered sugar before eating.

Apricot Tart with Thyme
Tastes of summer and sun

Makes 12 slices:

For the pastry:

1 ⅓ cups flour

Pinch of salt

3 tablespoons sugar

1 teaspoon grated lemon zest

1/2 cup (1 stick) cold unsalted butter

1 egg

1 tablespoon plain yogurt (or cold water)

For the filling:

24 ounces fresh apricots (about 15 to 20)

5-6 sprigs fresh thyme

2 tablespoons honey

1/4 cup (1/2 stick) unsalted butter

1/4 cup almonds

1 egg

2 tablespoons whipping cream

1 cup crème fraîche

1 For the pastry, mix the flour, salt, sugar, and lemon zest in a food processor (metal blade) and pulse the machine a few times to blend the ingredients. Cut the butter into pieces. Add the butter and pulse the machine about 30 times until the mixture is crumbly. Add the egg and yogurt, and pulse until the dough just starts to come together (you may need to add a little ice water—just a teaspoon or two should do). Shape the dough into a disk, wrap it in plastic wrap, and chill it for at least 1 hour.

2 Make the filling: Wash the apricots, cut them in half, and remove the pits. Wash and dry the thyme. Strip the thyme leaves off the stems. In a skillet, melt the honey and butter along with the thyme over medium heat. Add the apricot halves to the skillet, round side down, and simmer them for 3 for 4 minutes. Turn over the apricots and let them simmer for another 3 to 4 minutes. Remove the skillet from the heat.

3 Preheat the oven to 400°F. Roll out the pastry between 2 layers of plastic wrap until it is a circle about 1 ½ inches bigger than the pan. Transfer the pastry to an ungreased 10- or 11-inch tart or springform pan and trim the edges with a small knife.

4 Line the pastry with parchment paper and pie weights (or dried beans) and "blind bake" the pastry on the middle oven rack for about 15 minutes. Remove the pan from the oven and carefully lift out the parchment and pie weights.

5 Finely grind the almonds in the food processor (metal blade). In a small bowl, mix the egg, cream, and almonds until smooth, and spread the mixture evenly over the pastry. Place the tart in the oven and bake for another 20 minutes until the filling is golden. Cool slightly.

6 Stir the crème fraîche until smooth and spread it evenly over the almond filling. Distribute the apricots, round side up, on top of the crème fraîche. Serve the same day.

Time needed: 2 hours, including about 40 minutes doing something

Tarte Tatin
An upside-down delight invented by the French

Makes 12 slices:

1 sheet (1/2 package of a 17.3-ounce package) frozen puff pastry

2 pounds medium-sized tart apples (e.g., Granny Smiths)

1/2 cup (1 stick) unsalted butter

1 ½ cups powdered sugar

Crème fraîche, whipped cream, or vanilla ice cream for serving (if desired)

1 Follow the package's directions for thawing the puff pastry.

2 About halfway through the thawing time, peel the apples and cut them into eighths. Cut the core from each apple eighth. Cut the butter into pieces.

3 Put a 10-inch skillet on a burner. Add the butter and melt it over low heat. Thoroughly stir in the powdered sugar and simmer until it is just starting to turn brown. Add the apple pieces, stir well, and simmer for another 10 to 15 minutes until the apples are covered with a golden-brown caramel. Keep stirring and whatever you do don't walk away, because the apples burn easily. If it seems like there is too much liquid in the pan, increase the heat so that the liquid evaporates faster. Remember to keep stirring! Remove the pan from the burner and let the mixture cool slightly.

4 Preheat the oven to 450°F. Place the sheet of puff pastry on a work surface and roll it out so that it is a square slightly bigger than the diameter of the pan.

5 Loosely roll up the pastry around the rolling pin, move it over to the skillet, and then unroll it on top of the apples. Tuck the edges of the pastry inside of the pan all around and press it down a bit into the filling of the tart.

6 Put the skillet on the middle rack of the oven and bake it for about 25 minutes until the top crust is crispy and golden brown. Remove the skillet from the oven, wait 10 minutes, then carefully loosen the crust from the sides of the pan with a paring knife. Turn a large plate upside-down on top of the skillet, hold it securely, and turn the whole thing back over. The tart should now be sitting on the plate with the pastry on the bottom and the apples on the top. Tarte Tatin tastes best when lukewarm. And it's especially good with crème fraîche or slightly whipped cream. Vanilla ice cream isn't bad, either.

Time needed: 1 ½ hours, including about 55 minutes active

Pineapple Upside-Down Cake

Makes 8 slices:

For the topping:

1/2 cup (1 stick) unsalted butter

3/4 cup brown sugar

1 teaspoon ground cinnamon

1 can pineapple rings (20 ounces)

For the batter:

1/2 cup (1 stick) unsalted butter

1 ½ cups flour

2 teaspoons baking powder

Large pinch of salt

1 cup sugar

2 eggs

1 tablespoon rum

For garnish:

Maraschino cherries (if you're feeling kitschy!)

1 Preheat the oven to 375°F. For the topping, melt the butter over medium heat in a 10-inch skillet (nonstick is best, just make sure that it can go into the oven, i.e., doesn't have a plastic handle). Stir in the brown sugar and simmer for 3 to 5 minutes until the mixture is bubbling well and caramely. Remove the skillet from the heat and stir in the cinnamon.

2 Drain the pineapple rings and arrange them decoratively over the sugar—it's OK to overlap them.

3 For the batter, melt the butter in a small saucepan and remove it from the heat. In a bowl, combine the flour, baking powder, salt, and sugar. Add the eggs, and rum, and mix well with a wooden spoon. Pour in the melted butter and stir until well blended.

4 Spoon the batter over the pineapple, spreading it evenly. The batter is stiff, so it may take a little work to even it out. Bake the cake for about 45 minutes until it is done (do the toothpick test—see Tip on page 38).

5 Remove the cake from the oven and let it stand for about 10 minutes. Run the tip of a small knife around the edge of the cake to loosen it. Invert the cake onto a plate—now the pineapple will be on the top. If you're in a playful mood, put a maraschino cherry in the middle of each pineapple ring.

Time needed: About 1 ¼ hours

Blackberry Cobbler
Pure summer pleasure

Don't restrict yourself to blackberries. You can use peaches, nectarines, plums, or other similar fruits for this dessert, but remember to peel them and slice them before measuring. Blueberries also make terrific cobbler and they just need a quick rinse before using.

Makes 8 servings:

For the filling:

4 cups fresh blackberries

1/2 cup sugar, or more or less to taste

2 tablespoons cornstarch

Grated zest of 1/2 lemon

For the topping:

2 cups flour

2 tablespoons sugar

1 tablespoon baking powder

Pinch of salt

6 tablespoons (3/4 stick) cold unsalted butter

1 cup whipping cream, plus more for serving if desired

1 tablespoon coarse sugar (if you can't find it, see the Tip below)

1 Preheat the oven to 425°F. For the filling, pick over the berries to remove any leaves or other foreign material. Put the berries in a bowl and toss them with the sugar, cornstarch, and lemon zest; set aside.

2 For the topping, put the flour, sugar, baking powder, and salt in a bowl and mix well. Cut the butter into small cubes. Put the butter cubes into the flour mixture and, with a fork or your fingers, blend the mixture until it resembles cornmeal. Slowly add the 1 cup of cream, mixing just until the batter is moistened.

3 Pour the fruit into a 10-inch pie or springform pan. It's a good idea to put the pan on a foil-lined baking sheet to catch any drips—it's better than cleaning out the oven! Spoon the topping over of the fruit, letting some space remain between sections of topping. Sprinkle with the coarse sugar.

4 Bake the cobbler for 15 to 20 minutes until the topping is golden brown and the fruit is bubbly.

Basic Tip
If you can't find coarse sugar in the baking section of the supermarket, buy sugar cubes instead. Process them in a food processor until they look about the right texture. Or, put the sugar cubes in a heavy-duty locking plastic bag and pound on them with a rolling pin or other heavy object until they are coarsely broken up.

Italian Grape Flatbread
A treat from Tuscany

Makes 12 wedges:

1/2 cup raisins

2 tablespoons water

3/4 cup walnut pieces

2 sprigs fresh rosemary

1 teaspoon fennel seeds

1 cup milk

3 1/3 cups flour

2 tablespoons sugar

Pinch of salt

2 teaspoons rapid-rise yeast

1 tablespoon olive oil

About 2 pounds purple grapes

1 Soak the raisins in the water and set them aside. Coarsely break up the walnuts using your fingers. Wash the rosemary, pull off the leaves, and roughly chop the leaves. Slightly crush the fennel seeds with the side of a large knife or bottom of a heavy pan.

2 In a small saucepan, heat the milk to 120°F (an instant-read thermometer will help). In a food processor (metal blade or dough blade), combine the flour, sugar, and salt, and pulse to combine. Add the yeast and pulse to combine the ingredients. Pour the milk and oil into the food processor, and pulse 10 to 20 times until the dough comes together in a ball. Turn on the food processor and knead the dough for about 60 seconds (set the timer). Transfer the dough to a work surface and, with your hands, knead in the raisins (drained first), walnuts, rosemary, and fennel seeds. Transfer the dough to an oiled bowl. Cover the bowl with a clean dishtowel and let the dough rise for about 1 to 1 1/2 hours in a warm place with no drafts — the dough should about double in size.

3 In the meantime, wash the grapes, remove the stems, and cut them in half. If you don't like seeds, remove them with the point of a small knife. Preheat the oven to 375°F. Grease a baking sheet. Thoroughly knead the dough again, roll it out into a large circle (11 to 12 inches) on a bit of flour, and put it on the baking sheet.

4 Distribute the grapes evenly over the surface. Bake the flatbread on the middle oven rack for about 35 minutes. It should rise, turn nice and brown, and show reddish marks from the grapes.

Time needed: 3 hours, but a maximum of 1 hour doing something

63

Sunken Apple Cake
With a crispy top

Makes 12 slices:

1 lemon

4-5 tart apples (try Granny Smiths!)

3.5 ounces almond paste (1/2 of a 7-ounce tube—baking section of the supermarket or specialty foods store)

1 cup (2 sticks) unsalted butter, softened

6 tablespoons sugar

1 teaspoon vanilla extract

4 eggs

3 tablespoons apple brandy or milk

1 ⅓ cups flour

1/4 teaspoon salt

1 teaspoon baking powder

2 tablespoons sliced almonds

2 tablespoons powdered sugar

Powdered sugar

1 Scrub the lemon under hot water, dry it, and grate the zest. Cut the lemon in two and squeeze the juice from one half (save the remaining lemon half for another use). Peel the apples, cut them into eighths, and remove the cores from each piece. Mix the apple eighths with the lemon juice. Now, cut the almond paste into little cubes, and it's time to make the batter.

2 Preheat the oven to 350°F. Butter and flour a 10- or 11-inch springform pan.

3 With a mixer, mix the butter, sugar, vanilla, and lemon zest until the mixture is light and creamy. Add the eggs one after the other, beating each time until no trace of the egg can be seen. Stir in the brandy or milk. In another bowl, mix the flour, salt, and baking powder; if the mixture's lumpy, it should be sifted. Stir the flour mixture and the almond paste cubes into the butter mixture until the new mixture is smooth—except, of course, for the cubes of almond paste.

4 Spoon the batter into the pan and smooth it out with the back of the spoon or a spatula. If the batter sticks too much, hold the spoon under cold running water. Place the apples on the batter in a decorative, spiral pattern; they will sink into the cake during baking.

5 Put the cake on the middle oven rack and bake it for about 45 minutes. Do the toothpick test on a piece of the batter (see Tip on page 38). Remove the cake from the oven.

6 Now we'll give the cake a crispy top: Turn up the oven to broil and let it heat up. Mix the together the sliced almonds and powdered sugar, sprinkle the mixture evenly on the cake, and put the whole thing under the hot broiler for 1 to 2 minutes—only until the sugar melts and caramelizes! Always keep an eye on it, because it can quickly burn on you. If you don't have a broiler, turn the oven up to the highest temperature and leave the cake in the oven for a bit longer. It won't get as crispy, but it will still be good!

7 Remove the cake from the oven and leave it in the pan for about 10 minutes. Unhook the springform edge and let the cake cool on a rack. Sift more powdered sugar onto the cake before eating.

Time needed: 1 hour 20 minutes, including 45 minutes totally relaxed

Double-Crust Apple Pie
Better than Mom's!

Makes 8 to 10 slices:

For the pastry:

2 ⅓ cups flour

1 tablespoon sugar

1/4 teaspoon salt

6 tablespoons cold vegetable shortening (or, if you're a purist, you can use lard)

1/2 cup (1 stick) cold unsalted butter

1-2 tablespoons ice water

For the filling:

2 ¼ pounds tart apples (Granny Smiths are nice-sized)

1 tablespoon fresh lemon juice

1 tablespoon flour

5 tablespoons brown sugar

1/4 teaspoon ground cinnamon

1/4 teaspoon ground nutmeg

Tiny pinch of ground cloves

1-2 tablespoons melted butter

Whipped cream, vanilla ice cream, or vanilla sauce

1 Make the pastry: In a food processor (metal blade), mix the flour, sugar, and salt, and pulse the machine a few times to blend the ingredients. Cut the shortening and butter into little pieces and add them to the machine. Pulse the machine about 30 times, adding a little ice water if needed until the dough just starts to come together. Form the dough into a disk, wrap it in plastic wrap, and chill for 1 hour.

2 Make the filling: Peel the apples, quarter them, and remove the cores. Cut the apples into thin slices and mix them with the lemon juice.

3 Divide the pastry in half, putting one half in the fridge while you're working on the other. Form the pastry half into a ball and roll it out between two layers of plastic wrap until it is a circle about 1 inch bigger than the diameter of the pan. Carefully transfer the pastry to a 10- or 11-inch pie pan, letting the edges drape over the sides of the pan and discarding the plastic wrap.

4 Preheat the oven to 350°F. Mix the apples with the flour, brown sugar, cinnamon, nutmeg, and cloves, and pour the mixture into the pastry-lined pan. Follow the directions from step 3 to roll out the other half of the pastry. Place the second pastry half on top of the filling and trim the edges with a small knife. With your fingers, press the bottom and top of the pastry together. (Cut a few slits in the top for stream vents.)

5 Bake the pie on the middle oven rack for 35 minutes. Brush it with melted butter and bake for another 20 minutes until it is nice and brown. Serve the pie warm or at room temperature with whipped cream, vanilla ice cream, or vanilla sauce.

Drunken Apple Cake
Desert with a kick

Makes 12 slices:

For the crust:

1/2 cup (1 stick) unsalted butter, softened

2/3 cup sugar

1 teaspoon vanilla extract

1 egg

1 2/3 cups flour

1 1/2 teaspoons baking powder

1/2 teaspoon salt

For the filling:

3-4 crisp, tart apples (Granny Smiths are good and easy to find)

1 teaspoon fresh lemon juice

3 cups dry hard apple cider or white wine

1 cup sugar

1 box vanilla "Cook & Serve" pudding (4.6 ounces)

1 1/2 cups whipping cream

1 tablespoon sugar

1/2 teaspoon vanilla extract

1 For the crust, beat the butter and sugar with a mixer until they are light and creamy. Add the vanilla extract and egg and mix well. In another bowl, mix the flour with the baking powder and salt and mix it into the butter mixture. Shape the dough into a ball, wrap it in plastic wrap, and chill it for at least 30 minutes.

2 The filling: Peel, quarter, and core apples. Cut the quarters into slices about 1/4 inch thick and mix them with the lemon juice.

3 Measure out 2 1/2 cups of the apple cider and bring it to a boil with the 1 cup of sugar. In another bowl, mix the pudding powder and the remaining apple cider together until smooth. Take the hot apple mixture off the burner and stir in the pudding mixture. Return the pan to the heat and bring it to a full boil while stirring. Remove the pan from the heat and let the mixture cool slightly, stirring occasionally to prevent a skin from forming on the surface.

4 Preheat the oven to 350°F. Take the dough out of the refrigerator and press it flat. Line an ungreased 10- or 11-inch springform pan with the dough, flattening it with your hands and pushing it up on the edges to half the height of the pan—try to make the edges even.

5 Mix the apples with the pudding mixture and pour into the pan, spreading it evenly over the crust. Bake the cake on the middle oven rack for about 1 hour. Let the cake cool in the pan.

6 Whip the cream with the 1 tablespoon of sugar and the vanilla until stiff and spread it on the cake. Refrigerate the cake for 1 hour before serving.

Time needed: 2 3/4 hours, including only 45 minutes doing something

Peach Lattice Pie
With a hint of almonds

Makes 8 to 10 slices:

For the pastry:

2 cups flour

Pinch of salt

2 tablespoons sugar

1/2 cup (1 stick) cold unsalted butter

1 egg

1 egg yolk

For the filling:

4 large or 8 small ripe peaches

1/3 cup honey

2 tablespoons amaretto or milk

A few drops of almond extract

Grated zest of 1 lemon

1 tablespoon lemon juice

For the glaze:

1 egg yolk

1 tablespoon milk

1 tablespoon amaretto or milk

3-4 drops almond extract

1 Make the pastry: In a food processor (metal blade), mix the flour, salt, and sugar, and pulse the ingredients to mix them. Cut the butter into little pieces and add them to the machine. Pulse the machine about 30 times. Add the egg and egg yolk and pulse the machine just until the dough starts to come together; you may have to add a little bit of ice water. Form the dough into a disk, wrap it in plastic wrap, and chill it for 1 hour.

2 While the pastry is chilling, start the filling: Peel the peaches (see Tip on page 57). Cut the peaches in half, remove the pits, dice them finely, and mix them well with the honey, amaretto or milk, almond extract, lemon zest, and lemon juice.

3 Preheat the oven to 350°F. Divide the pastry into 3 parts. Shape two-thirds of it into a ball and roll it out into an 11-inch circle between two sheets of plastic wrap. Carefully transfer the pastry to an ungreased 11-inch tart pan, letting any excess dough drape over the edges and pulling off the plastic wrap. Roll out the remaining pastry on a lightly floured work surface to a thin rectangle, about 11-inches across. Use a knife to cut strips of pastry that are about 1/2 inch wide. Cool idea: Use a fluted pastry cutter to make decorative strips.

4 Dump the peach mixture into the pastry-lined pan. Place about half of the pastry strips on top of the peaches, evenly spaced. Then, place the remaining pastry strips on top of, and at right angles to, the first ones to make a lattice. Trim the pastry edges with a paring knife.

5 Make the glaze: In a small bowl, mix the egg yolk, milk, and amaretto, and brush it onto the edge of the pastry and the lattice, avoiding the filling. Bake the pie on the middle oven rack for about 45 minutes until the top is golden brown and crispy.

Time needed: 1 ½ hours, half of that with something to do

Strawberry Shortcake
Best in summer

Makes 12 slices:

For the batter:

4 eggs

1/2 teaspoon cream of tartar

5 tablespoons sugar

1 ⅓ cups flour

1/2 teaspoon baking powder

1/4 teaspoon salt

For the filling:

2 vanilla beans

1 heaping tablespoon cornstarch

3 egg yolks

1 cup milk

1/4 cup sugar

24 ounces fresh strawberries

2 tablespoons fresh lemon juice

2 tablespoons fruit syrup (such as strawberry)

For the topping:

1/2 cup whipping cream

1 teaspoon powdered sugar

1 Preheat the oven to 350°F. Coat a 10- or 11-inch springform pan first with butter, then with flour, shaking out the excess flour.

2 Separate the eggs. In a clean, grease-free bowl, beat the egg whites until stiff, adding the cream of tartar when the whites are foamy, and the sugar when the whites reach soft peaks. In another bowl, beat the egg yolks until light yellow in color. Heap the egg yolks onto the stiff egg white mixture, sift the flour, baking powder, and salt on top, and fold everything together with a hand whisk. Smooth the batter in the pan. Bake the cake on the middle oven rack for about 40 minutes until it feels springy and no longer sticky. Leave the cake in the pan for 5 to 10 minutes, release it from the springform, and let it cool for 1 to 2 hours.

3 The filling: With a small sharp knife, slit open the vanilla beans lengthwise, scrape out the seeds, and put everything (the bean pods and the seeds) in a saucepan. In a small bowl, whisk together the cornstarch, egg yolks, and half of the milk; set aside. Add the remaining milk and the sugar to the saucepan and heat until the milk is steaming, stirring to dissolve the sugar. Fish out the vanilla bean pods. Remove the pan from the heat and whisk in the egg yolk-cornstarch mixture. Put the pan back on the heat and cook over medium-low heat while stirring—don't let it boil! When the mixture thickens, pour it into a bowl and let it cool completely. Stir it occasionally to help the mixture cool fast.

4 Briefly wash the strawberries and shake them dry. Remove the stems, set aside a couple of particularly nice looking strawberries, and slice the rest.

5 Make one horizontal cut through the cake to make two even layers. Mix the lemon juice with the fruit syrup and brush it over the bottom cake layer. Mix the sliced strawberries into the cooled vanilla filling mixture. Spread half of the filling on the bottom cake layer. Arrange the second cake layer on top, lining up the edges.

6 Make the topping: Beat the whipped cream until stiff, sprinkling in the powdered sugar. Fold the sweetened whipped cream into the remaining vanilla filling mixture and spread it over the top and sides of the cake. Garnish the cake with the reserved strawberries, cut into pretty pieces.

Time needed: 2 hours, including 1 hour active–not counting resting time

Berry Tart
Too good to be true

Makes 8 slices:

For the crust:

1 tube prepared sugar cookie dough (17 ounces)

For the filling:

2 eggs

2 cups vanilla yogurt

1/4 cup flour

1/2 teaspoon grated lemon zest

4 cups fresh strawberries (you can also use an assortment of fruit, such as berries, sliced kiwi, sliced peaches, halved grapes)

For the glaze:

4 teaspoons cornstarch

3/4 cup water

1/4 cup sugar

1/4 cup fresh lemon juice

1 Preheat the oven to 400°F. Remove the cookie dough from the wrapper. With your fingers, press the cookie dough over the bottom and up the sides of a 9-inch tart or pie pan—one with fluted sides looks pretty. Try to keep the thickness of the dough even. Put the pan on the middle oven rack and bake it for 10 minutes. Remove it from the oven and let it cool a little bit.

2 In a bowl, beat the eggs slightly with a hand whisk. Add the yogurt, flour, and lemon zest, and mix well. Pour the yogurt mixture into the baked crust, spreading it evenly. Bake for 15 minutes until the filling is set. Completely cool the baked tart on a rack.

3 Briefly wash the strawberries, shake them dry, and remove the stems. Cut the strawberries into slices. Arrange the strawberry slices decoratively over the filling.

4 Make the glaze: Mix the cornstarch with the water in a small saucepan. Add the sugar, and lemon juice. Turn on the heat to medium and stir the mixture constantly until it thickens. Remove the glaze from the heat. When cool, spoon the glaze over the fruit, spreading it evenly.

5 Refrigerate the tart until you are ready to serve. Garnish with fresh mint leaves.

Savarin with Strawberries
Beautifully round and colorful

Named after a famous old food writer, this liqueur-soaked cake stands the test of ages because it is leavened with yeast, which helps the cake stand up to the long soaking time. You'll need a Savarin or ring pan to make this.

Makes 16 slices:

For the dough:

2 ⅔ cups flour

3 tablespoons sugar

Pinch of salt

Grated zest of 1 lemon

2 teaspoons rapid-rise yeast

About 1 ⅓ cups milk

1/2 cup (1 stick) unsalted butter, softened

3 eggs (room temp, please!)

For soaking:

2/3 cup orange juice (fresh squeezed, please!)

1/3 cup sugar

2 tablespoons orange liqueur (such as Grand Marnier)

For serving:

24 ounces fresh strawberries

1 cup whipping cream

3 tablespoons sugar

1 teaspoon vanilla extract

1 Coat savarin or ring pan first with butter, then with flour, shaking out the excess flour. For the dough, mix the flour, sugar, salt, and lemon zest in a food processor (metal blade or dough blade). Add the yeast and pulse the machine to mix it.

2 In a saucepan, heat the milk to about 120°F. Add the milk, butter, and the eggs to the machine and process until the dough comes together in a ball. Then, set the timer to 60 second and let the machine run (this will knead it).

3 Immediately put the dough in the prepared pan and distribute it evenly—a fork will help. Put a dishtowel over the pan and let the dough stand for about 1 to 1 ½ hours. The dough prefers things warm and with no drafts. While resting, the dough should more or less double in size.

4 Preheat the oven to 350°F. Put the savarin on the middle rack of the oven and bake it for about 30 minutes until it has risen well and is nice and brown.

5 While the cake is baking, make the soaking mixture: Pour the orange juice and the sugar into a saucepan, bring to a boil, and let it boil for about 5 minutes until it becomes syrupy. Stir the mixture occasionally to ensure that the sugar is dissolved. Remove the pan from the heat and stir in the orange liqueur.

6 After baking, leave the savarin in the pan for 5 to 10 minutes. Then, use a skewer or thin chopstick to make several holes in the savarin, nice and deep, but not all the way through. Turn the savarin out onto a plate, turn it back over onto another plate, and slowly pour the syrup over it, distributing it with a brush. Try to urge the syrup into the holes of the cake without letting it run out onto the plate. Now go do something else for 1 hour.

7 Just before serving, briefly wash the strawberries and blot them well on paper towels. Pull or cut off the stems and cut the strawberries into thin slices. Beat the cream, sugar, and vanilla extract together until the mixture is stiff and mix it gently with the strawberries. Spoon the strawberry-cream mixture into the middle of the savarin and serve it immediately.

Time needed: 3 hours, including 50 minutes active

Variation:

Coconut Savarin with Pineapple
Prepare and bake the dough is as described above (steps 1, 2, 3, and 4), but reduce the flour to 2 cups and add 5 ounces of flaked coconut. Also: Instead of the white sugar, use brown sugar. To soak the savarin, cook the sugar with lime juice instead of orange juice, and use coconut liqueur, or white rum instead of orange liqueur. Instead of the strawberries, peel 1 small pineapple, cut it into slices, and cut away the part around the hard center. Or, use a couple of 15-ounce cans of unsweetened, canned pineapple chunks (drain them first).

Tipsy Charlotte
Warms you up inside

Makes 8 servings:

24 ounces fresh raspberries

2/3 cup sugar

1/2 cup Grand Marnier or other orange liqueur

3 tablespoons sparkling wine or white wine

30 ladyfingers (look for them in a specialty foods store or bakery)

1 cup whipping cream

1 Clean the raspberries; in other words, remove all of the spoiled fruit, leaves, and anything that doesn't belong with the berries. (If you must rinse them, do so only briefly and very gently.) Carefully mix the berries in a bowl with the sugar, liqueur, and wine, and let stand for about 5 minutes until the sugar has dissolved. Put the berries into a strainer and collect the liquid in a bowl.

2 Choose a bowl that has steep sides, is a bit taller than the ladyfingers, and is not more than 8 inches in diameter at the upper edge. In batches, soak both sides of the ladyfingers in the raspberry liquid for 1 to 2 minutes. Be careful the ladyfingers don't fall apart! Lay the freshly-soaked ladyfingers on the sides and bottom of the bowl.

3 Now spoon a layer of raspberries about as thick as your finger into the bowl, followed by more freshly-soaked ladyfingers. It's OK if you have to cut or pull the ladyfingers into pieces in order to cover the surface. Then another layer of raspberries, ladyfingers, and so on—the last layer should be ladyfingers.

4 Cover the charlotte with plastic wrap and put it in the refrigerator. After 10 hours it is ready to be inverted onto a serving plate. Serve with the cream, whipped until stiff.

Time needed: 20 minutes, plus another 10 hours in the fridge

Miniature Summer Puddings
Good on hot days

Makes 4 servings:

24 ounces mixed fresh berries (such as strawberries, raspberries, and blueberries)

3 tablespoons sugar

About 12 slices thin, white sandwich bread (not necessarily fresh)

4 scoops vanilla ice cream

1 Pick over the berries and remove any leaves, stems, or anything odd looking. (Or, if you must, gently and briefly rinse them.) If you're using strawberries, remove the stems and cut them into slices. Mix the berries with the sugar in a saucepan and carefully heat them. Simmer the mixture for barely 1 minute—the sugar should be dissolved and some juice released, but the berries should still be whole. Pour the berries into a strainer, catch the liquid in a bowl, and let everything cool.

2 Remove the crusts from the bread. Cut 8 slices into circles that will cover the bottoms of 4 ramekins or small bowls (they should hold about 1 cup of liquid). Cut the remaining bread into strips about 1 inch wide. Briefly dip the round bread pieces into the berry juice and put half of them in the ramekins. Dip the bread strips into the juice and use them to line the sides of the ramekins, arranging the bread so that it slightly overlaps.

3 Half-fill the ramekins with berries, then add another layer of soaked bread circles, and strips. Fill with the remaining berries and finish with the remaining soaked bread strips. Cover the tops of the ramekins with plastic wrap and lightly weight the pudding (another ramekin half-filled with water works well). Refrigerate everything overnight.

4 The next day, remove the plastic wrap, turn out the puddings onto serving plates, and serve them with vanilla ice cream.

Time needed: 30 minutes

OJ Cake
Doesn't require heat

Makes 10 slices:

1 quart orange juice (good quality, please!)

1/4 cup apricot jam

1 large readymade sponge cake base
(sometimes packaged as shortcake; look for
it in the produce section of the supermarket)

1 box vanilla "Cook & Serve" pudding
(4.6 ounces)

1/4 cup plus 1 tablespoon sugar

1 cup whipping cream

1/2 teaspoon vanilla extract

About 20 ladyfingers

4 ounces bittersweet chocolate

1 Set aside 1 cup of the orange juice.
Combine 2 tablespoons of the set aside juice
with the jam and stir until smooth. Brush the
mixture over the sponge cake base.

2 Mix 1/2 cup of the remaining orange juice
with the pudding powder, stirring until
smooth. In a saucepan, bring the remaining
2 1/2 cups of the orange juice to a boil with
the 1/4 cup of sugar, remove it from the heat,
and stir in the pudding mixture. Return the
pan to the heat and bring it to a full boil
while stirring—the mixture should thicken
when it comes to a boil. Remove the pan
from the heat and let the mixture cool
completely (stir it occasionally to help along
the cooling process).

3 Spread the orange-pudding mixture in a
thick layer on the sponge cake base. In a
bowl, beat the whipping cream with the 1
tablespoon of sugar and the vanilla extract
until stiff and spread it over the orange-
pudding mixture.

4 Dunk the ladyfingers into the leftover
orange juice (set aside from step 1) and
press them slightly into the whipped cream
until all of the ladyfingers have been used
up—or the cake is completely covered
(anything leftover can be a snack).

5 Chop the chocolate and melt it in a water
bath, stirring it until smooth. Use a teaspoon
to drizzle the melted chocolate over the
ladyfingers in a decorative manner. Chill the
cake for 1 hour before serving.

Time needed: 35 minutes, plus 1 more hour
for chilling

Chocolate Cookie Cake
"Baked" in the refrigerator

Though this recipe doesn't have any fruit, it,
just like the others on this page, doesn't
require an oven.

Makes 16 slices:

4 ounces bittersweet chocolate

1/2 cup (1 stick) unsalted butter

6 tablespoons powdered sugar

3 tablespoons chopped almonds

About 24 Petit Beurre cookies (buy 2
packages and eat the leftovers)

Cocoa powder for sprinkling

1 Chop the chocolate, cut the butter into
cubes, and melt them together in a saucepan
over low heat. Stir them from time to time so
that everything comes out smooth.

2 Mix together the powdered sugar and
almonds.

3 Line an 8 1/2- x 4 1/2-inch loaf pan with a
layer of the cookies. Pour a layer of the
chocolate mixture—not too thick—over it
and spread it out evenly with a spatula.
Continue the layering process with the
cookies and chocolate until everything has
been used. You may have to cut or break the
cookies to make them fit.

4 Refrigerate the cake for at least 1 hour. To
take it out of the pan, dip it briefly into a pan
of really hot water, run a paring knife around
the edges, and flip it over onto a cutting
board. Sprinkle the cake with cocoa. Unlike
most cakes, this one looks best after it is cut
into slices.

Time needed: 1 1/4 hours, but only 15 minutes
is active

Raspberry-Almond Galettes
Little free-form tarts

Makes 4 galettes:

For the pastry:

2 cups flour

Pinch of salt

1/4 cup sugar

1/2 cup (1 stick) cold unsalted butter

1 egg

1 egg yolk

Ice water

For the filling:

1/2 pint fresh raspberries

2 tablespoons amaretto

1/2 package almond paste (7-ounce package—baking section in the supermarket or specialty foods store)

1/4 cup (1/2 stick) unsalted butter, softened

1 egg

1/4 cup flour

1/4 cup raspberry jam (seedless, if desired)

For the topping:

1 egg

1 tablespoon water

1/4 cup sliced almonds, finely chopped

2 tablespoons coarse sugar (see Tip on page 62)

1 Make the pastry: Put the flour, salt, and sugar in a food processor (metal blade) and pulse to mix the ingredients. Cut the butter into small pieces and add them to the bowl. Pulse the mixture 25 to 40 times until it resembles cornmeal. Add the egg, and egg yolk, and pulse a few times. If the mixture doesn't seem like it's coming together, add a tablespoon or so of ice water. Dump the mixture onto a work surface and gently push the pastry together with your hands. Form the dough into a disk, wrap it in plastic wrap, and chill for about 1 hour.

2 Make the filling: Pick over the raspberries, removing any leaves or other stuff that you don't want to end up in your galettes. Mix the raspberries and amaretto in a bowl, and set aside. Combine the almond paste, butter, egg, and flour in a food processor (metal blade), and process until the mixture is smooth.

3 Preheat the oven to 400ºF. Roll out the pastry until it is about 1/8 inch thick. Cut the pastry into four 6-inch circles. Tip: Look in your cupboard for a glass or jar that's about the right size, invert it onto the rolled-out pastry, and press down to make an indentation. Use a paring knife to cut out the circle.

4 Spread the almond paste mixture over the pastry circles, leaving a 2-inch border. Spread the raspberry jam over the almond paste. Divide the soaked raspberries among the pastry circles. Fold the pastry over the filling in a free-form manner. With a metal spatula, carefully transfer the galettes to a parchment-lined baking sheet.

5 Make the topping: Beat the egg with the water. With a pastry brush, brush the egg mixture over the crust. Sprinkle the exposed filling with the almonds and coarse sugar.

6 Bake the galettes for about 30 to 40 minutes, until the crust is golden brown and the filling is bubbly.

Time needed: About 1 ¾ hours

Choco-Almond-Mango Cake
Something for everyone

Makes 12 slices:

4 ounces bittersweet chocolate

1 large—but still firm—mango

2 tablespoons lemon juice

5 eggs

1/2 teaspoon cream of tartar

2/3 cup sugar

1/2 teaspoon vanilla extract

2 cups almonds

1 cup flour

1 ½ teaspoons baking powder

1/2 cup crème fraîche or whipping cream

1/4 cup grated coconut

1 Finely chop the chocolate. Peel the mango and make the prettiest and thinnest possible slices from a quarter or half mango; the slices will be used as a garnish later. It doesn't matter how the rest of the fruit is cut—just get it off the pit, then cut it into little cubes. Sprinkle the mango slices with 1 tablespoon of the lemon juice and cover them with plastic wrap; mix the mango cubes with the remaining 1 tablespoon of lemon juice in a bowl.

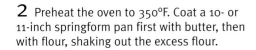

2 Preheat the oven to 350°F. Coat a 10- or 11-inch springform pan first with butter, then with flour, shaking out the excess flour.

3 Separate the eggs. In a clean, grease-free bowl, beat the egg whites until stiff. While beating, sprinkle in the cream of tartar when the egg whites are foamy, and drizzle in 1/3 cup of the sugar when the egg whites reach soft peaks. Refrigerate the mixture.

4 Combine the remaining 1/3 cup of sugar, and vanilla extract with the egg yolks, and beat them well until foamy. The mixture should get lighter in color and increase slightly in volume.

5 In a food processor (metal blade), process the almonds until finely ground. Add the flour and baking powder, and pulse to combine the ingredients. Mix the almond-flour mixture into the egg yolk mixture along with the crème fraîche until everything is blended.

6 Add the mango cubes (not the slices), and the chopped chocolate to the batter, and mix well. Put the egg white mixture on top, and mix all of it with a hand whisk, gently, but thoroughly. Pour the batter into the pan and smooth the top.

7 Bake the cake on the middle rack of the oven for 45 to 55 minutes (do the toothpick test to see if it is done—see Tip on page 38). Leave the cake in the pan for 5 to 10 minutes, then release the pan's edge, and let the cake

cool completely on a cooling rack. Sprinkle the grated coconut on the cake, and arrange the mango slices on top.

Time needed: 1 ½ hours, including 40 minutes doing something

Cherry Streusel Cake
Pan-full of pleasure

Makes 20 slices:

For the filling and streusel:

2 pounds cherries, preferably sour cherries

3/4 cup (1 ½ sticks) unsalted butter

1 ⅓ cups flour

6 tablespoons sugar

Pinch of salt

1 teaspoon ground cinnamon

For the batter:

3/4 cup (1 ½ sticks) unsalted butter, softened

5 tablespoons sugar

3 eggs

Grated zest of 1 lemon

2 ½ cups flour

3 teaspoons baking powder

1/4 teaspoon salt

1/2 cup milk

1 Wash the cherries and remove the stems. And now the great question, to pit or not to pit? Without pits, the cherries release more juice and the cake gets redder and moister. But pitting cherries can be a pain (you can substitute frozen cherries for ease). With pits, as they would do in Europe, you can have spitting contests later. But make sure to warn your guests! Pit or not to pit? We say do what you want!

2 To make the streusel, cut the butter into small pieces. Add it to a food processor (metal blade) with the flour, sugar, salt, and cinnamon, and pulse the machine until the mixture is uniformly crumbly. (You can also make this by hand by dumping all the ingredients into a bowl and blending them together with a fork, pastry blender, or use your hands.)

3 Preheat the oven to 400°F. Butter an 11-x-7-x-2-inch baking pan and coat it with flour. Shake off anything that doesn't stick.

4 Now for the batter: With a mixer, beat the butter and sugar until they are light and creamy. Mix in the eggs one after the other, blending each one well before adding the other. Mix in the lemon zest.

5 Mix the flour with the baking powder and salt, then slowly mix the flour mixture into the butter mixture alternately with the milk. The batter should be heavy, falling slowly off the beaters when they are lifted.

6 Scrape the batter into the baking pan and spread it evenly using a moistened rubber scraper, or a broad cake spatula. Scatter the cherries over the top, and sprinkle with the streusel.

7 Slip the baking pan onto the middle oven rack and bake the cake for about 35 minutes until it has risen somewhat and browned. Let the cake cool before cutting it into squares.

Time needed: 1 ½ hours, of which 50 minutes is active (including pitting the cherries)

Plum Streusel Yeast Cake
Don't let summer end without it

Makes 20 slices:

For the dough:

2 ⅓ cups flour

Pinch of salt

2 ½ tablespoons sugar

1 tablespoon rapid-rise yeast

About 2/3 cup milk

1/4 cup (1/2 stick) unsalted butter, softened

1 egg (room temp)

For the filling and topping:

4 pounds fresh plums

1/2 cup (1 stick) cold unsalted butter

2/3 cup flour

1/2 cup walnuts, ground

1 teaspoon ground cinnamon

2/3 cup brown sugar

Whipped cream, sweetened if desired

1 For the dough: Mix the flour, salt, and sugar in a food processor (metal blade or dough blade). Add the yeast and pulse to combine the ingredients. In a saucepan, heat the milk to 120°F. Cut the butter into pieces and add it to the milk.

2 Add the milk mixture and the egg to the machine and process until the ingredients come together in a ball. Set your timer for 60 seconds, then let the machine run for the allotted time—this will knead it. Now the dough needs only rest and warmth. So transfer it to an oiled bowl, cover it with a dishtowel, and let it stand in a warm, draft-free place for 1 to 1 ½ hours. It should rise to about twice its original size.

3 In the meantime, start the topping: Wash the plums, cut them in half, and remove the pits. Cut off a small slice at the bottom of each half so that they can stand up straight in the pan.

4 Brush a pan with butter. The broiler pan that comes with your oven is the perfect size—just make sure it's clean. Or, you can use a small jellyroll pan. Briefly knead the dough, place it in the middle of the baking sheet, and distribute it evenly on all sides using floured fingers, by pulling and stretching the dough out on all sides. Put the towel back over the dough and let the dough stand for another 20 to 30 minutes.

5 In the meantime, make the streusel topping: Cut the butter into small pieces. Use your fingertips to rub it together with the flour, nuts, cinnamon, and sugar, pressing the ingredients lightly until a fine-textured mixture is produced. To make the streusel faster, put all of the ingredients into a food processor (metal blade) and pulse the machine until they are crumbly.

6 Preheat the oven to 400°F. Pack the plums close together on top of the dough so that the plum halves are standing up. Sprinkle the streusel over the tops of the plums.

7 Put the pan on the middle oven rack and bake for about 35 minutes until the plums are soft and the dough is browned at the edges. Cool the cake and eat while it is lukewarm with lots of whipped cream.

Time needed: 2 hours, including about 40 minutes active

Banana-Lemon Cake
Fast, square, good

Makes 20 slices:

3 lemons

4 ripe bananas

1 cup (2 sticks) unsalted butter, softened

2/3 cup brown sugar

4 eggs

2 ⅓ cups flour

2 teaspoons baking powder

1/4 teaspoon salt

2 tablespoons rum (or leave it out)

1 Thoroughly scrub the lemons under hot water. Dry them and grate the zests. Squeeze the juice from all of the lemons.

2 Preheat the oven to 400°F. Butter a broiler pan or small jellyroll pan. Peel the bananas and thoroughly mash them with a fork.

3 With a mixer, beat the butter and sugar until they are light and creamy. Add the eggs, mixing each one in completely before adding the next one. Mix in the bananas, lemon zest, and juice. In a separate bowl, mix together the flour, baking powder, and salt, then stir them into the butter mixture along with the rum.

4 Spread the batter in the pan. Bake the cake on the middle oven rack for about 30 minutes, until the cake is nice and brown. Cool and cut into squares.

Time needed: 50 minutes, including 30 minutes waiting

Pear-Chocolate Sheetcake
Super-moist, super-good

Makes 20 slices:

For the batter:

5 ounces cream cheese, softened

6 tablespoons vegetable oil

1 egg

1 teaspoon vanilla extract

2 tablespoons sugar

2 cups flour

3 teaspoons baking powder

Pinch of salt

1 tablespoon cocoa powder

1-2 tablespoons water (optional)

For the filling:

3 ⅓ pounds ripe, juicy pears (try Anjous)

Grated zest and juice of 1 large lemon

3 eggs

1/4 teaspoon cream of tartar

8 ounces cream cheese, softened

1 cup sour cream

1/2 teaspoon vanilla extract

1/4 cup sugar

1 tablespoon cornstarch

Pinch of ground cloves

1 Make the batter: In a food processor (metal blade) combine the cream cheese, oil, egg, vanilla, and sugar, and process until the mixture is completely smooth. In a bowl, stir together the flour, baking powder, salt, and cocoa. Add it to the machine in two batches, processing briefly just until the mixtures are incorporated. If the dough is too thick, blend in a little water. Butter a broiler pan or small jellyroll pan. Roll the dough out on it in all directions using a rolling pin.

2 Make the filling: Peel the pears, cut them lengthwise into quarters, and remove the cores. Cut the pears into slices that are not too thin, otherwise, they will fall apart when baking. Carefully mix them with the lemon zest and the lemon juice. Preheat the oven to 400°F.

3 Separate the eggs. In a clean, grease-free bowl, beat the egg whites until stiff, adding the cream of tartar when the whites turn foamy. In another bowl, beat the egg yolks, cream cheese, sour cream, vanilla extract, sugar, cornstarch, and ground cloves until smooth. Heap the egg whites onto the cream cheese mixture. Gently mix everything together using a hand whisk.

4 Lay the pears on the dough and spread the filling over them, smoothing the top. Bake the cake on the middle oven rack for about 30 minutes, until the filling is completely set. Let the cake cool.

Time needed: 45 minutes active, 30 minutes very relaxed

Rhubarb Meringue Tart
Pretty and pink

Makes 20 slices:

For the pastry:

2 ⅔ cups flour

5 tablespoons sugar

Pinch of salt

2 sticks (1 cup) cold unsalted butter

2 eggs

2 tablespoons plain yogurt

For the filling:

4 ½ pounds fresh rhubarb stalks

6 tablespoons sugar

1/2 cup hazelnuts

4 eggs

1 vanilla bean

2 cups milk

1 tablespoon cornstarch

1/4 teaspoon cream of tartar

For the meringue:

1/4 teaspoon cream of tartar

1/3 cup sugar

1 Make the pastry: In a food processor (metal blade), combine the flour, sugar, and salt, and pulse until the ingredients are blended. Cut the butter into small cubes, add it to the machine, and pulse about 30 times until the mixture looks evenly crumbly. Separate the eggs. Add the egg yolks and yogurt, and pulse until the dough just comes together—you may need to add a little ice water in order to get things to adhere to each other. Shape the dough into a ball, wrap it with plastic wrap, and chill for about 30 minutes.

2 Make the filling: Wash the rhubarb. Cut off a piece at the top and bottom and if the skin starts to loosen, pull it off. If not, cut the rhubarb stalks as-is into pieces about 1/2 inch long. Mix the rhubarb with 2 tablespoons of the sugar and let them stand until the juice starts to leach out. Process the hazelnuts in a food processor (metal blade) until they're finely ground. Separate the eggs. Put 3 of the egg whites in a bowl; add the remaining egg white to the egg whites leftover from making the pastry.

3 Slit the vanilla bean lengthwise and scrape out the seeds. Set aside 2 to 3 tablespoons of the milk. Add the vanilla seeds and pods to a saucepan along with the remaining milk, and the remaining 4 tablespoons of sugar. Mix the cornstarch with the set-aside milk, then add it to the saucepan, mixing well. Stir in the ground hazelnuts, and egg yolks, and cook the mixture over medium heat while stirring constantly until it thickens. Remove the saucepan from the heat and take out the vanilla pods. Transfer the mixture to a bowl and let it cool to room temperature, stirring from time to time to aid the cooling process.

4 In a clean, grease-free bowl, beat 2 egg whites until stiff, adding the cream of tartar when the egg whites turn foamy. Fold the egg whites into the cooled, vanilla filling mixture.

5 Preheat the oven to 400°F. Roll out the pastry on an ungreased baking sheet, pulling up a small edge to make a crust. Bake the pastry on the middle oven rack for 10 minutes.

6 Drain the rhubarb and put it on the pastry. Pour on the vanilla filling and spread it out evenly. Bake for another 20 minutes.

7 After about 10 minutes of baking time, make the meringue: Beat the 3 egg whites in a clean, grease-free bowl, and with clean beaters, adding the cream of tartar when the egg whites turn foamy. When the meringue is almost stiff, gradually sprinkle in the sugar and keep beating until the egg whites stand in very firm peaks. Spoon the meringue into a pastry bag (see page 23).

8 Pipe the meringue onto the rhubarb in a criss-cross pattern and return the pan to the oven. Bake for another 10 to 15 minutes—the meringue will turn firm and brown on top. Cool and serve .

Time needed: 1 ½ hours, 50 minutes active

Chocolate-Cherry Pudding Cake
Layers of appeal

Makes 20 slices:

For the batter:

2 jars sour cherries (22 ½ ounces each)

1 cup (2 sticks) unsalted butter, softened

1/2 cup sugar

6 eggs

2 ⅔ cups flour

3 teaspoons baking powder

Pinch of salt

1/4 cup milk

2 tablespoons cocoa powder

2 teaspoons rum or milk

For the filling:

1 box vanilla "Cook & Serve" pudding (3.4 ounces)

2 cups milk

1 tablespoon sugar

1 cup (2 sticks) unsalted butter, softened

1/3 cup powdered sugar

For the topping:

8 ounces semisweet chocolate

2 tablespoons unsalted butter

1 Preheat the oven to 350°F. Butter an 11-x-7-x2-inch baking pan.

2 Make the batter: Drain the cherries. With a mixer, beat the butter and sugar until the mixture is light and creamy. Add the eggs one at a time, mixing them in completely before adding the next one. Thoroughly stir together the flour, baking powder, and salt, add the flour mixture to the butter mixture, and mix until blended. Mix in the milk.

3 Pour half of the batter onto the baking sheet and spread it out evenly using a moistened rubber scraper. Add the cocoa, and rum (or milk) to the remaining batter, and mix well. Spread the dark batter onto the light batter, spreading it out evenly using a moistened rubber scraper. Pour on the cherries and push them slightly into the batter. Bake the cake on the middle oven rack for approximately 30 minutes. Let the cake cool in the baking pan.

4 While the cake is cooling, make the filling: Mix the pudding powder with 1/4 cup of the milk and the sugar until smooth. Put the remaining 1 ¾ cups of milk in a saucepan and thoroughly mix the pudding mixture into it. Over medium heat, heat the mixture, stirring constantly until it comes to a full boil. Remove the pan from the heat, transfer the pudding to a bowl, and let it cool (stir the pudding occasionally to help along the cooling process).

5 In a bowl, beat the butter and powdered sugar until nice and creamy. Add the cooled pudding to the butter mixture one spoonful at a time, beating until smooth. Spread this mixture onto the cooled cake.

6 Make the topping: Cut the chocolate and butter into small pieces and melt them in a saucepan, stirring until smooth. Carefully pour a thin layer of the chocolate mixture over the filling and spread it out with a spatula or knife. Chill the cake until ready to serve.

Time needed: 1 ¾ hours, of which only 1 ¼ hours is actually active

Strawberry-Lemon Roulade
Light and luscious

Perfect or imperfect doesn't matter here! This roll tastes great even when it doesn't look like it came from the bakery.

Makes 20 slices:

For the batter:

4 eggs

1/2 teaspoon cream of tartar

3 tablespoons sugar

1/2 teaspoon vanilla extract

2 egg yolks

1 cup flour

1/4 teaspoon baking powder

Pinch of salt

For the filling:

1 large lemon

24 ounces fresh strawberries

1/4 cup powdered sugar

2 cups whipping cream

1 teaspoon vanilla extract

Powdered sugar

1 Preheat the oven to 400°F. Line a jellyroll pan with parchment paper.

2 Separate the eggs. Put the egg whites in a clean, grease-free bowl and beat well with an electric mixer. When they become foamy, add the cream of tartar and keep beating. When the egg whites start to stiffen, sprinkle in the sugar and vanilla extract and keep beating until the egg whites stand in stiff peaks and the mixture is glossy.

3 Gradually stir in all 6 egg yolks, mixing with a hand whisk until they are incorporated. Mix the flour with the baking powder, and salt, and sprinkle it over the top of the egg mixture. Mix the whole thing, gently, but thoroughly with a hand whisk.

4 Immediately pour the batter onto the pan, smoothing the surface with a rubber scraper or broad knife. It should be almost 1/2 inch thick.

5 Bake the cake on the middle oven rack for 8 to 10 minutes. When you push it with a finger, the cake should bounce back and feel light and moist. Very important: While the sponge cake is in the oven, moisten a clean, smooth dishtowel under hot water, wring it out well, and lay it on a large cutting board or your countertop.

6 Pull the cake out of the oven and immediately turn it out onto the dishtowel. Remove the pan. Loosen the parchment paper at one corner with the point of a knife, and carefully pull it off. Starting from a long side, tightly roll up the cake with the towel (we know, this seems weird, but it's necessary). Let the cake cool completely while rolled up.

7 In the meantime, make the filling: Wash the lemon under hot water and dry it. Finely grate the zest. Cut the lemon in half, and squeeze out the juice.

8 Briefly wash the strawberries, dry them, and pull off or cut out the stems. Set a few strawberries aside. Crush the remaining strawberries with a fork in a bowl. Add 3 tablespoons of the powdered sugar and mix well.

9 Beat the whipping cream until stiff with the remaining 1 tablespoon of sugar and the vanilla. Thoroughly mix the strawberries, lemon zest, and lemon juice. Fold in the whipped cream.

10 Now unroll the sponge cake, spread the strawberry whipped cream on it, not too thick and not all the way to the edge, or too much will run out when it's rolled up. It's better to spread the leftovers around the outside later. Lift the towel and roll the cake up again—this time the towel is used as a guide, securely holding the cake while you're rolling, rather than being rolled up inside the cake. Slide the cake roll onto a platter, seam-side down. If desired, spread the roll with the remaining strawberry-whipped cream filling, and sprinkle it with powdered sugar. Slice the remaining strawberries and use them to garnish the roll.

Time needed: 45 minutes

Variations:

Cream Cheese-Lemon Roulade

Make the batter as directed above (steps 1 through 6). For the filling, whip 2 cups of whipping cream until stiff. In another bowl, mix the grated zest, and juice of 2 lemons with 8 ounces of softened cream cheese until light and creamy. Add the whipped cream and mix well. Fill and roll the cake as directed above (step 10).

Chocolate Roulade

Make the batter as directed above (steps 1 through 6). Melt 6 ounces of your favorite chocolate over a water bath (chop the chocolate first) and then cool it to room temperature. Mix the melted chocolate with 8 ounces of softened cream cheese, ricotta cheese, or mascarpone cheese until light and creamy. Beat 2 cups of whipping cream with 1 tablespoon of sugar, and 1/2 teaspoon vanilla extract until stiff, and fold in a pinch of cinnamon. Add the whipped cream to the chocolate mixture and mix well. Fill and roll the cake as directed above (step 10).

Fruited Ricotta Cake
A good summertime cake

Makes 12 slices:

4 nectarines

2 tablespoons fresh lemon juice

1 ¼ cups almonds

4 eggs

1/2 teaspoon cream of tartar

2 egg yolks

1/3 cup sugar

1/2 teaspoon vanilla extract

Grated zest of 1 lemon

2 cups ricotta cheese

12 ounces raspberries

1 package fruit glaze (look for it in the

produce section of the supermarket)

Fruit juice (as directed on the fruit glaze

package)

1 Wash the nectarines, cut them in half around the pit, and rotate each half in opposite directions until they come loose. Pull the pits out of their halves. Cut the nectarines into 1/4 to 1/2 inch slices and sprinkle them with the lemon juice. Process the almonds in a food processor (metal blade) until finely ground.

2 Preheat the oven to 350°F. Line a 10- or 11-inch springform pan with parchment paper: Cut out a parchment circle for the bottom and a long parchment strip for the sides and place them in the pan.

3 Separate the eggs. First beat the egg whites in a clean, grease-free bowl until stiff, adding the cream of tartar when the whites turn foamy. In another bowl, beat all 6 egg yolks with the sugar, vanilla extract, and lemon zest until they are nice and foamy, about 2 minutes on medium speed. The egg yolk mixture will gradually get lighter in color and increase in volume. Stir in the ricotta one spoonful at a time, followed by the ground almonds. Dump the beaten egg whites on top of the batter and fold everything together, gently, but thoroughly, using a hand whisk.

4 Pour half of the batter into the pan, cover it with the nectarines, then add the rest of the batter, smoothing the surface. Bake the cake on the middle oven rack for almost 1 hour until everything is set and slightly browned. Leave the cake in the pan to cool.

5 And now for a little something on top: Please don't wash the raspberries, just inspect them carefully and remove any that are spoiled. Lay the raspberries on the cake while it is still in the pan.

6 Use the fruit juice to prepare the glaze according to the instructions on the package and pour it evenly over the raspberries. Let it set, after which the cake can be removed from the pan. Use the paper on the bottom to lift the cake onto a plate, while keeping it in one piece. Serve soon!

Time needed: 1 hour 50 minutes, including 50 minutes of something to do

Caramelized Lemon Tart
Make this year 'round

Makes 8 to 10 slices:

For the pastry:

1 ⅓ cups flour

1/4 teaspoon salt

1/4 cup sugar

Grated zest of 1/2 lemon

1/2 cup (1 stick) cold unsalted butter

1 egg yolk

1/2 teaspoon vanilla extract

1-2 tablespoons ice water (optional)

For the filling:

2 ½ lemons

4 eggs

1 egg yolk

1/2 cup sugar

1/2 cup whipping cream

1 tablespoon powdered sugar

1 For the pastry, mix the flour, salt, sugar, and lemon zest in a food processor (metal blade) and pulse the machine a few times to blend the ingredients. Cut the butter into pieces, add it to the machine, and pulse about 30 times until the mixture is crumbly.

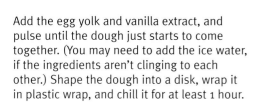

Add the egg yolk and vanilla extract, and pulse until the dough just starts to come together. (You may need to add the ice water, if the ingredients aren't clinging to each other.) Shape the dough into a disk, wrap it in plastic wrap, and chill it for at least 1 hour.

2 Preheat the oven to 350°F. Roll out the pastry between 2 layers of plastic wrap into a circle that is 1 inch larger than the diameter of the pan. Carefully transfer the pastry to an ungreased 10- or 11-inch tart pan and trim the edges. Poke a fork into the bottom of the pastry a few times. Line the pastry with parchment paper, then with pie weights or dried beans. Bake the pastry on the middle oven rack for 10 minutes.

3 Make the filling: Wash the lemons, dry them, and grate the zests. Squeeze out the juice. Beat the whole eggs, the egg yolk, and the sugar with an electric mixer until they are nice and foamy, then stir in the lemon zest and juice. In another bowl, beat the whipping cream until stiff; fold it into the lemon mixture with a hand whisk.

4 Remove the beans or peas and parchment from the pastry. Pour the lemon filling onto the pastry and return the tart to the oven. Bake at 300°F for approximately 50 minutes. The tart should not be brown (yet), but the filling should be set. Take the tart out of the oven and cool it in the pan.

5 Before serving, turn on the broiler. Sift the powdered sugar over the tart, slip it under the hot broiler, and brown it for about 1 minute. But keep watching, because this can go pretty fast, and sugar burns easily!

Time needed: being active 35 minutes, relaxing 1 ¾ hours

Quick Choco-Pear Tart
For sudden cravings

Makes 12 slices:

1 sheet (1/2 of a 17.3 ounce package) frozen puff pastry

1 box chocolate "Cook & Serve" pudding (3.4 ounces)

2 tablespoons sugar

2 cups milk

1/2 cup whipping cream

1 teaspoon vanilla extract

1 tablespoon cocoa powder

1 can pear halves (15 ounces)

1 Follow the package directions for thawing the puff pastry.

2 Thoroughly mix the pudding powder with the sugar, and 1/2 cup of the milk. Put the remaining 1 ½ cups of milk in a saucepan, add the pudding mixture, and stir until smooth. Stirring constantly, bring the mixture to a boil over medium heat. Remove the pan from the heat, transfer the pudding mixture to a bowl, and let it cool to room temperature; stir the pudding from time to time to help the cooling process.

3 Beat the whipping cream until stiff. Fold the whipped cream and the cocoa powder into the pudding until the ingredients are well blended. Drain the pear halves and cut them into slices.

4 Preheat the oven to 400°F. Rinse a 10- or 11-inch tart pan with cold water and do not dry it.

5 On a lightly floured work surface, roll out the puff pastry so that it will fit the pan, even at its shortest part. Transfer the pastry to the pan, trimming the edges with a small knife. Poke several holes into the bottom of the pastry with a fork, then line the pastry with parchment paper and pie weights (or dried beans). Bake the pastry on the middle oven rack for about 12 minutes. Remove the pastry from the oven, take out the pie weights, and parchment paper, and let it cool completely.

6 Spoon the chocolate filling into the cooled pastry and top with the sliced pears—arranged in a decorative pattern. Chill for 1 or 2 hours before serving.

Time needed: 50 minutes, including 20 active

Small
swee

Big things come in small packages...of cream, butter, and chocolate!

&t

"Big things come in small packages." Heard that before? OK, it may be a tired, old cliché, but in the case of this chapter it's true. On the following pages you'll find lots of little things to satisfy your large sweet tooth— or teeth, as the case may be. Think blueberry muffins, brownies, and chocolate chunk cookies. Or how about some miniature chocolate cakes, or raspberry tartlets? Would a lemon napoleon or chocolate-filled cream puff do the trick?

If you're not a domestic goddess and you don't have a cake stand in the house, or if you hate it when the black forest torte messes up your backpack, this is the chapter for you.

Coffee Corner

Coffeehouses are confusing—it seems that the coffee drinks are different in every store. So what to order? Here's a quick reference to common names of coffee drinks and what they mean.

Espresso:
One shot of thick, strongly flavored steam-brewed coffee. If brewed properly, the espresso will have a layer of caramel-colored foam on the top. If the foam's not there, send it back!

Espresso dopio:
A double shot of espresso

Espresso ristretto:
An espresso made with less water than usual for the amount of coffee grounds

Espresso lungo:
An espresso made with more water than usual for the same amount of coffee grounds

Espresso macchiato:
Espresso "marked" with a dollop of foamed milk

Espresso con panna:
Espresso topped with a dollop of whipped cream

Café Americano:
Espresso diluted with hot water to approximate the strength of American coffee

Cappuccino:
1/3 espresso, 1/3 hot milk, 1/3 foamed milk. A dry cappuccino has more foam and less milk. A wet cappuccino uses more milk and less foam.

Cafè latte:
Espresso in a tall glass, filled with a lot of hot milk; it should contain little or no foam.

Café au lait (pronounced "olé"):
Equal parts of drip-brewed coffee and steamed milk (no foam)

Café mocha:
A caffé latte with the addition of chocolate syrup and whipped cream

Nowadays, each coffeehouse has their own names and sizes for the different drinks that are offered. If you're confused, here's some advice: Tell the barista what you want and ask him or her what they call it!

84

Aunt Betty's Baking Bits

Dear Aunt Betty:
I just started baking and I find a lot of recipes that call for puff pastry. But I'm wondering...How do I make it? How do I handle it? What kinds of things can I make out of it? My mom says it's ok to use frozen puff pastry. Is she right?

Curious in Columbus

Dear Curious:
You are an inquisitive fellow, my dear. So let's begin at the end: Do you actually know what's in puff pastry? Up to 200 layers of butter and flour, rolled out and folded together in a very complicated manner. With all due respect, honey, you'll never have the patience to make it from scratch. And I don't say that because I have a contract with the puff pastry company.

When you get the frozen puff pastry home, take it out of the box and lay the sheets next to each other on the countertop. Let them stay there for about 15 to 20 minutes to thaw. Then, before the pastry gets too soft, get going with the recipe. If the whole thing is to be combined into one rectangle, you have two possibilities. Either overlap two edges that have been brushed with water and roll them out on a floured work surface—this will tend to give you a flat piece of pastry. Or, you can brush one sheet of pastry with water, stack the other one on top, and roll out the two sheets of pastry together. This will give you a lighter result.

Carefully lift the pastry so it doesn't stretch and get distorted during baking. Pricking the pastry with a fork will help it keep its shape if the holes aren't a problem in the final product. When cutting the pastry, use a sharp knife; a dull one will press the edges together, keeping it from puffing up properly when baked. Be careful, too, when using egg yolk as "glue" for turnovers, because it can also cause the pastry to stick together and impede the puffing action.

A lot of recipes will tell you to get the baking sheet wet before putting the pastry on it. I know this seems strange, but when the water evaporates it will make the pastry rise. In other words, it will make the puff pastry puffier.

The possibilities are endless: Tarts, turnovers, pizzas, pies...And remember to always listen to your mother.

A Detour into the Universe of the Cookie

A glance at the universe shows that nature abhors a straight line and is full of curves. Every sunbeam that is still speeding as straight and fast as an arrow will curve some day, and if the material is left to itself for a few millennia, it will clump into planets that are as perfectly round as balls.

This phenomenon can also be observed in the everyday life of the oven, in which the collision of material and energy occurs in small format. Let's take the following experiment as an example:

Take a blob of raw cookie dough, throw it any old way onto a baking sheet, and slide the whole thing into a nice hot oven. Soon the irregular heap will turn into a round disk that will be transformed into a delicious, cookie.

Fascinating. Now why isn't the earth a disk? Because it isn't subject to gravity. If ovens were equipped with anti-gravity machines, you could throw the batter right in and it could hover and be baked into a ball just like a doughnut floating in hot fat. However, the problem of cutting cake into equal slices would be expanded by one dimension. And it doesn't look like ovens will be equipped with anti-gravity machines anytime soon.

What have we learned? Whether cookies, doughnuts, or muffins, the perfection of baking lies in the circle. If it is broken, the human hand is at play—as it is in Cream Cheese Pockets, Pastry Crescents, Quick Nut "Croissants," or Vanilla Moons. Do we need to know all of this? Not really. But it is interesting, isn't it?

Blueberry Muffins
Easier than pie!

Makes 12 muffins:

2 cups fresh blueberries (or frozen and thawed blueberries)

1 ⅔ cups flour

2 teaspoons baking powder

1/4 teaspoon salt

1 egg

6 tablespoons sugar

1/2 teaspoon vanilla extract

1 ¼ cups buttermilk

1 tablespoon unsalted butter, melted, or vegetable oil

1 Briefly rinse the blueberries in a strainer and let them drain. Preheat the oven to 400°F. Butter a muffin tin.

2 In a bowl, mix the flour with the baking powder and salt. Crack the egg into another bowl, add the sugar and vanilla, and stir with a wooden spoon until well blended. Stir in the buttermilk, then add the flour mixture to the buttermilk mixture one spoonful at a time, mixing just until the ingredients are blended. At the end, mix the melted butter into the batter, adding the blueberries.

3 Spoon the batter into the muffin cups, filling them two-thirds full so the batter will have room to rise. Be sure to clean up any drips so that they don't burn. Bake the muffins on the middle rack of the oven for about 20 minutes, until they've all risen and browned. Cool them or serve them warm.

Time needed: 40 minutes, including 20 minutes just watching

Lemon Muffins
Morning refreshment

Makes 12 muffins:

2 lemons

1/2 cup unsalted shelled pistachios or chopped almonds

1 ²⁄₃ cups flour

2 teaspoons baking powder

1/4 teaspoon salt

2 eggs

2/3 cup brown sugar, packed

1/2 cup milk

3/4 cup plain yogurt

1 Wash the lemons under hot water and dry them. Finely grate the zests. Completely peel 1 of the lemons, cutting away the white pith, too. Cut out the lemon flesh between the membrane walls. Dice it, removing all of the seeds. Chop the pistachios semi-coarsely; set a few aside.

2 In a bowl, stir together the flour, baking powder, and salt. Preheat the oven to 400°F. Butter a muffin tin.

3 In another bowl, blend the eggs and the brown sugar with a wooden spoon. Add the milk and yogurt and stir thoroughly. Add the

flour mixture a small amount at a time, stirring just until blended. At the end, fold in the lemon zest and the bits of lemon with the chopped pistachios.

4 Use a spoon to add the batter to the cups of the muffin tin. But don't fill them to the top, or the batter will overflow while baking. Sprinkle the rest of the pistachios on top.

5 Bake the muffins on the middle rack of the oven for about 20 to 25 minutes, until they are brown and have risen. Let them stand briefly, take them out of the pan, and put them on a rack to cool completely.

Time needed: 50 minutes, including 30 active

Chocolate Muffins
Chock full of chocolate

Makes 12 muffins:

8 ounces semisweet chocolate

1/4 cup (1/2 stick) unsalted butter

3/4 cup milk

1 egg

1/2 cup sour cream

2 ½ tablespoons brown sugar, plus more for the pan

1 ²⁄₃ cups flour

1 tablespoon cornstarch

2 teaspoons baking powder

3 tablespoons cocoa powder

1/4 teaspoon salt

1 Set aside 1 ounce of the chocolate. Cut the remaining chocolate into small pieces. Melt the butter and the reserved 1 ounce of chocolate in a saucepan. Use a whisk to mix the milk, egg, sour cream, and brown sugar in a medium bowl.

2 Preheat the oven to 350°F. In a small bowl, mix the flour with the cornstarch, baking powder, cocoa, and salt. With a wooden spoon, stir the flour mixture, chocolate-butter mixture, and chopped chocolate into the egg-milk mixture. Stir just until the batter is blended.

3 Butter a muffin tin and sprinkle the bottoms with a little bit of brown sugar. Pour the batter into the muffin cups and carefully smooth the tops—the muffin cups should not be completely filled.

4 Bake the muffins on the middle rack of the oven for 20 to 25 minutes. Remove them from the oven and let them stand in the pan for about 5 minutes. Remove the muffins from the pan and cool them on a rack.

Time needed: 40-45 minutes, of which only half the time is active

Cream Cheese Pockets
These freeze well

Makes 16 pockets:

For the pastry:

5 ounces cream cheese, softened

6 tablespoons vegetable oil

1 egg

2 tablespoons sugar

2 cups flour

3 teaspoons baking powder

1/4 teaspoon salt

For the filling:

12 ounces cream cheese, softened

3 tablespoons sour cream

1 egg

1/4 cup sugar

2 tablespoons orange marmalade

For the glaze:

1 egg yolk

1 tablespoon milk

1 The pastry: In a medium bowl, blend the cream cheese, oil, egg, and sugar with an electric mixer until smooth. In a small bowl, mix the flour, baking powder, and salt. Stir the flour mixture into the egg mixture until a smooth dough forms. If desired, you can use your hands to knead the dough until smooth.

2 Preheat the oven to 400°F. Line a baking sheet with parchment paper.

3 Make the filling: Beat the cream cheese with the sour cream, egg, sugar, and orange marmalade until smooth.

4 Make the glaze: Thoroughly blend the egg yolk with the milk.

5 Sprinkle flour on a work surface, place the pastry on top of it, and roll it out with a floured rolling pin until you have a very thin rectangle–about as thick at the back of a knife. Cut out squares measuring about 3 1/2 x 3 1/2 inches. Heap about 1 tablespoon of the cream cheese filling in the middle of each square. Brush the corners of the pastry with the glaze. Fold each corner toward the middle, gently pressing the edges of the pastry together and turning them slightly.

6 Transfer the cream cheese pockets to the baking sheet, preferably using a spatula to prevent tearing. Brush the tops of the pockets with the remaining glaze and bake on the middle rack of the oven for about 20 minutes, until they are nice and brown. Cool them before eating.

Time needed: 1 hour, including 40 minutes doing something

Quick Nut "Croissants"
Eat these immediately!

Makes 16 crescents:

1 package (17.3 ounces) frozen puff pastry

1 1/2 cups hazelnuts or almonds

5 tablespoons whipping cream

1/4 cup honey

1 teaspoon ground cinnamon

Grated zest of 1/2 lemon

1 tablespoon lemon juice

1-2 tablespoons unsalted butter

Powered sugar

1 Remove the puff pastry from the package and thaw it at room temperature for 20 to 30 minutes. Process the nuts in a food processor (metal blade) until finely ground.

2 Mix the nuts with the cream, honey, cinnamon, lemon zest, and lemon juice. Preheat the oven to 400°F. Rinse the baking sheet with cold water; do not dry it. Melt the butter and remove it from the heat.

3 On a lightly floured work surface, roll out each sheet of puff pastry into a large square. Cut each square into quarters, then cut each quarter in half diagonally—each square will yield 8 triangles. Distribute the nut filling on the middles of the triangles. Roll up the pastry around the filling, beginning with the longest side of the triangles, bend them slightly into crescents, and put them on the baking sheet. Brush the crescents with the melted butter.

4 Bake the crescents on the middle rack of the oven for about 20 minutes, until they are nice and brown. Cool them. Sprinkle them with powdered sugar, and eat right away.

Time needed: 1 hour, including 25 minutes doing something

Baby Brioches
Très français!

Makes 12 brioches:

3 ⅓ cups flour

1 ½ teaspoons sugar

Generous pinch of salt

1 tablespoon rapid-rise yeast

5 eggs (room temperature)

1 cup (2 sticks) unsalted butter, softened

1 egg yolk

Butter and jam

1 Combine the flour, sugar, and salt in a food processor (metal blade or dough blade). Pulse the machine a couple of times to mix the ingredients. Add the yeast and pulse to mix. Add the eggs and process until the mixture forms a smooth dough (you may need to add 1 to 3 tablespoons of hot tap water to achieve the right consistency).

2 Cut the butter into small pieces, add them to the food processor, and process until the pieces of butter have disappeared (it should take 30 to 60 seconds). Put the dough in a bowl, cover it with plastic wrap, and refrigerate it overnight.

3 The next day, transfer the dough to a floured work surface and knead it vigorously with your hands for about 5 minutes. Divide the dough into 12 equal pieces. Remove one quarter of each piece and roll the pieces into small balls. Roll the other pieces into larger balls. Place one paper muffin cup inside another for each brioche and place on a baking sheet—in other words, you should have 12 double-thick paper muffin cups on the baking sheet. Put one of the larger dough balls into each cup, then place the smaller balls on top, and press them down slightly. The brioches now have to rise, for about 1 to 1 ½ hours in a warm, draft-free place.

4 Preheat the oven to 425°F. Brush the brioches with the egg yolk, which has been slightly beaten. Bake the brioches on the middle rack of the oven for about 20 minutes, until they have risen and are nice and brown. Eat them while fresh with butter and jam. Time needed: 2 hours, of which only about 35 minutes is active—not including the resting time overnight

Almond Tea Cakes
Parisian style

Makes 12 tea cakes:

3/4 cup (1 ½ sticks) unsalted butter

1 ¼ cups sliced almonds

2 cups powdered sugar

6 tablespoons flour

Pinch of salt

6 egg whites

1 Melt the butter in a small saucepan over medium heat. After the butter stops foaming, watch it closely. As soon as it takes on a nice golden brown color, remove it from the heat to prevent scorching. Set the butter aside to cool slightly. Preheat the oven to 400°F.

2 Set aside 1/4 cup of the almonds. Process the remaining almonds in a food processor (metal blade) until finely ground. In a bowl, mix the powdered sugar, flour, ground almonds, and salt together. In another bowl, stir the egg whites, but please don't beat them—you don't want to incorporate any air. Mix the egg whites with the sugar-flour mixture to form a smooth batter.

3 Now stir in the butter, followed by the reserved almonds. Generously butter a muffin tin or 12 large barquette pans (ask for these at a kitchenware store), and fill them three-quarters full with the batter. Bake the tea cakes on the middle rack of the oven for 5 minutes. Turn down the oven heat to 350°F and bake the cakes for about 20 minutes, until they are brown and crispy. Turn off the oven and let the cakes stand for 5 more minutes. Open the oven and pull them out, but leave the cakes in their pans for another 10 minutes before taking them out and cooling them on a rack.

Time needed: 55 minutes, including 30 minutes active

water bath, and stir it until smooth. Dip the edges of the nut triangles in the melted chocolate and place them on a rack to dry.

Time needed: 1 ½ hours, including about 1 hour active

Variation:

Coconut Triangles

In a food processor (metal blade), mix together 2 ½ cups flour, 3/4 cup (1 ½ sticks) butter (cut into pieces first), 3 tablespoons sugar, 1 egg, and 1 pinch salt until a smooth dough forms. Chill the dough for about 30 minutes. Preheat the oven to 350°F. Spread the pastry on a jellyroll pan with your hands or a floured rolling pin. Mix together 4 eggs, 1 cup whipping cream, 2/3 cup sugar, 2 teaspoons grated lemon zest, and one 7-ounce bag of shredded coconut. Spread the coconut mixture onto the pastry. Bake on the middle oven rack for about 30 minutes. Cool, cut into squares, and then into triangles, as directed above. Melt 4 ounces of semisweet chocolate in a water bath, stirring until smooth. Dip the edges of the triangles in the melted chocolate and place them on a rack to dry.

Nut Triangles
Stay delicious for a few days

Makes 20 to 30 triangles:

For the pastry:

1 cup (2 sticks) unsalted butter, softened

1 cup powdered sugar

1 egg

1 egg yolk

1 teaspoon grated lemon zest

2 ½ cups flour

1 ½ teaspoons baking powder

1/2 teaspoon salt

For the topping:

4 cups hazelnuts or almonds

1 cup shelled pistachio nuts

1/2 cup honey

1 cup (2 sticks) unsalted butter

8 tablespoons whipping cream

1/2 teaspoon ground cinnamon

3/4 cup slivered almonds

For the coating:

10 ounces semisweet chocolate

1 Make the pastry: In a food processor (metal blade), combine the butter, powdered sugar, egg, egg yolk, and lemon zest and process until smooth. Add the flour, baking powder, and salt and process briefly until the mixture forms a smooth dough. Wrap the dough in plastic wrap, chill it for about 30 minutes, then spread the pastry out on an ungreased jellyroll pan using your hands or a floured rolling pin.

2 Preheat the oven to 350°F. Make the topping: Set aside 3 cups of the hazelnuts. Coarsely chop the remaining hazelnuts along with the pistachios. In a food processor (metal blade), process the 3 cups hazelnuts until finely ground. Mix the honey, butter, and whipping cream with the ground nuts and the cinnamon in a saucepan. Heat the mixture until it looks like thick mush.

3 Stir the chopped hazelnuts, pistachios, and slivered almonds into the mush and cool the whole thing for 5 minutes. Spread the nut mixture onto the pastry, smoothing the surface evenly. Bake the whole thing in the oven on the middle rack for 20 to 25 minutes. Remove the pan from the oven and cool on a rack. Cover the pan with foil and let stand overnight.

4 Cut the baked rectangle into squares approximately 3 ½ inches on each side, and then cut them diagonally into triangles. Make the coating: Chop the chocolate, melt it in a

Brownies
To die for!

Makes 40 brownies:

1 ½ cups (3 sticks) unsalted butter

2 ¼ cups sugar

2 tablespoons vanilla extract

5 eggs

1 cup flour

1 cups cocoa powder

1 teaspoon salt

Optional: 1 ½ cups chopped peanuts, walnuts, or pecans

1 Line a jellyroll pan with parchment paper. Preheat the oven to 350°F.

2 In a saucepan, melt the butter. Transfer the butter to a medium bowl, add the sugar,

and mix well with a spoon. Stir in the vanilla and blend well. Add the eggs one at a time, completely incorporating them before adding the next egg.

3 In another bowl, mix together the flour, cocoa, and salt. Add the flour mixture to the butter mixture and mix until blended. If desired, stir in the nuts.

4 Pour the batter into the pan, smoothing the surface. Bake for 40 to 45 minutes, until the edges begin to draw away from the sides of the pan. Remove from the oven and cool before cutting into bars.

Time needed: About 1 hour, including 40 minutes waiting for them to be done

Crispy Apricot Bars
Bring your energy back

Makes 18 bars:

1/3 cup dried apricots

3/4 cup (1 ½ sticks) unsalted butter

2-3 tablespoons honey

2 cups Rice Crispies cereal

1 cup chopped almonds

1 egg

1 egg yolk

2/3 cup flour

3/4 cup apricot jam

1 tablespoon lemon juice

1 Dice the apricots. Heat them in a saucepan with the butter and honey over low heat until the butter melts. Process the cereal in a food processor (metal blade) until it is reduced to fine crumbs (or you can put the cereal in a locking plastic bag and roll it with a rolling pin into fine crumbs). Mix the cereal crumbs in a bowl with the almonds, egg, egg yolk, and flour. Preheat the oven to 350°F. Butter an 11-x-7-x-2-inch baking pan.

2 With a wooden spoon, mix the cereal mixture and the butter-apricot mixture. Put half of it in the baking pan and press down with the spoon to compact it slightly. In a small bowl, mix the jam and lemon juice, and spread it on top of the cereal mixture in the pan. Press the remaining cereal mixture on top evenly.

3 Bake on the middle oven rack for about 30 minutes, until the surface is nice and brown. Cool them to lukewarm, then cut them into 2 inch squares.

Time needed: 50 minutes, including 20 active

Crunchy Chocolate Bars
No oven necessary

Makes 16 bars:

4 ounces bittersweet chocolate

4 ounces milk chocolate

6 tablespoons (3/4 stick) unsalted butter

1 tablespoon honey

2 tablespoons whipping cream

3/4 cup shelled walnuts

3/4 cup crumbled vanilla wafers

2 tablespoons shredded coconut

1 Chop the chocolates. In a saucepan, melt the chocolates with the butter, honey, and cream over low heat, stirring until everything is smooth.

2 Finely chop the walnuts. Stir the walnuts and vanilla wafers into the chocolate mixture and pour the whole thing into an 8-inch square pan. Sprinkle the top with the coconut and chill until firm. Cut into bars.

Time needed: 15 minutes (not including cooling)

Apple Fritters
Super as a snack

Makes about 14 fritters:

3 large tart apples

2 tablespoons sugar

2 tablespoons lemon juice

3/4 cup flour

Pinch of salt

1 egg

1/2 cup beer or mineral water

1 egg white

1/4 teaspoon cream of tartar

2 ½ cups canola or vegetable oil

Cinnamon sugar (sugar flavored with ground cinnamon to taste—about 1/4 teaspoon cinnamon per 1 tablespoon sugar)

1 First, peel the apples. Now you have to take out the core. Experienced fritter makers use an apple corer. If you don't have one, do this: Use a small knife to cut a round hole in the apple from both the blossom and stem ends and push out the core. But be very careful when doing this!! If there are still bits of core inside, get them out using the point of a potato peeler or a melon baller. And, if you end up without a nice-looking, coreless apple, cut the apple into small pieces. You can batter and fry the little apple pieces and they'll still taste good.

2 Once the apples have been cored, cut them crosswise into 1/2-inch-thick rings. Sprinkle the apple rings with the sugar and lemon juice and set them aside.

3 In a bowl, mix the flour with the salt. Separate the egg. Stir the egg yolk and beer into the flour mixture until it's smooth. The batter should be thick. In a clean, grease-free bowl, beat both egg whites until stiff, adding the cream of tartar when they turn foamy. Fold the stiff egg whites into the batter.

4 In a large, deep-sided saucepan, heat the oil until it is about 350°F (see the Tip below). A few at a time, draw the apple rings through the batter, letting the excess batter drip off, and add them to the hot oil (you don't want to add any more than can float in one layer on top of the oil). Fry the fritters on both sides for about 1 minute each, until they are golden brown. Remove the fritters from the oil using a skimmer or tongs, and drain them on paper towels. Ideally, eat the fritters while they're warm, sprinkled with cinnamon sugar.

Time needed: 30 minutes

Basic Tip
Fat for frying

To keep fried foods from being too greasy, the fat needs to be nice and hot. When it's at the right temperature, the oil will immediately form a crust on the outside of the food that you're frying and will prevent the food from absorbing any of the oil. Be careful: Not every fat can stand that much heat. Good choices are canola, soybean, safflower, and other vegetable oils. In fact, the stuff labeled plain old "vegetable oil" is perfect.

The best way to test the temperature of the oil is to use a candy thermometer. Here's how to tell whether the oil's hot enough without the thermometer: Hold a wooden kitchen spoon in it, and if lots of small bubbles immediately rise along the spoon, you can go ahead with the frying. Or, drop a cube of white bread into the hot oil. It should take no more than 1 minute for it to turn brown and crispy. Note that you will probably have to adjust the burner's heat throughout the frying process in order to maintain the right level of heat. Or, if you have an electric stove, you may have to take the pan off the burner from time to time so that it doesn't get too hot.

Miniature Chocolate Cakes
Almost flourless

Makes 6 cakes:

8 ounces semisweet chocolate

1 cup (2 sticks) unsalted butter

4 eggs

1/2 teaspoon cream of tartar

1/4 cup granulated sugar

1/4 cup powdered sugar

1/4 cup flour

Powdered sugar

Lightly sweetened whipped cream

Lemon Napoleons
Good anytime

Makes 10 slices:

1 package (17.3 ounces) frozen puff pastry

4 lemons

4 eggs

3 tablespoons unsalted butter, softened

1 cup powdered sugar

1 cup whipping cream

1 Remove the puff pastry from the package and thaw it at room temperature for 20 to 30 minutes.

2 Meanwhile, thoroughly wash one lemon, dry it, and finely grate the zest. Squeeze the juice from all of the lemons.

3 Preheat the oven to 425°F. Stack the sheets of puff pastry on a lightly floured work surface and roll them out with a rolling pin into a thin rectangle. Cut the rolled-out pastry into three equal-sized rectangles. Run cold water over the baking sheet and do not dry it. Put the rectangles of puff pastry on the wet baking sheet. Bake the pastry on the middle rack of the oven for about 15 minutes, until it is puffed and golden brown. Cool the pastry briefly, then cut one of the rectangles crosswise into 10 pieces.

4 Fill a large bowl with cold water and ice cubes. Put the eggs, butter, powdered sugar, lemon zest, and lemon juice in a saucepan. Set the heat to just under medium and cook while stirring constantly until the mixture thickens somewhat. Take care: The filling shouldn't boil, or the eggs will curdle. Put the saucepan in the ice water bath (don't let the water get inside the pan) and keep stirring the mixture with a wooden spoon until it has cooled.

5 In another bowl, beat the cream until very stiff (be careful not to overbeat or it will look like cottage cheese!) and fold it into the cooled lemon filling. Spread about half of the filling neatly onto one puff pastry rectangle. Place the second rectangle onto it and spread it with the remaining filling. Set the 10 small pieces of puff pastry on top of the filling, standing them up on one long side, and placing them slightly askew. Let the napoleons rest for about 30 minutes.

6 To serve, use a serrated knife to carefully cut the napoleons into serving portions—try not to press too hard or you'll squish them.

Time needed: 45 minutes active, 15 minutes resting

1 Chop the chocolate. Melt the chocolate and butter in a saucepan over low heat; stir the mixture until it's smooth, and set it aside. Separate the eggs. In a clean, grease-free bowl, beat the egg whites until stiff, sprinkling in the cream of tartar when the whites turn foamy, and the granulated sugar when the whites reach soft peaks. In another bowl, beat the egg yolks and the powdered sugar until they make a thick, foamy mixture that is light yellow in color.

2 Preheat the oven to 350°F. Coat six 4½-inch tartlet pans first with butter, then with flour, shaking out the excess flour. Fold the chocolate mixture into the egg yolk mixture. Heap the egg white mixture on top, sift the flour over it, and fold everything together using a hand whisk. Divide the batter among the pans, smoothing the tops. Bake the cakes on the middle oven rack for about 30 minutes. Leave the cakes in the switched-off oven with the door ajar for 10 minutes. Cool the cakes on a rack before serving. Sprinkle them with powdered sugar and serve them with whipped cream.

Time needed: 1 hour, half of that time active

Berry Tartlets
A midsummer day's dream

Makes 6 tartlets:

For the pastry:

1 ⅓ cups flour

Pinch of salt

2 tablespoons sugar

1/4 cup (1/2 stick) cold unsalted butter

1/2 teaspoons vanilla extract

1-3 tablespoons ice water

For the filling:

2 vanilla beans

1 cup milk

2 ½ tablespoons sugar

2 egg yolks

1 ½ tablespoons cornstarch

1/2 cup whipping cream

1 teaspoon grated lemon zest

12 ounces fresh raspberries, blackberries, or blueberries

1 Make the pastry: In a food processor (metal blade), combine the flour, salt, and sugar and pulse the machine to blend the ingredients. Cut the butter into cubes and add them to the machine. Pulse for 25 to 30 times, until the mixture is evenly crumbly.

Add the vanilla and 1 tablespoon of the water and pulse just until the dough starts to come together, adding more water if necessary. Wrap the dough in plastic wrap, and chill it for about 1 hour.

2 Preheat the oven to 400°F. Divide the pastry into 6 equal pieces and, with your hands, press each piece into a 4 ½-inch tartlet pan up to the edges. Line each pan with a square of parchment paper, lightly pushing it down onto the pastry. Fill the tartlet shells with dried beans or pie weights.

3 Bake the tartlet shells on the middle oven rack for about 18 to 22 minutes, until the pastry is golden brown. Then, remove the beans and the paper. Cool the tartlet shells on a rack.

4 Make the filling: Slit the vanilla beans lengthwise, scrape out the seeds, and add the seeds along with the pods to a saucepan with the milk. Heat the milk until just under the boiling point and remove it from the heat. Fish out the vanilla pods. In a bowl, thoroughly whisk the sugar, egg yolks, cornstarch, and 1/4 of the vanilla-infused milk. Then, whisk the whole thing into the remaining vanilla-milk in the saucepan and heat slowly, stirring constantly with a wooden spoon. When everything has thickened slightly and begins to gel, remove the pan from the heat. Transfer the filling to a bowl and let it stand until cool, stirring from time to time.

5 In a bowl, beat the whipping cream until stiff, adding the lemon zest. Fold the lemon whipped cream into the cooled cream filling. Pick over the berries, removing any leaves or spoiled berries. Pop the tartlet shells out of the pans and put them on serving plates. Spread the vanilla cream filling evenly in the tartlet shells, then arrange the berries on top. Serve immediately.

Vanilla Tartlets
Great with coffee

Makes 6 tartlets:

1 sheet (1/2 of a 17.3-ounce package) frozen puff pastry

1 vanilla bean

5 egg yolks

1 cup whipping cream

1 tablespoon cornstarch

1/4 cup sugar

Pinch of salt

Grated zest of 1/2 lemon

For sprinkling:

2 teaspoons powdered sugar

1/4-1/2 teaspoon ground cinnamon

1 Remove the pastry from the package and thaw it at room temperature for 20 to 30 minutes. Slit the vanilla bean along its length and scrape out the seeds. Put the egg yolks in a saucepan and stir in the vanilla seeds.

2 In a small bowl, mix 2 tablespoons of the whipping cream with the cornstarch. Pour the remaining cream, the sugar, and salt into the pan and whisk well. Mix in the lemon zest. Slowly heat the mixture over low heat, stirring constantly. When the mixture is warm, stir in the cornstarch mixture. Once it begins to steam, it will slowly get thicker. Take care not to let the mixture boil or the egg yolk will curdle. Remove the thickened filling from the heat and let it cool to lukewarm, stirring occasionally.

3 Preheat the oven to 425°F. Rinse six 4 ½-inch tartlet pans with cold water but do not dry them. Roll out the puff pastry on a floured work surface until it's big enough so that you can cut out 6 circles for the pans. To do so, turn the pans upside down on the pastry and cut around them with a small knife leaving 1/4 inch extra space on all sides. Line the pans with the pastry circles, pushing the pastry into any grooves.

4 Transfer the pastry-lined pans to a baking sheet. Fill each pastry shell almost up to the edge with vanilla filling. Bake the tartlets on the middle oven rack for about 10 minutes, until the filling sets and the surface gets a few brown spots on it. Cool the tartlets and sprinkle with powdered sugar and cinnamon.

Doughnuts
Deep-fried on the stovetop

OK, so they don't have holes in the middle. But you won't care after tasting them. Plus, they're a lot quicker to make than the ones with holes. A simple trick will make these especially puffy: When frying the first side, cover the pot so the steam that is produced will really inflate them.

Makes about 10 doughnuts:

Almost 1/2 cup milk

2 tablespoons unsalted butter, softened

1 ⅓ cups flour

2 tablespoons sugar

Pinch of salt

2 teaspoons rapid-rise yeast

2 egg yolks (make sure they are at room temperature)

Canola or other mild-flavored vegetable oil

Vanilla sugar (see Tip) or powdered sugar for rolling

1 In a saucepan, heat the milk with the butter until the milk reaches 120°F (check it on an instant-read thermometer).

2 Put the flour, sugar, and salt in a food processor (metal blade) and pulse until the ingredients are blended. Add the yeast and pulse to mix. Add the egg yolks and milk-butter mixture and process until the mixture forms a smooth, slightly stiff dough. Process the dough for 45 to 60 seconds.

3 Transfer the dough to a lightly oiled bowl, cover the dough with a clean dishtowel, and let it rise in a warm, draft-free place for 15 to 20 minutes. Punch down the dough, knead it again, and let it rise in a warm spot for another 15 to 20 minutes.

4 On a floured work surface, and with a floured rolling pin, roll out the dough and cut out portions with a drinking glass (3 ½ to 4 inches in diameter), as if it were a cookie cutter. Place the doughnuts on a piece of parchment paper, cover them with a towel, and let them rise again for 20 to 30 minutes—they should double in size.

5 Into a deep-sided saucepan, pour about 2 to 3 inches of the oil. Heat the oil over medium to high heat until it reaches 350°F (if you don't have a candy thermometer to test it, see the Tip on page 92). Carefully add as many doughnuts as can float next to each other to the hot oil. Quickly cover the pan, and fry the doughnuts for about 1 to 1 ½ minutes on one side, until they are golden brown. With tongs or a couple of wooden spoons, turn over the doughnuts and finish frying them without the lid for another 1 to 1 ½ minutes.

6 With a skimmer or tongs, remove the doughnuts from the pan, drain them briefly on paper towels, and roll them in vanilla sugar while still warm (or sift powdered sugar over the cooled doughnuts). Fry the remaining doughnuts in the same manner. Note: You'll probably have to adjust the heat throughout the cooking process in order to keep it at an appropriate level. Electric stoves are harder to control than gas stoves.

Time needed: About 2 hours, including 50 minutes doing something

Basic Tip

Homemade Vanilla Sugar
Don't throw away your vanilla beans after they've been slit open and the seeds have been scraped out. Instead, rinse the beans and let them dry. Cut the beans into pieces about 1 inch long and mix them with granulated sugar in a screw-top jar, sealed tightly. After about 2 weeks, the vanilla-infused sugar will be ready to use in any recipe just as you would use any type of regular sugar.

Chocolate Cream Puffs

Caution: Danger of addiction!

Makes 16 puffs:

For the choux paste:

1 cup water

6 tablespoons (3/4 stick) unsalted butter

1 tablespoon sugar

Pinch of salt

1 cup flour

4 eggs

1 teaspoon baking powder

For the filling:

1 box chocolate "Cook & Serve" pudding (3.4 ounces)

2 cups milk

2 ½ tablespoons sugar

2 tablespoons crème fraîche

1 tablespoon grated chocolate

Pinch of ground cinnamon

Powdered sugar or cocoa powder

1 Make the choux paste (which will turn into the cream puffs): Pour the water into a heavy saucepan. Cut the butter into pieces and add it to the pan with the sugar and salt. Bring the water to a boil. Reduce the heat to a very low setting.

2 Pull the pan off the heat and pour the flour into the butter-water mixture all at once, stirring well with a wooden spoon. Return the pan to the heat and keep stirring the mixture until it becomes a solid lump that can barely be stirred anymore, and a thin white layer can be seen on the bottom of the pan.

3 Transfer the mixture to a bowl. Cool it to lukewarm, for about 15 minutes, then mix in the eggs one at a time until they are incorporated into the dough. Add the baking powder along with the last egg.

4 Preheat the oven to 350°F. Line a baking sheet with parchment paper. Use 2 teaspoons to portion generous heaps of the choux paste on the baking sheet, placing them at least 1 inch apart. Bake them on the middle rack for about 35 minutes, until they have risen and browned. Do not open the oven door for the first 20 minutes no matter what happens, or the dream will collapse!

5 In the meantime, make the filling: Mix the pudding powder with 1/2 cup of the milk, and the sugar. Pour the remaining 1 ½ cups milk into a saucepan. Stir the pudding mixture into the milk in the saucepan and place it over medium heat, until it comes to a boil, stirring the whole time. Remove the mixture from the heat, pour it into a bowl, and let it cool. Keep stirring to prevent formation of a skin on the pudding and to aid the cooling process.

6 Remove the cream puffs from the oven. Immediately cut open the cream puffs using kitchen scissors or a serrated knife, then cool them to room temperature.

7 Stir the crème fraîche, grated chocolate, and cinnamon into the cooled pudding. Spread the cream puff bottoms with the filling mixture, dividing evenly. Put the cream puff tops over the filling like a sandwich. Sprinkle the cream puffs with powdered sugar or cocoa, and eat them immediately.

Time needed: 2 hours, including 35 minutes doing something

Christmas Cookies
Simply sweet!

Makes about 40 cookies:

For the dough:

6 tablespoons (3/4 stick) unsalted butter, softened

1 cup sugar

1/2 teaspoon vanilla extract

1 egg

2 tablespoons whipping cream

1 ⅔ cups flour

1/3 cup cornstarch

2 teaspoons baking powder

1/4 teaspoon salt

For decorating:

1 egg white (optional)

1 ⅔ cups powdered sugar (optional)

2 tablespoons lemon or orange juice, rum, coffee, or other flavorful liquid (optional)

Food coloring (optional)

Tubes of purchased icing (optional)

Sprinkles and other cookie garnishes (optional)

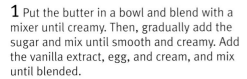

1 Put the butter in a bowl and blend with a mixer until creamy. Then, gradually add the sugar and mix until smooth and creamy. Add the vanilla extract, egg, and cream, and mix until blended.

2 In another bowl, mix the flour with the cornstarch, baking powder, and salt. With a wooden spoon, quickly stir half of the flour mixture into the butter mixture. Add the rest of the flour mixture and stir or knead with your hands until a smooth dough forms. Wrap the dough in plastic wrap and refrigerate it for at least 1 hour.

3 Preheat the oven to 350°F. Line a baking sheet with parchment paper. Sprinkle a work surface with flour. With a lightly floured rolling pin, roll the dough out on the work surface until it is about 1/8 inch thick. Dip Christmas-themed cookie cutters into the flour and press them into the dough to make shapes. Keep dipping the cookie cutters into the flour between cuts. With a metal spatula, transfer the cookie shapes to the baking sheet. Knead the dough scraps together, roll them out again, and cut additional shapes.

4 Bake the cookies for about 8 to 12 minutes, until they are light brown—don't let them get too dark. Cool them on a rack. Cover the cookies and let them stand overnight before decorating.

5 For the decorating, we're not going to tell you what to do. After all, beauty's in the eye of the beholder. If you choose to frost the cookies, stir together the egg white, powdered sugar, and your preferred liquid until smooth and color it as desired with food coloring. Otherwise, pile the cookies high or low with your favorite decorations.

Time needed: 3 hours, including 2 hours active—not counting the cooling time overnight

Vanilla-Moons
Short and sweet

Makes about 50 cookies:

1 cup almonds

3/4 cup (1 ½ sticks) cold unsalted butter

6 tablespoons sugar

1 teaspoon vanilla extract

1 ⅔ cups flour

1/4 teaspoon salt

About 1 tablespoon whipping cream

Sugar or vanilla sugar (see Tip on page 96)

1 Put the almonds in a food processor (metal blade) and process until they're finely ground. Cut the butter into pieces. With your hands or with a food processor, knead the butter, sugar, vanilla extract, almonds, flour, and salt together until a smooth dough forms, adding the whipping cream if necessary to bind the ingredients. Wrap the dough in plastic wrap and chill it for at least 1 hour.

2 Line a baking sheet with parchment paper. Preheat the oven to 350°F. Shape walnut-sized pieces of dough into cylinders with pointed ends. Bend the cylinders into crescents and put them on the baking sheet.

3 Bake the vanilla moons on the middle oven rack for about 12 minutes, taking care

---

that they don't get too dark. Carefully roll the warm cookies in the sugar and cool completely before serving.

Time needed: 2 hours, 1 hour active

Cinnamon-Hazelnut Rounds
Crispy and gooey

Makes about 50 cookies:

2 ½ cups hazelnuts

2 teaspoons ground cinnamon

4 egg whites

1/2 teaspoon cream of tartar

1 ¼ cups powdered sugar

1/2 teaspoon vanilla extract

1 In a food processor (metal blade) process the hazelnuts until they're very finely ground. Add the cinnamon and pulse to combine.

2 Preheat the oven to 325°F. Line a baking sheet with parchment paper.

3 In a clean, grease-free bowl, beat the egg whites. When the egg whites turn foamy, add the cream of tartar and continue beating. When soft peaks form, slowly sprinkle in the sugar and vanilla extract. Keep beating until stiff peaks form and the mixture turns glossy.

4 Fold in the nut mixture using a hand whisk. Use two teaspoons to transfer small mounds of batter to the parchment paper. Bake the cookies on the lower oven rack for about 20 minutes, until crispy. Cool before eating.

Oatmeal Cookies
Almost healthy

Makes about 50 cookies:

1 cup (2 sticks) unsalted butter, softened

1 ½ cups brown sugar

2 eggs

1 teaspoon vanilla extract

2 cups old-fashioned oats

1 ½ cups flour

1 teaspoon baking soda

1/2 teaspoon salt

1/2 teaspoon ground cinnamon

3/4 cup raisins

1 Preheat the oven to 350°F. Line a baking sheet with parchment paper.

2 Put the butter in a bowl with the brown sugar and beat until the mixture is light and creamy. Mix in the eggs one at a time, then blend in the vanilla extract.

3 In another bowl, mix together the oats, flour, baking soda, salt, and cinnamon. Add the flour mixture to the butter mixture and mix until everything is blended. Stir in the raisins at the end.

4 Using a tablespoon, place portions of the dough 1 ½ inches apart on the baking sheet. Bake the cookies for about 12 to 15 minutes, until golden brown. Cool on a rack.

Choco-Nut Bars
So easy to make

Makes about 60 bars:

10 ounces bittersweet chocolate

2 ½ cups sliced almonds

2/3 cup flour

1 cup (2 sticks) unsalted butter, softened

1 ¼ cups sugar

6 eggs

8 ounces semisweet chocolate

1 Cut the bittersweet chocolate into pieces. In a food processor (metal blade), process the almonds until they're finely ground. Transfer the almonds to a bowl. Add the chocolate to the food processor and process until it is finely ground. Return the almonds to the machine along with the flour and pulse with the chocolate until everything is blended.

2 Preheat the oven to 350°F. Line a jellyroll pan with parchment paper. With a mixer, beat the butter and sugar until it is light and creamy. Mix in the eggs one after the other. Mix in the chocolate mixture.

3 Transfer the batter to the pan, smoothing the surface evenly with a spatula. Bake it on the middle oven rack for 35 to 40 minutes. Take the pan out of the oven, and while still hot, cut everything into bars about 1 inch wide and 2 inches long. Cool the bars, then remove them from the baking sheet.

4 Chop the semisweet chocolate into pieces, then melt it in a water bath, stirring until smooth. Spread the chocolate over the bars. Let the bars stand until the chocolate has set.

Time needed: at least 1 hour, about half of which is active

Triple Almond Cookies
Eat these immediately

Makes about 35 cookies:

1 cup blanched almonds

2 tubes marzipan (7 ounces each)

1 egg

6 tablespoons powdered sugar

2 tablespoons amaretto or almond syrup (try a coffeehouse for the almond syrup)

1 ½ cups flour

1 egg yolk

1-2 tablespoons chopped almonds

1 In a food processor (metal blade), process the almonds until they're finely ground. Transfer the almonds to a bowl. Cube the marzipan and process it until it is finely ground. Add the almonds back to the machine with the marzipan, along with the egg, powdered sugar, amaretto, and flour, and process until everything is just blended.

2 Preheat the oven to 300°F. Line a baking sheet with parchment paper. Shape walnut-size pieces of the dough into balls, place them on the baking sheet, and press them until they are a bit flatter. Moistening your hands from time to time will help keep things from sticking.

3 Brush the cookies with the egg yolk, slightly beaten, and sprinkle them with the chopped almonds. Bake the cookies on the middle oven rack for 12 to 15 minutes. Cool before eating.

Orange-Ginger-Nut Diamonds
With an Asian flair

Makes about 40 cookies:

3/4 cup candied ginger

3 oranges

3 ½ cups blanched almonds

1/2 cup sugar

2 eggs

2 tablespoons chopped pistachio nuts

1 Chop the candied ginger, then grate the zest from the oranges (remember to wash them first). Squeeze out the orange juice and strain it to get rid of the seeds.

2 Preheat the oven to 325°F. In a food processor (metal blade), process the almonds until they're finely ground. Set aside 1 tablespoon of the sugar. Beat the eggs with the remaining sugar until foamy. Stir in the ground almonds, orange zest, and candied ginger to make the dough.

3 Roll out the dough between 2 sheets of plastic wrap until it is about 1 inch thick. Cut the dough into diamond shapes. Put half of the diamonds on a parchment-lined baking sheet and bake them on the middle oven rack for 10 to 12 minutes. Transfer the baked cookies to a cooling rack. Bake the remaining half of the cookies in the same manner.

4 In a saucepan, vigorously boil the reserved 1 tablespoon of sugar with the orange juice until it turns syrupy, about 5 minutes, then cool the mixture. Put each of the cookies in the orange mixture and let them stand for 1 minute. Remove the cookies, let them dry slightl, and dunk them again as before. Place the cookies on a rack, sprinkle them with the pistachios, and let them stand for 1 to 2 days before eating.

Ladyfingers
Just like Paris

Makes about 60 ladyfingers:

4 eggs

1/2 teaspoon cream of tartar

1 cup sugar

1 teaspoon vanilla extract

1 ¼ cups flour (sifted!)

Pinch of salt

2 tablespoons powdered sugar

1 Line a baking sheet with parchment paper and preheat the oven to 350°F. Then, separate the eggs.

2 In a clean, grease-free bowl, beat the egg whites. When the whites are foamy, add the cream of tartar and keep beating. When the whites form soft peaks, drizzle in 1/3 cup of the sugar and keep beating until the mixture is very stiff and glossy.

3 In another bowl, beat the egg yolks, vanilla extract, and the remaining 2/3 cup sugar until the mixture is nice and foamy and light yellow in color. Mix the flour with the salt. Fold the flour mixture and egg whites into the egg yolk mixture in two installments.

4 Carefully add the batter to a pastry bag (see page 23) and pipe "fingers" about 4

inches long onto the baking sheet. The ends should be a bit thicker than the middle of each finger. Sift powdered sugar over them and bake the ladyfingers on the middle oven rack for about 12 minutes. They should turn only light golden brown. Transfer the ladyfingers to a rack to cool.

Time needed: 50 minutes, including 35 active

Chocolate Chunk Cookies
A classic

Makes about 50 cookies:

4 ounces semisweet chocolate

3/4 cup (1 ½ sticks) unsalted butter, softened

1 cup granulated sugar

3/4 cup brown sugar, packed

2 eggs

1 teaspoon vanilla extract

1 ¾ cups flour

1 teaspoon baking powder

1/4 teaspoon salt

1 Cut the chocolate into medium chunks. Put the butter in a bowl and mix it until smooth with an electric mixer. Add the sugars and beat until the mixture is light and creamy. Add the eggs and vanilla and mix well.

2 Preheat the oven to 325°F. Line a baking sheet with parchment paper. In another bowl, mix the flour with the baking powder and salt. Add the flour mixture to the butter mixture and mix well. Stir in the chocolate chunks with a wooden spoon.

3 Drop teaspoonfuls of dough 1 ½ inches apart onto the baking sheet. Bake the cookies on the middle oven rack for about 20 minutes. Let them stand for a few minutes, then carefully transfer them using a spatula to a baking rack to cool.

Time needed: 50 minutes, including 30 active

Variations:

Thicker, Chewier Chocolate Chunk Cookies
Substitute vegetable shortening for at least half of the butter. Use cake flour (available in the baking section of most supermarkets) instead of regular (all-purpose) flour.

Peanut-Chocolate Chunk Cookies
Substitute peanut butter for 1/4 cup of the butter. Omit the granulated sugar and increase the brown sugar to 1 ¾ cups. Add 2 tablespoons cocoa powder with the flour and 1 cup chopped peanuts (unsalted!) with the chocolate chunks.

Amaretto Cookies
Worthy of an Italian pasticceria

Makes about 35 cookies:

2 ½ cups blanched almonds

Pinch of salt

3 egg whites

1/4 teaspoon cream of tartar

2/3 cup sugar

1/2 teaspoon pure almond extract

1 Preheat the oven 275°F. Line 2 baking sheets with parchment paper.

2 In a food processor (metal blade), process the almonds until they are very finely ground, almost like flour. Add the salt and pulse the machine to mix it.

3 In a clean, grease-free bowl, beat the egg whites until they are very stiff and glossy, adding the cream of tartar when the egg whites turn foamy, and the sugar (slowly, please!) when the egg whites reach soft peaks. Stir the ground almonds and the almond extract into the egg white mixture.

4 Shape the dough into walnut-sized balls—using two teaspoons or your fingers—

and put them on the baking sheets an inch or two apart.

5 If you suddenly remember that you have to go somewhere, you can leave the baking sheet until the next day. The cookies will even get better if they have dried on the outside. But be sure you turn off the oven! If you're impatient, go right ahead and bake. Bake the cookies on the middle oven rack for about 30 minutes, until they're very dry and golden brown.

Time needed: 50 minutes, of which 20 are active

White Chocolate-Ginger Cookies
Extra spicy with 2 types of ginger

Makes about 50 cookies:

6 ounces good-quality white chocolate

1 piece fresh ginger (about 1 inch long)

1 tablespoon shelled pistachios

3/4 cup (1 ½ sticks) unsalted butter

2 cups flour

1 teaspoon vanilla extract

1/4 cup chopped candied ginger

Powdered sugar (optional)

1 Cut 2 ounces of the white chocolate into little cubes and set them aside. Chop the rest of the white chocolate and melt it over a water bath. Let the chocolate cool slightly.

2 Peel the fresh ginger and chop very finely. Or, press the ginger through a garlic press (be sure the press is clean so that it doesn't smell like garlic!). Finely chop the pistachios.

3 Cut the butter into cubes and add it to a food processor (metal blade). Add the flour, melted white chocolate, and vanilla extract, and process until a smooth dough forms. Dump the dough onto a work surface and knead in the pistachios, candied ginger, and white chocolate cubes with your hands. Form the dough into a ball, wrap it with plastic wrap, and chill it for 1 hour.

4 Preheat the oven to 350°F. Line a baking sheet with parchment paper. Shape the dough into walnut-sized balls, press them slightly flat, and put them on the baking sheet. Bake the cookies on the middle oven rack for approximately 10 minutes. Remove them from the baking sheet and cool them on a rack before eating. Roll the cookies in powdered sugar if desired.

Time needed: 1 ¾ hours, including about 35 minutes active

Elegan
but

So elegant you'd like to scoop the whole thing right off the plate...

t
easy

Jane: "What makes a torte a torte, instead of a cake?"
Joe: "When it's stuffed full of pastry cream."
Jane: "Then how do you explain the Lemon Napoleon?"
Joe: "Well,...a torte has to be round, too, I guess."
Jane: "Like Linzertorte? Sorry, but it doesn't have any pastry cream!"
Joe: "OK, Smart One. How do you explain Sachertorte then?"
Jane: "Well...it's just too rich to be called a cake."

Confused? We know. The definition of torte is pretty hard to pin down. But you'll know it when you see it: Rich, dense, or multi-layered, stuffed with luscious fillings or made with top-quality ingredients. And it's so elegant you'd like to scoop the whole thing right off the serving plate.

Chocolate

Chocolate can be intimidating to Basic cooks, because it is so temperamental. Don't worry: Once you get used to working with it, you will feel like a pastry chef in training. Here are a few things to remember.

As we said in chapter 1, always buy top-quality chocolate for your desserts—you won't be sorry. Don't just pick up a candy bar off the drug store shelf because it probably doesn't have enough cocoa solids and cocoa butter to behave itself in these recipes.

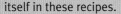
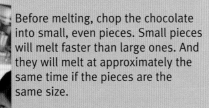

Before melting, chop the chocolate into small, even pieces. Small pieces will melt faster than large ones. And they will melt at approximately the same time if the pieces are the same size.

When melting pure chocolate, make sure the bowl and utensils are completely dry. Even a drop of water will cause the chocolate to "seize." In lay terms, this means that it will clump together and refuse to melt properly. If your chocolate seizes on you, you can still save it by adding cream or butter (1 tablespoon for every 2 ounces of chocolate) to it before continuing to melt it. You can use this mixture for a glaze or filling, but you'll have to start over melting your pure chocolate.

The best way to melt chocolate is over a water bath. If you're lucky enough to have your Grandma's double boiler in the house, get it out. Otherwise, you can improvise. Pick a bowl, preferably stainless steel, and dry it with a paper towel. Chop the chocolate into little pieces and put it in the bowl. Set the bowl over a saucepan filled with an inch or two of simmering (not boiling) water. Make sure the bowl can sit comfortably in the pan without touching the water below. Turn off the heat and let the chocolate melt, stirring it until it is smooth. Remember: Chocolate only needs a little bit of heat to melt it. Too much heat will cause its components to separate or burn. Stirring it constantly will keep the temperature even.

A Brief Guide to the Architecture of Tortes

Like most fascinating structures, a well-built torte is made of only a few contrasting materials. What steel and concrete are to skyscrapers, the cake layers and fillings are to tortes. Following are the most popular types of tortes from an architectural point of view (with a little fast food theory thrown in).

Open-Faced Sandwich Style
Simple in structure, and often built with opulent materials. This style requires good engineering, because the filling stands alone on a layer of pastry (at most supported by the edge of the pastry). The base is usually made of rich flaky pastry, and the filling is often reinforced with gelatin. A typical structure: Rice Pudding Torte (page 122).

Regular Sandwich Style
A continuation of the sandwich style, in which a more solid filling rises between two pastry layers. It's hard to cut if the top floor is too solid, which is usually not the case for the normal sponge cake sandwich. Otherwise, the top floor is pre-cut before installation (A typical structure: Orange-Meringue Torte, page 121).

Club Sandwich Style
This is the most popular style. Like its namesake, this torte includes at least one intermediate layer. The additional layer(s) gives heavy tortes some strength and reduces their kinetic energy (e.g., Walnut-Buttercream Torte, page 124). The objective of this type of structure is the separation of the different fillings, or the interplay between the filling and the layers (e.g., Crêpe Gâteau, page 113). Club sandwich style tortes are often frosted, usually with the same material that comprises the filling (e.g., Baby Black Forest Torte, page 112).

Club Sandwich Deluxe Style
This is used only for certain particularly festive structures and is characterized by a tower made of several club sandwich style tortes,

with an exterior design that in some cases runs riot to the point of kitsch. It is beloved of large families. A typical structure: Wedding cake from a bakery.

Loaf-of-Bread Style
This is the exact opposite of the CSD style, renouncing any bric-a-brac and allowing intense individual materials to express themselves. The result is a solid torte made of one piece, at most refined by a glaze and/or frosting. A typical structure: Sachertorte (page 110).

Five Quick Ideas for Decorating Tortes

People who decorate their cakes only with chocolate sprinkles and sugar flowers live the rest of their lives like accountants: Everything is carefully classified, thoroughly calculated, and always logical. People who avoid such compartmentalized thinking get their cake decorating ideas from all over. Here are five places for cake decorators who think outside the pastry box:

The candy aisle
Chocolate candies on chocolate tortes and licorice candy when there is an exotic fruit filling can mark the individual slices. So can cubes of nougat-filled candy bars, or halved purchased chocolate truffles. Chocolate chips can go anywhere. Use your imagination!

The baked goods section
Ladyfingers are always good, if you can find them. Leave them whole and arrange them like a star. Or, cut them into pieces and arrange them around whipped cream rosettes like flower petals. Even use ladyfingers as a cake border. Really elegant: Partially cover ladyfingers with melted chocolate and let them dry before using. Cute little cookies make cute little details. Sponge cake or pound cake can be cut into cubes or other shapes and either soaked or dipped in melted chocolate before using as a garnish.

The frozen foods section
Brush pieces of frozen puff pastry with egg yolk, sprinkle it with sugar, and cut it into a decorative shape. Then bake it and use it solo covered with frosting or melted chocolate for decoration. Mini-cream puffs can be halved and used to garnish finished tortes.

The produce department
Of course, you already know that fresh fruit makes a perfect garnish. But why not decorate tortes with fresh herbs, too? Mint goes with chocolate, thyme goes with stone fruits, and basil (put it on right before serving) tastes delicious with strawberries, cherries, and nectarines. Cool idea: Cut carrots into thin strips and simmer them in apricot jam. Use to decorate lemony desserts. Or coarsely grate the carrots, put them in a strainer, cover them with melted chocolate, and dry them on parchment paper—guilt-free chocolate sprinkles!

The rest of the store
Roast whole beans of your favorite coffee in a 200°F oven for at least 5 minutes. Transfer them to parchment paper, cool, and dip them in melted dark or white chocolate. Dry them on the parchment paper and dust them lightly with cocoa powder or ground cinnamon. You can also coat dried fruits, nuts, or seeds with melted chocolate.

Aunt Betty's Baking Bits

Dear Aunt Betty:
Cutting a cake—I've done it a hundred times, but it's not always 100 percent straight. A lot of times the slices come out uneven. Sometimes the whole thing looks horribly squished afterwards! The fact that everybody's watching me do it doesn't make it any easier. How do you do it, Aunt Betty?

Flustered in Fayetteville

Dear Flustered:
First, my dear bewildered one, I cut the cake in the kitchen. Obviously, in theory everyone should see how pretty it is. But should they also see how nervous you get when you're fiddling with it? Of course not. So here's the plan: Show them the cake at the table, but then bring it back to the kitchen for cutting. Your knife should be at least as long as the diameter of the cake, sturdy enough to cut straight, and not too wide—and of course, it has to be very sharp. Before cutting, it is important that the cake has cooled thoroughly. If there is a soft core under a solid frosting, it's better to saw than to press. But after that, firm cutting in one stroke is advised. Important: After every cut, rinse the knife in hot water and wipe it dry to ensure that the cut is smooth. And be careful to draw the blade all the way down to the plate and to go past the middle of the cake, or part of the slice will stick to the cake.

Now for the specifics. First count to see whether you want to cut the whole cake (advisable for six or more people) or only want part of it (then the rest stays fresher). For a large table of guests, the cake is cut crossways once and then again, to make quarters. Cut the quarters in half again, making eight slices of cake—for a large cake, these are still huge portions. If they are each cut in half again, there will be 16—petite servings. To cut a cake into 12 slices, cut one slice out of the middle of each quarter, producing three equal-sized slices.

Unbelievably Easy Wedding Cake
Perfect for eloping friends

Since you'll need three tiers, you'll see why your nesting set of springforms comes in handy. You'll need an 8-inch, 9-inch, and 10- or 11-inch pan for this recipe. A wedding cake simply must have at least that many layers, otherwise, it's only a cake, even if it looks pretty good.

Makes 30 to 40 slices:

For the cake layers:

2 boxes "butter recipe" yellow cake mix, plus the ingredients you'll need to make the cake (check the box panel for the additions)

For the filling:

2 boxes vanilla or raspberry "Cook & Serve" pudding (3.4-ounces each)

4 cups milk

7 tablespoons sugar

5 cups whipping cream

2 teaspoons vanilla extract

3 ½ ounces grated coconut (use 1/2 of a 7-ounce bag)

Sugar flowers and candies for decorating—your choice!

1 Make the cake layers: Preheat the oven according to the instructions on the package. Follow the package directions for greasing the pans and mixing the batter. Mix each batch in a separate bowl. Divide the batter among the three pans, filling each pan up to approximately the same level—even if you have to pour some of the batter from both bowls. Bake them according to the package directions in two stages: First bake the largest cake, testing it for doneness with the toothpick test (see Tip on page 38). Next, bake the remaining two cakes, rotating their positions in the oven halfway through the baking time. Remove the cakes from the oven, let them stand for about 10 minutes, then release them from the pans. Let the cakes cool while you're making the filling. If you have the time, let the cakes sit for a few hours before proceeding.

2 Make the filling: Mix the pudding powder (both boxes) with about 1 cup of the milk and 5 tablespoons of the sugar. Pour the remaining 3 cups milk into a large saucepan. Stir the pudding powder mixture into the milk in the saucepan and turn the heat to medium. Bring the mixture to a boil, stirring constantly. Pour the pudding into a bowl and let it cool completely. Stir the pudding occasionally to aid the cooling process. When the filling reaches room temperature, chill it, stirring it from time to time to keep a skin from forming.

3 Beat the whipping cream in a large bowl until stiff with the vanilla extract and the remaining 2 tablespoons sugar. Fold about 1/4 cup of the whipped cream into the filling to lighten it. Spread the top of each cake layer with the filling. Place the biggest cake layer on a serving platter. Carefully stack the remaining 2 cake layers on top of the first, centering them—a long spatula will help this process. If you don't have a platter, you can use a thick, stable piece of cardboard and cover it with a nice-looking piece of foil.

4 Spread the remaining whipped cream all over the cake. It doesn't have to be super-smooth and beautiful. Sprinkle the grated coconut over it like snowflakes—it will hide the flaws.

5 Now, let the decoration begin! Decorate with anything that occurs to you, particularly anything that the bride and groom like. And let the party begin!

Time needed: About 1 ¼ hours, not including sitting time

Sachertorte
An authentic Viennese dessert

This is an Austrian classic, simple and delicious. For authenticity, serve it with lightly beaten whipping cream.

Makes 14 slices:

For the batter:

8 ounces semisweet chocolate

10 eggs

1 ¼ teaspoons cream of tartar

2/3 cup sugar

1 cup (2 sticks) unsalted butter, softened

1/3 cup powdered sugar

1 teaspoon vanilla extract

1 ¼ cups flour

Pinch of salt

For the coating:

1 cup apricot jam

1 recipe Chocolate Glaze (see Tip)

1 Make the batter: Chop the chocolate and melt it in a water bath (see page 106); set it aside. Separate the eggs. In a clean, grease-free bowl, beat the egg whites until they are very stiff, adding the cream of tartar when the egg whites turn foamy. In another bowl, beat the butter, powdered sugar, and vanilla extract until the mixture is light and creamy. Mix in the egg yolks. Separately mix the flour with the salt.

2 Preheat the oven to 400°F. Butter a 10- or 11-inch springform pan. Mix the melted chocolate into the butter mixture. With a hand whisk, fold in 1/3 of the egg white mixture. Pour the remaining egg white mixture on top, sprinkle it with the flour mixture, and fold everything together using the hand whisk.

3 Pour the batter into the pan, smooth the top, and bake it on the middle rack of the oven for 15 minutes. Reduce the heat to 350° and bake for another 45 minutes (do the toothpick test to check for doneness—see Tip on page 38). Cool the cake overnight in the pan and then turn it out onto a rack.

4 Make the coating: Heat the jam in a saucepan until it turns liquidy. If it seems too thick, dilute it with a little water. Strain the jam, then spread a thin layer of it all over the cake. Let it dry. Set the cake on a cooling rack with a baking sheet under it. Prepare the chocolate glaze; it should be nice and thin so it can run smoothly over the surface of the cake.

5 Pour the glaze over the cake so the top and sides are covered. It helps to hold the torte at a slight angle and turn it. If this is all too complicated for you, you can simply smooth out the glaze with a spreader after it is poured on. But work quickly, because it doesn't stay liquid for long. Let the cake stand until the glaze hardens.

Time needed: 2 hours, including 1 really relaxed—not counting the standing time

Basic Tip
Chocolate Glaze

Chop 5 ounces of semisweet chocolate and melt it in a water bath. Bring 1 cup sugar and 1/2 cup water to a boil and boil for 1-2 minutes. Let the sugar mixture cool until it is slightly more than lukewarm and carefully stir in the melted chocolate until smooth. Now cool the glaze until it is just beginning to harden. Then, carefully heat it to lukewarm again. Now it's ready to use, but use it quickly!

Double-Chocolate Mud Cake
It doesn't get any chocolatier than this!

Makes 16 slices:

For the batter:

1 ¼ cups (2 ½ sticks) unsalted butter

10 ounces bittersweet chocolate

5 eggs

5 tablespoons sugar

1 tablespoon warm water

1 cup flour

1/2 teaspoon baking powder

Pinch of salt

For the filling and frosting:

2 cups whipping cream

14 ounces semisweet chocolate

2 tablespoons unsalted butter

1 Preheat the oven to 325°F. Line the bottom of a 10- or 11-inch springform pan with a circle of parchment paper.

2 Make the batter: Melt the butter with the chocolate (chopped first) in a saucepan over low heat. Cool.

3 In a large bowl, beat the eggs, sugar, and water. The mixture will increase in volume, turn light yellow in color, and become very foamy (this will take several minutes). In a small bowl, mix the flour with the baking powder and salt. Stir about 1 cup of the egg mixture into the chocolate mixture and fold it in until incorporated. Transfer this mixture back to the bowl with the egg mixture and fold everything together. About halfway through, sift the flour mixture over the surface and fold it in with a hand whisk until it's incorporated. Be gentle—the key is to try and keep as much air in the batter as possible.

4 Pour the batter into the pan, smooth the surface, and bake it for 35 to 45 minutes (toothpick-test it—see Tip on page 38). Carefully transfer the cake to a rack to cool, removing the outside of the springform after about 5 minutes.

5 Make the filling and frosting: Warm the whipping cream in a saucepan over low heat. Cut the chocolate into pieces and melt them in the whipping cream, stirring until smooth. Divide the chocolate-cream mixture into two parts. Stir the butter into one part until it has melted. Let the cake and cream mixtures rest wrapped overnight, the creams in the refrigerator, labeled clearly.

6 Cut the cake crosswise into two layers, using a knife or thin string. Beat the chocolate-cream mixture without the butter until it is stiff; spread it on one of the layers and place the other layer on top, lining up the edges. Gently warm the remaining chocolate-cream mixture until it has just turned liquid and spread it all over the cake. Let the cake stand for 2 hours before serving.

Time needed: 1 ½ hours, including 50 minutes active—not including cooling time

Baby Black Forest Torte
Small and elegant

Makes 6 slices:

For the batter:

4 eggs

1/2 teaspoon cream of tartar

1/3 cup sugar

2 teaspoons water

1/2 cup flour

2 tablespoons cornstarch

2 tablespoons cocoa powder

For the filling:

1 jar morello cherries or other sour cherries (24.7 ounces; specialty foods store)

4 teaspoons cornstarch

1 tablespoon sugar

2-3 tablespoons kirsch (optional)

1 ¾ cups whipping cream

1 ½ teaspoons powdered sugar

1 teaspoon vanilla extract

Grated chocolate

1 Butter an 8-inch springform pan on the bottom only. Preheat the oven to 350°F.

2 Make the batter: Separate the eggs. In a clean, grease-free bowl, beat the egg whites until stiff, adding the cream of tartar when the whites turn foamy, and sprinkling in the sugar when the whites reach soft peaks. Once they are nice and firm, fold in the egg yolks and water. In another bowl, mix the flour with the cornstarch and cocoa and sprinkle it on top of the egg mixture. Carefully fold everything together using a hand whisk.

3 Pour the batter into the pan, smoothing the surface. Bake the cake on the middle rack of the oven for about 30 minutes. Don't forget to do the toothpick test (see Tip on page 38). Cool the cake in the pan, transfer to a rack, and let it stand, covered, overnight.

4 Make the filling: Drain the cherries, saving the juice. Stir the cornstarch into about 1/4 cup of the juice. Bring the remaining juice to a boil in a saucepan with the sugar. Whisk in the cornstarch mixture and bring it back to a boil, whisking constantly, until it thickens. Remove it from the heat. Set aside a couple of nice cherries for garnish and mix the rest into the thickened juice mixture. Cool it completely.

5 With a string or a long knife, cut horizontally through the cake two times (you should end up with 3 cake layers). Place the bottom layer on a serving plate and brush it with the kirsch (if using). Beat the whipping cream with the powdered sugar and vanilla until stiff. Spread half of the cherry mixture on the bottom cake layer. Put the second cake layer on top, centering it. Brush it with kirsch (if using), spread the rest of the cherries on it, and top with some of the whipped cream. Place the last cake layer on top, centering it, and brush it with kirsch (if using). Spread the top and sides of the torte with the rest of the whipped cream. Decorate the cake with the reserved cherries and grated chocolate.

Crêpe Gâteau
AKA pancake torte

Makes 8 to 10 slices:

For the crêpes:

1/2 cup (1 stick) unsalted butter

4 eggs

1 1/3 cups cold milk

1/4 teaspoon salt

1/4 cup sugar

1 cup flour

Juice of 1/2 lemon

For the filling:

2 egg yolks

3 tablespoons cornstarch

1 2/3 cups cold milk

4 ounces bittersweet chocolate

3/4 cup (1 1/2 sticks) unsalted butter, softened

1 cup powdered sugar

For the glaze:

6 ounces semisweet chocolate

2/3 cup whipping cream

1 tablespoon unsalted butter

1 Make the crêpes: Melt 1/2 of the butter (1/4 cup) in a small saucepan and let it cool slightly. In a bowl, whisk the eggs, then stir in the milk. Add the salt and sugar and mix well. Add the flour a little at a time, whisking until the batter is smooth. Stir in the lemon juice and melted butter. Cover the batter and refrigerate it for at least 30 minutes.

2 Melt the remaining 1/4 cup butter in the saucepan and remove it from the heat. Brush an 8- or 10-inch crêpe pan or skillet with a little of the melted butter, and set it over medium heat. Add about 1/4 cup of the batter to the pan and quickly swirl it around so that the batter is completely covering the surface of the pan. Put the pan back on the burner and let it cook for 1 1/2 to 2 minutes. When ready, the crêpe will form small bubbles on the top and be golden brown on the underside. With a fork or your fingers flip the crêpe and cook the other side. Transfer the cooked crêpe to a plate and continue the cooking process with the remaining batter.

Tip: As you make them, stack the cooked crêpes slightly askew on the plate. This will help you get them apart later.

3 Make the filling: Stir together the egg yolks, cornstarch and a bit of milk in a saucepan, then add the rest of the milk. Place the pan over medium heat until the entire thing thickens, stirring the whole time. Remove the pan from the heat as soon as it thickens—boiling will cause the mixture to curdle. Transfer the filling to a bowl. Cut the chocolate into pieces, drop them in the bowl with the filling, and stir until it melts. Let the filling cool, stirring it from time to time.

4 In another bowl, beat the butter and the powdered sugar until light and creamy. Add the cooled chocolate filling one spoonful at a time, beating until smooth. Spread the filling on each of the crêpe layers, except for the top one, and stack them one on top of the other. (Note: You may not need all of the filling—this will depend on the size of the crêpe pan you used.)

5 Make the glaze: Chop the chocolate into pieces and put them in a saucepan with the cream and butter over medium-low heat. Stir until the chocolate is melted, then remove from the heat. Pour the glaze over the crêpes, making the glaze even. Refrigerate until the glaze has hardened.

Time needed: 3 hours, of which only 2 1/4 are really active

Espresso Mascarpone Torte
Tiramisu, basically

Makes 12 slices:

2 cups hazelnuts

For the batter:

8 eggs

1/2 teaspoon cream of tartar

2/3 cup sugar

1 teaspoon vanilla extract

2 tablespoons strong cold espresso

Grated zest of 1 lemon

1 cup flour

1/2 teaspoon baking powder

1/4 teaspoon salt

For the filling:

18 ounces mascarpone cheese (look for it in a specialty food store or Italian deli)

5-6 tablespoons milk

1 tablespoon lemon juice

1 cup whipping cream

3 tablespoons sugar

1 teaspoon vanilla extract

2 tablespoons grated chocolate

For soaking:

1/2 cup strong cold espresso

2 tablespoons rum (optional)

Grated chocolate and chocolate-covered coffee beans

1 Line a 10- or 11-inch springform pan with parchment paper. Put the hazelnuts in a food processor (metal blade) and process until they are finely ground. Preheat the oven to 350°F.

2 Make the batter: Separate the eggs. In a clean, grease-free bowl, beat the egg whites until stiff. Sprinkle in the cream of tartar when the egg whites turn foamy, and about one-third of the sugar when the egg whites turn to soft peaks. In another bowl, beat the egg yolks with the remaining sugar and the vanilla extract, until they are thick and light yellow in color. Mix in the espresso and the lemon zest.

3 Mix half of the nuts into the egg yolk mixture. Heap the egg white mixture on top. Mix the remaining nuts with the flour, baking powder, and salt, and put the mixture on top of the egg whites. Fold everything together gently, but thoroughly, using a hand whisk. Pour the batter into the pan and smooth out the surface. Bake the cake on the lower rack of the oven for approximately 1 hour. Don't forget the toothpick test (see Tip on page 38). Leave the cake briefly in the pan, remove it, and let it stand overnight, wrapped well after it's completely cooled.

4 The next day, make the filling and soaking mixtures: With a mixer, blend the mascarpone with the milk and lemon juice. In another bowl, beat the cream until stiff, sprinkling in the sugar and vanilla. Fold the whipped cream and grated chocolate into the mascarpone mixture. In a small bowl or cup, mix the 1/2 cup of espresso with the rum (if you're using it).

5 Horizontally cut through the cake two times using a long knife or a string. Place the bottom cake layer on a serving plate and brush it generously with the espresso-rum mixture. Spread one-quarter of the mascarpone filling on the bottom cake layer. Place the middle cake layer on top of the mascarpone mixture, lining up the edges, and brush it generously with the espresso-rum mixture. Spread another one-quarter of the mascarpone mixture on top. Place the top cake layer over the mascarpone mixture, lining up the edges. Use the remaining half of the mascarpone mixture to spread over the top and sides of the torte. Decorate the torte with grated chocolate and chocolate-covered coffee beans.

Time needed: 1 ¾ hours, including 45 minutes with something to do, plus the standing time overnight

Pear-Caramel Torte
Nostalgically good

Makes 16 slices:

For the batter:

5 eggs

5 tablespoons cold water

1/2 teaspoon cream of tartar

2/3 cup sugar

1 cup flour

1/2 cup cornstarch

1 teaspoon baking powder

1/4 teaspoon salt

For the topping:

2 firm, ripe pears (try Anjou)

2 tablespoons lemon juice

1/2 cup white wine

1 tablespoon sugar

1/2 cinnamon stick

For the filling:

1/2 cup sugar

3/4 cup water

3 1/3 cups milk

2 vanilla beans

4 egg yolks

1/4 cup cornstarch

For garnish:

2/3 cup whipping cream

2 teaspoons sugar

1/2 teaspoon vanilla extract

2 ounces amaretto cookies

1 Preheat the oven to 350°F. Line just the bottom of a 10- or 11-inch springform pan with parchment paper.

2 Make the batter: Separate the eggs. In a clean, grease-free bowl, beat the egg whites with the cold water until stiff. While beating, add the cream of tartar when the whites turn foamy, and slowly add the sugar when the whites reach the soft-peak stage. Set the mixer to low speed and stir in the egg yolks just until no more trace of yellow can be seen.

3 In a bowl, mix the flour, cornstarch, baking powder, and salt, sprinkle it on the egg mixture, and gently fold it in using a hand whisk. Pour the batter into the pan and smooth the surface. Bake the cake on the lowest oven rack for about 50 minutes (don't forget to do the toothpick test—see Tip on page 38). Let the cake rest in the pan for 5 to 10 minutes, then remove it from the pan and let it stand overnight (wrap it in plastic wrap as soon as it's cool).

4 Make the topping: Peel the pears, cut them into quarters, and cut out the cores.

Now cut the pears along their length into slices about 1/4 inch thick. Bring the lemon juice, white wine, sugar, and cinnamon to a boil in a saucepan. Reduce the heat to low, add the pear slices, and simmer them for about 5 minutes. Transfer the pears with their juice to a bowl and let them cool.

5 Make the filling: Heat the sugar in the same pan over medium heat until it melts, browns lightly, and foams. Keep stirring it. Pour in the water. Don't worry—the mixture will sizzle and the sugar will get hard. But if you stir, it will turn to liquid again.

6 Set aside 1/3 cup of the milk. Pour the rest of the milk into a saucepan. Slit the vanilla beans lengthwise and scrape out the seeds. Add the vanilla pods, the seeds, and the caramel to the milk and heat it over medium-low heat. In a bowl, thoroughly mix the egg yolks, remaining 1/3 cup milk, and the cornstarch. Fish the vanilla pods out of the hot milk mixture. Remove the pan from the heat and stir in the egg yolk mixture. Return it to the heat and bring it to a boil again while stirring—the mixture will thicken as it gets hotter. When it just boils, immediately remove the pan from the heat, dump the filling into a bowl, and cool it. Stir it from time to time to aid cooling.

7 With a string or long knife, cut the cake horizontally into three layers. Place the bottom cake layer on a serving plate and brush it generously with some of the pear cooking liquid. Spread about one-quarter of the caramel filling over the cake. Place the middle cake layer on top of the filling, lining up the edges, and brush it generously with the pear cooking liquid. Spread the cake with another one-quarter of the caramel filling. Place the top cake layer over the filling, lining up the edges. Cover the entire torte— top and sides—with the remaining filling.

8 Drain the pears and distribute them decoratively over the top of the torte. In a bowl, beat the whipping cream, sugar, and vanilla until stiff. Put the amaretto cookies in a locking plastic bag and crush them into coarse crumbs using a rolling pin or other heavy object. Sprinkle the cookie crumbs over the torte. Garnish with small dollops of whipped cream.

Very Berry Yogurt Torte
Cool on hot days

Makes 14 slices:

For the pastry:

1 ⅔ cups flour

1/4 teaspoon salt

1/4 cup sugar

1/2 cup (1 stick) cold unsalted butter

1 egg

1-2 tablespoons ice water

For the filling:

24 ounces mixed berries (such as strawberries, raspberries, and red currants)

2/3 cup sugar

1/2 cup red fruit juice

2 envelopes unflavored gelatin

1 ¾ cups plain yogurt

4 ounces cream cheese, softened

For garnish:

2/3 cup whipping cream

1 tablespoon sugar

1 Make the pastry: In a food processor (metal blade), combine the flour, salt, and sugar and pulse the machine to blend the ingredients. Cut the butter into cubes and add them to the machine. Pulse for 25 to 30 times, until the mixture is evenly crumbly. Add the egg and 1 tablespoon of the water and pulse just until the dough starts to come together, adding more water if necessary. Transfer the dough to an ungreased 10- or 11-inch springform pan. With your fingers, push the dough out so that it covers the entire bottom of the pan and goes about 1 to 1 ½ inches up the sides (try to keep the sides even). Refrigerate the pastry in the pan for 1 hour.

2 Preheat the oven to 400°F. Line the pastry with parchment paper and fill it with pie weights or dried beans. Bake the pastry on the middle oven rack for about 25 minutes, until it is nice and brown. Remove the dried beans and the paper. Let the pastry cool in the pan, remove it, and put it on a serving plate.

3 Make the filling: Pick over the berries, removing the damaged fruit, leaves, or other unwanted stuff. It's best not to wash the berries. Set aside about one-quarter of them for garnish. Finely crush the remaining berries in a bowl, using a fork or pastry blender, and adding about 2 tablespoons of the sugar.

4 Put the fruit juice in a saucepan, sprinkle the gelatin on top, and let it stand for 5 minutes. In a bowl, thoroughly beat the yogurt with the cream cheese and the remaining sugar. Heat the gelatin mixture over low heat, stirring, until the gelatin completely dissolves—it should take about 2 minutes. Let the mixture cool slightly, then stir in 1 tablespoon of the yogurt mixture. Pour the contents of the saucepan into the bowl with the yogurt. Gently fold in the crushed berries, but don't mix them in totally—you want the whole thing to have streaks, like marble. Pour the berry-yogurt mixture into the pastry. Chill it for about 3 hours, until it is firm enough to cut.

5 In a bowl, beat the whipping cream with the sugar until stiff. Distribute the remaining berries on top of the torte and garnish it with dollops of whipped cream.

Time needed: 2 ¼ hours, including a good 2 hours doing something—not counting chilling time

Basic Tip

Afraid of gelatin? People who have never made anything with it often refuse to touch it. That's too bad, because working with gelatin is really easy. All it wants is a brief soak in cold liquid until it gets soft (takes five minutes) and a bit of heat until it liquefies (takes about 2 minutes). Just make sure the gelatin doesn't get too hot or it won't set. Once it has liquefied, stir the gelatin into 1 to 2 tablespoons of whatever it's going to be mixed with in order to help it blend properly. Then, you can go ahead and stir it into the rest of the ingredients.

Pink Cheesecake
Easy and impressive

Makes 16 slices:

20 ounces frozen raspberries

For the pastry:

1 cup flour

Pinch of salt

2 tablespoons sugar

1/2 cup (1 stick) cold unsalted butter

3-4 tablespoons ice water

For the filling:

18 ounces cream cheese, softened

2/3 cup sugar

1 tablespoon fresh lemon juice

3 very fresh eggs

1/2 cup red fruit juice

2 envelopes unflavored gelatin

1/4 teaspoon cream of tartar

2 ½ cups whipping cream

For garnish:

Fresh raspberries

Powdered sugar

1 First, pour the raspberries into a strainer, hang them over a bowl, and let them thaw—they'll go into the filling later. The thawing will take about 4 hours, so plan ahead.

2 Preheat the oven to 400°F. Make the pastry: In a food processor (metal blade), combine the flour, salt, and sugar and pulse the machine to blend the ingredients. Cut the butter into cubes and add it to the machine. Pulse 25 to 30 times, until the mixture is evenly crumbly. Add 3 tablespoons of the water and pulse just until the dough starts to come together, adding more water if necessary. Use your fingers to spread the pastry over just the bottom of an 8- or 10-inch ungreased springform pan (it's not necessary to have the sides of the pan attached). Roll a rolling pin over it to make it nice and flat. Prick the pastry with a fork a few times and bake it on the middle rack of the oven for about 10 minutes, until it is golden brown. Cool it.

3 In the meantime, do something for the filling: Put the cream cheese, sugar, and lemon juice in a large bowl and beat everything with a mixer until it is light and creamy. Separate the eggs. Set the egg whites aside. Add the egg yolks to the cream cheese mixture and beat them in well.

4 Put the juice in a small saucepan, sprinkle the gelatin over the top, and let it stand for 5 minutes to soften. Heat the mixture over low heat for about 2 minutes, stirring, until the gelatin is dissolved. Cool slightly.

5 Finely crush the thawed raspberries in a bowl using a fork or pastry blender. Thoroughly mix the crushed raspberries into the cream cheese mixture. Stir a couple of spoonfuls of the cream cheese mixture into the gelatin mixture, mixing well. Then, transfer the gelatin mixture to the bowl with the cream cheese mixture and mix everything well. Put the bowl in the refrigerator for about 5 minutes, until the filling starts to set.

6 Now it's time to clamp the edge of the springform around the pastry-lined pan bottom. In a clean, grease-free bowl, and with clean beaters, beat the egg whites, adding the cream of tartar when they turn foamy, until they reach stiff peaks. In another bowl, beat the whipped cream until it is very stiff.

7 Fold the whipped cream and egg whites into the raspberry-cream cheese mixture, blending gently, but evenly. Pour the mixture onto the pastry-lined pan and smooth the surface. Refrigerate it for at least 2 hours until the filling is completely set. Then, release the edge of the springform, decorate the cheesecake with raspberries and dust it with powdered sugar.

Time needed: 1 ¼ hours including approximately 45 minutes active, plus the cooling time

Snowflake Torte with Fruit
As light as freshly fallen snow

Makes 12 slices:

For the choux paste:

1 cup water

1 tablespoon sugar

Pinch of salt

6 tablespoons (3/4 stick) unsalted butter

1 cup flour

4 eggs

For the filling:

About 2 pounds of fruit (fresh figs and purple grapes, or berries, peaches, or nectarines)

2 ½ cups whipping cream

2 tablespoons sugar

2 teaspoons vanilla extract

Grated zest of 1 lemon

Powdered sugar

1 Make the choux paste: Pour the water, sugar, and salt into a saucepan. Cut the butter into cubes, add them to the pan, bring the mixture to a boil, and remove it from the heat.

2 Add the flour all at once and stir everything well. Return the pan to the heat and keep stirring, until the dough forms a lump that can barely be stirred anymore and a thin white layer can be seen on the bottom of the pan. Transfer the dough to a bowl and let it cool for 15 minutes. Then, thoroughly mix in the eggs one after the other with a wooden spoon.

3 Preheat the oven to 425°F. Line two baking sheets with parchment paper. With a pencil, draw one 10-inch circle on each piece of paper. Spread one-quarter of the choux paste onto each circle. Bake the layers one at a time on the middle oven rack for 15 minutes each, until they're golden brown. If the choux paste gets a blast of cold air too soon, it will collapse. Remove the choux paste circles from the pans, cool the pans slightly, and repeat the baking process with the remaining choux paste batter. Cool the four layers.

4 Make the filling: Wash the fruit. Cut figs into eighths; cut grapes in half and remove the seeds. Or pick over the berries and cut the large ones into smaller pieces. Or, skin the peaches and nectarines (see page 57), cut them in half, remove the pits, and cut them into cubes.

5 Beat the whipping cream until stiff with the sugar, vanilla, and lemon zest. Place one of the choux paste layers on a serving plate, spread it with one-third of the whipped cream, and top it with one-third of the fruit. Repeat this process two more times, placing another choux paste layer in between each section. Top with the last layer of choux paste and dust the top with powdered sugar. To serve, use a serrated knife to gently cut through the layers. Eat soon!

Time needed: 1 hour 20 minutes, including 1 hour active

Triangular Torte
Oddly shaped, but easy

Makes 16 slices:

For the batter:

4 eggs

1/2 teaspoon cream of tartar

3 ½ tablespoons sugar

2 egg yolks

1/2 teaspoon vanilla extract

1 cup flour

1/4 teaspoon baking powder

Pinch of salt

For the filling:

8 ounces bittersweet chocolate

2 cups whipping cream

10 ounces seedless green grapes

12 ounces blackberries

1/2 cup seedless raspberry jam

Cocoa powder

1/2 cup blanched slivered almonds

1 Preheat the oven to 400°F. Line a jellyroll pan with parchment paper.

2 Separate the eggs. In a clean, grease-free bowl, beat the egg whites until they form stiff peaks, adding the cream of tartar when they turn foamy and sprinkling in the sugar when they reach the soft-peak stage. Gradually mix in all 6 egg yolks and the vanilla extract. Mix the flour with the baking powder and salt, sprinkle it over the top of the eggs, and fold together, gently, using a hand whisk.

3 Immediately smooth the batter in the pan, smoothing it with a rubber scraper. Bake the cake on the middle oven rack for 10 to 12 minutes. When you press on it with your

finger, the cake should bounce right back to its starting point.

4 While the cake is in the oven, spread a clean dishtowel on the countertop. After baking, immediately turn the baked sponge cake out onto the towel, pulling off the parchment paper. Cool the cake completely.

5 Make the filling: Chop the chocolate into pieces and melt it over a water bath, stirring until smooth. Set the chocolate aside to cool.

6 In a bowl, beat the whipping cream until stiff. Stir about one-third of it with the melted chocolate, and fold the rest in using a hand whisk. Put the chocolate whipped cream in the fridge. Wash the grapes and cut them in half. Pick over the blackberries.

7 Arrange the cake so that one of the long ends is facing you. Starting at the upper left hand corner, make one diagonal cut down to the lower right hand corner to form two triangles. Then, starting from the upper right hand corner, make a straight, diagonal cut down to the midline of the triangle. You should now have three triangles: One large one at the bottom left and two smaller ones at the top right. Spread the raspberry jam over the surface of the largest triangle. Spread just under half of the chocolate whipped cream on top of the jam.

8 Pay attention—this is the confusing part. Take the uppermost smaller triangle, turn it over so that its point is facing up instead of down, then flip it over to the other side. You should now be able to position it so that the points line up across the bottom of the larger triangle. Now take the remaining small triangle, turn it over so that its point is facing right instead of left, then flip it over to the other side. You should now be able to position it so that the points line up along the left side of the triangle.

9 Spread the top and sides of the torte with the remaining chocolate whipped cream and dust the surface with cocoa powder (a mesh sieve works well). Press the almonds into the sides of the torte all around, then decorate the top of the torte with the fruit.

Time needed: 50 minutes

Orange-Meringue Torte
Refreshing and light

Makes 14 to 16 slices:

4 eggs

1/2 cup (1 stick) unsalted butter, softened

1 1/3 cups sugar

1/4 cup milk

1 cup flour

2 teaspoons baking powder

1/4 teaspoon salt

1/2 teaspoon cream of tartar

1/4 cup sliced almonds

2 cans Mandarin oranges (11-ounces each)

2 cups whipping cream

1 Separate the eggs. Beat the butter with 5 tablespoons of the sugar until it is light and creamy. Gradually stir in the egg yolks, followed by the milk, beating well. In another bowl, mix the flour, baking powder, and salt, and then mix everything together.

2 Preheat the oven to 400°F. In a clean, grease-free bowl, and with clean beaters, beat the egg whites until stiff. While beating, sprinkle in the cream of tartar when the egg whites turn foamy, and the remaining sugar when the egg whites form soft peaks. Line a 10- or 11-inch springform pan with parchment paper.

3 Pour half of the batter into the pan, smoothing the surface. Top it with half of the egg white mixture, making "waves" in it with a moistened teaspoon. Sprinkle with half of the almonds and bake the cake in the oven for 25 to 30 minutes, until it is lightly browned. Remove the cake from the springform. Bake the other cake layer in the same way as above, making sure the pan is cool first. Cool both of the layers.

4 Drain the oranges. Beat the whipping cream until stiff. Distribute the oranges on one of the cake layers, and spread the oranges with the whipped cream. Cut the second layer into 14 to 16 pieces and set them on top of the whipped cream. Eat the cake the same day you make it.

Time needed: 1 1/2 hours, including about 35 minutes doing something

Rice Pudding Torte
With exotic fruits

Makes 16 slices:

For the pastry:

1/4 cup (1/2 stick) cold unsalted butter

1 cup flour

3 tablespoons sugar

Pinch of salt

1 egg yolk

1-2 tablespoons cold water

For the filling:

1 lime

1 mango

1 papaya

1 can pineapple chunks (5 ½ ounces)

1 ¼ cups milk

1/2 cup Arborio rice

1/2 cup cold water

2 envelopes unflavored gelatin

2-4 tablespoons sugar

1 teaspoon vanilla extract

1 cup whipping cream

1 envelope light-colored fruit glaze (optional)

Orange juice (optional)

1 Make the pastry: Cut the butter into cubes. In a food processor (metal blade), pulse together the flour, sugar, and salt. Add the egg yolk and pulse to combine. Add the butter cubes and pulse until the dough comes together, adding the water as necessary (it will take 30 to 40 times). Push the pastry over the bottom of the springform pan and chill for 1 hour.

2 Preheat the oven to 350°F. Cover the pastry with a piece of parchment paper and weigh it down with pie weights or dried beans. Bake the unfilled pastry on the middle oven rack for 15 minutes, then remove the beans and paper, and bake the pastry for another 10 minutes. Remove the pan from the oven and cool.

3 Make the filling: Wash the lime under hot water and thinly grate the zest; squeeze out the juice. Peel the mango, cut the fruit from the pit, and dice it. Cut the papaya in half, remove the seeds, and peel and dice the fruit. Drain the pineapple. Mix the lime juice in a bowl with all of the fruit.

4 Bring the milk to a boil with the lime zest and let the rice swell in it over low heat for 25 to 30 minutes. At about the 20-minute mark, put the water in a bowl, sprinkle the gelatin over the top, and let it stand for about 5 minutes to soften. Dump the gelatin mixture into the pan with the rice, along with 2 tablespoons of the sugar and the vanilla extract. Stir well, and let the mixture simmer

for the last 5 minutes. Transfer the rice pudding mixture to a bowl and place it in the refrigerator.

5 In another bowl, beat the whipping cream until stiff. When the rice pudding starts to get firm, stir in the fruits and their juice, and then, fold in the whipping cream. Pour the mixture onto the pastry in the pan, smooth the surface, and refrigerate.

6 If desired, prepare the glaze with orange juice and the remaining sugar according to the package instructions, cool slightly, and spread it on top of the torte. Chill the torte for at least 2 hours before eating.

Time needed: 45 minutes active, 3 hours relaxed

Meringue Torte with Berries
Nearly melts in your mouth

Makes 10 slices:

For the meringue:

4 very fresh egg whites

1/2 teaspoon cream of tartar

1 cup sugar

For the filling:

18 ounces mixed berries

4 ounces cream cheese, softened

2 teaspoons lemon juice

1 ½ cups whipping cream

2 tablespoons powdered sugar

1 Preheat the oven to 250°F. Line a baking sheet with parchment paper.

2 Make the meringue: Pour the egg whites into a clean, grease-free bowl and beat them until stiff with a mixer. While beating, add the cream of tartar when the whites turn foamy. When the whites reach the soft-peak stage, sprinkle in half of the sugar, one spoonful at a time, while continuing to beat. Keep beating until the meringue is very stiff, smooth, and glossy. If you turn the bowl upside down, nothing should drip out.

3 Transfer the meringue to a pastry bag with a smooth tip (see page 23). With a pencil, draw two circles on the parchment paper, using the bottom of a 9-inch springform pan as your guideline. Pipe the meringue into the circles, working in a spiral from the inside to the outside.

4 Put the meringue layers on the middle rack of the oven and leave them there for 45 minutes to 1 hour. Remove them from the baking sheet along with the paper and cool completely. The meringue layers should be very dry and crispy.

5 Make the filling: Carefully pick through the berries and discard any that have spoiled. It is best not to wash the berries. Set aside a few berries for garnish. Finely crush about one-third of the remaining berries in a bowl with a fork or pastry blender. Leave the other berries whole or cut them into pieces, depending on their size.

6 Put the cream cheese in a bowl and beat it until it is smooth. Add the berry puree, mix well, and then stir in the other berries and the lemon juice. In another bowl, beat the cream with the powdered sugar until very stiff. Fold the whipped cream into the cream cheese-berry mixture.

7 Put one of the meringue layers on a serving plate and spread half of the berry filling on it. Put the other meringue layer on top of it, lining up the edges, and spread it with the remaining filling. Garnish the torte with the reserved whole berries.

8 To serve, quickly cut through the torte with a very sharp knife. If you have your mom's old electric knife, haul it out of storage. It's great for cutting this torte. Serve immediately after assembling so that the meringue layers don't soften.

Time needed: 1 ½ hours, including 50 minutes doing something

Tip
This torte makes a great dessert during the summer months and it can even be prepared in advance. Bake the meringue the day before and all you'll have to do before serving is quickly mix the berry filling.

Walnut-Buttercream Torte
So small, nothing will be left over

Makes 8 slices:

For the batter:

3 eggs

1/4 teaspoon cream of tartar

3 tablespoons sugar

1/2 teaspoon vanilla extract

1/4 cup flour

1/2 teaspoon cinnamon

1 level tablespoon cornstarch

1/2 teaspoon baking powder

For the filling:

1 tablespoon shelled walnuts

1 egg yolk

2 tablespoons cornstarch

1 cup milk

1/2 cup (1 stick) unsalted butter, softened

1/4 cup powdered sugar

For garnish:

2 tablespoons walnut pieces

1 tablespoon honey or maple syrup

1 Preheat the oven to 350°F. Line the bottom of an 8-inch springform pan with parchment paper.

2 Separate the eggs. In a clean, grease-free bowl, beat the egg whites until stiff along with the cream of tartar. Once they reach soft peaks, sprinkle in the sugar and keep beating. Stir in the egg yolks, one after the other (if two slip into the meringue at once, it's not all that serious), adding the vanilla with the last one. Mix the flour with the cinnamon, cornstarch, and baking powder and sprinkle it onto the egg mixture. Gently fold everything together using a hand whisk.

3 Pour the batter into the pan and smooth out the surface. Bake the cake on the middle rack of the oven for about 25 minutes. Do the toothpick test to make sure it's done (see Tip on page 38). Leave the finished cake in the pan for 5 to 10 minutes, remove it, and let it stand overnight, or for at least a couple of hours. Wrap the cake with plastic wrap as soon as it has cooled.

4 Make the filling: Finely grate the walnuts using the small holes of a cheese grater. Thoroughly mix them with the egg yolk, cornstarch, and a bit of the milk in a saucepan. Now stir in the remaining milk.

5 Put the pan over medium heat and bring the mixture to a boil while stirring constantly. Remove the pan from the heat and cool the mixture. Keep stirring or a thick skin will be floating on it afterward.

6 With a mixer, beat the butter and the powdered sugar until creamy. Stir in the cooled walnut mixture one spoonful at a time.

7 With a string or long knife, horizontally cut the cake into three layers. Place the bottom cake layer on a serving plate and spread about one quarter of the filling on top. Place the middle cake layer on top of the filling, lining up the cake edges, and spread with another one quarter of the filling. Place the third cake layer on top of the filling, lining up the cake edges. Spread the remaining filling over the top and sides of the torte. Break the walnuts into small pieces and heat them in a skillet over medium heat, until they give off a pleasant aroma. Stir in the honey, or maple syrup. Cool the walnuts slightly and then distribute them over the top of the torte.

Time needed: At least 1 hour, including 40 minutes doing something—not counting standing times

Basic Tip

Here's a nice, rich bonus for you: Chocolate Truffles. Though elegant, these satisfying treats are easy to make.

Makes 30 truffles:
Cut 12 ounces of chocolate (half semisweet and half bittersweet) into pieces. In a saucepan, warm 2/3 cup whipping cream and melt the chocolate in it over low heat, stirring until everything's smooth. Transfer the mixture to a bowl, cool it completely, cover it with plastic wrap, and chill it overnight.

The next day, beat the mixture until it is smooth and creamy, yet still slightly firm. Pick a baking sheet that fits in the fridge and line it with parchment paper. Divide the truffle mixture into teaspoon-sized portions, place them on the baking sheet, and chill them for one hour.

Shape the portions into balls with cold hands (if your hands tend to be warm, dip them frequently into a bowl of ice water; don't forget to dry them before proceeding) and place them back on the baking sheet. Chill. Melt 8 ounces chopped semisweet chocolate in a water bath. Dip the truffles into the melted chocolate, remove them with a fork, and let them drain on a cooling rack. Put the truffles on the baking sheet with a fresh sheet of parchment paper, and chill until firm again. Keep them cold for as long a possible before eating.

Savory Snack

Life as a couch potato can really be a pleasure...

s

Pomme de chaiselounge, patata di veranda, Sofakartoffel—it doesn't matter where you live, couch potatoes are everywhere. They just sit around, eat anything but what's good for them, nibbling on one enticing tidbit after another.

If you go to Italy, you'll see him with his feet in the sand eating focaccia. In France, she's sitting in a sidewalk café and brazenly biting into a baguette. If you stumble into a Beer Garden in Munich, the pretzel eaters will be grinning at you from every corner. Bagels in New York delis, blinis in a datscha in the Crimea, and spanikopita in a Greek taverna: Couch potatoes are always sitting where things are nicest. Even if there's no couch!

But there's a couch at home, which is really the nicest place of all to sit—especially with a couple of homemade rolls. Who needs potatoes? This leisurely life can really be a pleasure. And we have the recipes to make it happen.

Five Quick Bread Spreads

Tangy Turkey Spread

Cut 6 ounces of turkey breast into small pieces and mix them with 2 teaspoons of grainy mustard and chopped fresh chives to taste. Heap the stuff on a sliced baguette. You can also use lean roast beef or ham in place of the turkey.

Creamy Carrot Spread

Peel and grate 1 carrot and finely chop 4 green onions. Mix them with 6 ounces of softened cream cheese, 2 tablespoons plain yogurt, 1/4 cup grated cheese of your choice, and a bit of chopped fresh parsley. This tastes great on whole-grain bread.

Potato-Herb Spread

Smash boiled, peeled potatoes with a fork and add a bit of olive oil, chopped fresh basil, and garlic to make a stiff spread. Spread it on toasted country bread and top with toasted pine nuts.

New-Style Tuna Salad Spread

Thoroughly drain one 6-ounce can of water-packed tuna and break up the fish into a bowl. Add 2 minced spicy pickles, 1 small peeled and grated apple, 1 tablespoon mayonnaise, 1 tablespoon plain yogurt, and chopped fresh dill to taste. Try it on rye bread.

Chocolate-Hazelnut Spread

In a saucepan, warm 5 tablespoons honey and 3 tablespoons whipping cream with 3 tablespoons each of butter and Nutella (chocolate-hazelnut spread) and stir until everything's smooth. Stir in 2 ounces of chopped hazelnuts or almonds and 1 tablespoon cocoa powder. Spread it on dinner rolls for a snack or impromptu dessert.

Aunt Betty's Baking Bits

Dear Aunt Betty:
I like bread, preferably when it's very fresh. But I often have to buy a new loaf of bread before the first one is gone, because it just seems stale to me. I know that's not a good thing, and it's straining my pocketbook. How long does bread actually stay fresh, and is there anything I can do with the leftovers?

Wondering in Wichita

Dear Wondering:
Ponder this, my sweet: What does "fresh" actually mean? It depends on your point of view. Some people don't like to cut into sourdough bread until three days after they buy it, because that's when it's supposed to have the right taste. Other people, like you, prefer a crispy crust and a moist, aromatic interior. But the right time to eat it depends on the bread and your preference. For example, a baguette won't last overnight, because it quickly gets hard and dry. Other white breads can stay fresh for two days, and if it contains some rye flour it could last 3 to 4 days. Ditto for whole-grain breads.

Try this trick with breads that seem stale: Cut them into slices and put them in a 350° to 400°F oven for a few minutes to toast. Give them a slather of butter or a drizzle of olive oil and you have the perfect snack or accompaniment to a hearty soup or salad.

As for bread leftovers, there are countless ways to use them. For example, pull out your favorite Italian cookbook and make some bread salad with tomatoes or a nice bread and vegetable soup. Or, do what the Swiss do and cut the stale bread into cubes to dip into cheese fondue. Or, you can use this very book to take care of your stale bread by cutting it into pieces and using it for baked French toast or bread pudding (see pages 160). If worse comes to worse, grind your rock-hard bread in a food processor—cut it into pieces first—and make your own homemade bread crumbs!

Name that Loaf

Go to a bakery and you might be overwhelmed with the selection, and confused about the attributes of each loaf. Here's a quick guide to help you choose the perfect loaf for the occasion.

Name	Description	Good For
Brioche	Light-textured bread enriched with egg yolks and butter	Breakfast (toasted first), grilled sandwiches, bread pudding
Challah	Similar to brioche; traditionally served on Jewish holidays	See Brioche
Ciabatta	Lean light bread that is formed into the shape of a slipper. The crust is crisp, while the crumb is soft and spongy.	Side dish, sandwiches, bread pudding
Focaccia	Spongy Italian flatbread often drizzled with olive oil and sprinkled with toppings such as fresh rosemary and coarse salt	A snack, enclosing sandwich fillings (try vegetable spreads or Italian meats and cheeses), an accompaniment to hearty soups and salads
Fougasse	Similar to focaccia. Made with a lean white dough, shaped into a leaf, and topped with different herbs, spices, or other toppings	A snack accompanied by soft cheeses and other savory spreads, a companion to hearty soups and salads
French bread	Light textured and light colored bread made without any fat. Crispy texture. Doesn't stay fresh for long. The baguette is its most popular shape.	Anything—try it spread with butter and jam for breakfast just after you bring it home from the bakery; garlic bread
Pullman loaf (AKA sandwich bread)	A loaf of bread shaped like a pullman railroad car—a long rectangle—with a firm, finely crumbed texture. Usually found sliced.	Sandwiches (duh!), croutons, canapés
Rye bread	Bread that contains some light, medium, or dark rye flour; available with or without caraway seeds.	Sandwiches, croutons
Semolina bread	A mild flavored loaf made with some coarsely ground hard wheat flour. The loaf is slightly yellow in color and the flavor has a hint of nuttiness.	Side dish (serve the day it's baked), sandwiches, croutons
Sourdough bread (AKA levain in French)	Bread that uses a starter (a fermented mixture of flour, water, and yeast) for leavening and has a tangy flavor	Sandwiches, side dishes, croutons

More Ideas for Leftover Bread

Don't panic: Stale bread can be a good thing, as long as you use it to make something. Following are some examples:

• Layer slices of it in a casserole with fresh tomatoes, mozzarella, and basil. Then pour a vinaigrette over it and after 20 minutes you can serve it as a great luncheon salad.

• Cut the crusts off of stale sandwich bread, cut them in cubes, mix them with ham, cheese, and chopped fresh sage, and pour the mixture into a pie pan. Pour on a custard mixture (4 eggs to every 2 cups milk) seasoned with salt and pepper and throw them in a 375°F oven until the custard is set. Voila—savory bread pudding!

• Soak slices of multigrain bread in pancake batter and fry them. Serve them with butter and pure maple syrup and you have a new take on breakfast that's kind of a cross between pancakes and French toast. Give it your own name!

Cheese Straws
Great for snacking

Makes about 40 straws:

1 package (17.3 ounces) frozen puff pastry

4-ounce chunk of cheese (such as Gruyère, Emmentaler, or Gouda)

2-ounce chunk of Parmesan cheese

2 tablespoons Dijon mustard

Cayenne pepper

1 Take the squares of pastry out of the package, set them next to each other on the counter, and cover them with a dishtowel so they won't dry out. Thawing will take 15 to 30 minutes.

2 Grate the cheeses, but keep them separate. Cut each square of puff pastry into 3 rectangles, using the fold lines as a guide.

3 Brush a bit of mustard on one rectangle of pastry, sprinkle with a dash of cayenne, and cover with about 1/4 of the first kind of cheese. Place another puff pastry rectangle on top of the cheese, brush it, and sprinkle it. Put a third puff pastry rectangle on top. Make another stack of puff pastry squares using the other three puff pastry rectangles, and the rest of the mustard, cayenne, and the first cheese.

4 Put the two stacks of pastry in the refrigerator, covered, if you still have a while to wait for your guests. When ready to bake, roll out the stacks on a lightly floured countertop until they have approximately doubled in length and width.

5 Preheat the oven to 425°F. Line a baking sheet with parchment paper. Cut the rectangles into 1/2 inch strips. Twist each strip several times and place on the baking sheet, pushing down the edges slightly so that they keep their twisted shape. Sprinkle the cheese straws with the Parmesan cheese and bake them on the middle oven rack for about 15 to 20 minutes, until browned. Let them cool before eating.

Time needed: 50 minutes

Cheese-Walnut Coins
For wine, for beer, for a good time

Makes about 40 coins:

1 ⅔ cups flour

Salt, black pepper to taste

Cayenne pepper to taste

4 ounces Roquefort or Gorgonzola cheese (make sure it's the good stuff)

1/2 cup (1 stick) cold unsalted butter

1/2 cup walnut pieces

2 eggs

1 In a food processor (metal blade), combine the flour and the salt (not too much, because cheese is salty), pepper, and a little bit of cayenne pepper and pulse the machine to blend them together. Cut the cheese and butter into cubes. Break the walnuts into small pieces.

2 Add the butter and eggs to the machine and process until the mixture is blended. Add the walnuts and pulse—don't process—until the nuts are incorporated into the mixture (you want the walnuts to remain in slightly large pieces). Transfer the dough to a work surface. With floured hands, divide the dough into 2 equal pieces. Roll each dough piece on the work surface into a cylinder about 1 ½ inches in diameter. Wrap both cylinders in plastic wrap and chill in the refrigerator for about 1 hour.

3 Preheat the oven to 400°F. Line a baking sheet with parchment paper.

4 Unwrap the rolls of dough, cut them into slices about 1/4 inch thick, and put the slices on the baking sheet.

5 Bake the cheese coins on the middle rack of the oven for about 15 minutes, until they are golden brown. Cool before eating.

Time needed: 40 minutes, including 15 minutes in peace

131

Spinach and Feta Turnovers
An easier approach to spanakopita

Remember: Spinach takes a while to thaw, so take it out of the freezer early enough (it takes at least 3 to 4 hours).

Makes 9 turnovers:

1 box frozen chopped spinach (10 ounces)

1 sheet (1/2 of a 17.3-ounce package) frozen puff pastry

2 cloves garlic

8 ounces feta cheese

1/2 bunch fresh Italian parsley

1/4 cup peperoncini rings (optional)

2 eggs

2 tablespoons plain yogurt or sour cream

Salt, black pepper to taste

1/2 teaspoon ground coriander

1 egg yolk

1 tablespoon milk

1 Take the spinach out of the package, put it in a strainer, and put it in a sink to thaw—about 3 to 4 hours should do it.

2 Take the puff pastry out of the package, unroll it on a work surface, cover it with a dishtowel, and let it thaw for about 15 to 30 minutes.

3 Meanwhile, peel the garlic and cut it into fine slices. Drain the feta cheese and crumble it. Wash and dry the parsley, cut off the leaves, and chop them finely.

4 Preheat the oven to 400°F. Rinse a baking sheet under cold water; do not dry it.

5 Thoroughly squeeze the water out of the thawed spinach—it might take a while to get out all of the liquid—and coarsely chop it. Mix it in a bowl with the garlic, feta, parsley, peperoncini (if using), eggs, and yogurt in a bowl and season the mixture with salt (not too much, because the cheese is salty), pepper, and coriander.

6 On a floured work surface, roll out the puff pastry sheet to a 15- by 15-inch square. Cut the pastry into nine 5-inch squares. Imagine that the squares are 2 triangles. Spread the spinach mixture over one triangle of each square, but not all the way to the edge. Fold the other half over the filling. Press the pastry edges together with the tines of a fork. Note: You may not need to use all of the filling. Try not to overfill the turnovers or you'll have seeping problems (but even messy turnovers taste good!). If you do have extra filling, put it into an ovenproof dish and bake it at 400°F for 10 to 15 minutes; serve it as a side dish.

7 Transfer the turnovers to the baking sheet, preferably using a spatula. Whisk the egg yolk and milk and brush the mixture over the tops of the turnovers.

8 Bake the turnovers on the middle oven rack for approximately 25 minutes, until the pastry has risen and browned nicely. Cool slightly (to avoid burned tongues) or completely before eating.

Time needed: 1 hour, including 35 minutes doing something

More Turnovers

With Bean and Leek Filling:
Drain one 15-ounce can of kidney beans. Mash 1/2 of the beans well, then mix them with the remaining whole beans. Trim, wash well, and finely chop 1 small leek. Mix it with the beans, 2 minced cloves of garlic, 3 tablespoons sour cream, and 2 eggs. Finely chop 1/2 bunch of fresh chives, mix them in, and season to taste with plenty of salt, pepper, and paprika. Fill and bake the turnovers as described above (see steps 2, 4, 6-8).

With Ham & Cheese Filling:
Mix together 2 ounces of ham, cut into cubes, 1 bunch of green onions, sliced into rings, 1 diced tomato, 8 ounces of softened cream cheese, and 1 egg. You may need to thin the mixture with a little milk or cream. Season the mixture to taste with plenty of salt, pepper, and cayenne pepper. Fill and bake the turnovers as described above (see steps 2, 4, 6-8).

With Sauerkraut Filling:
Cook 4 ounces of bacon until crisp, drain it well, and crumble it. Drain and finely chop 8 ounces of sauerkraut and mix it with the bacon, 2 chopped green onions, 1 tablespoon chopped fresh Italian parsley, 1 tablespoon Dijon mustard, 2 tablespoons sour cream, and 2 eggs. Season with salt, pepper, and paprika. Fill and bake the turnovers as described above (see steps 2, 4, 6-8).

Mini Meat Pies
Freeze for emergencies

Makes 12 pies:

For the filling:

12 ounces cooked turkey breast

2 green onions

2 ounces prosciutto

For the sauce:

1 clove garlic

1 tablespoon unsalted butter

1 ½ tablespoons flour

1 cup chicken broth

Salt, black pepper to taste

For the pastry:

1/2 cup milk

1/2 cup water

3/4 cup (1 ½ sticks) unsalted butter

1 teaspoon salt

3 ⅓ cups flour

2 egg yolks

1 Make the filling: Cut the turkey into approximately 1/2 inch cubes. Wash and trim the green onions and cut them into rings. Coarsely chop the prosciutto.

2 Make the sauce: Peel and chop the garlic and sauté it in the butter briefly. Add the flour and brown it slightly, stirring. Stir in the broth and bring it to a boil. Season the mixture with plenty of salt and pepper, simmer for 10 minutes, and cool slightly. Add the sauce to a bowl, let it cool slightly, then mix in the turkey, green onions, and prosciutto.

3 Make the pastry: Bring the milk, water, and butter to a boil along with the salt. Place the flour in a food processor (metal blade). Pour the hot liquid into the machine and process briefly, until a smooth dough forms. Let the dough cool to lukewarm.

4 Coat 12 muffin cups with butter. On a floured work surface, roll out two-thirds of the dough until very thin—about 1/8 to 1/4 inch thick. You'll need a circular template about 4 1/2 inches in diameter to cut 12 circles into the rolled-out dough. You can find cutters for this purpose in kitchenware stores, but you can also use a drinking glass or jar with the same diameter. Line each buttered muffin cup with a circle of pastry—the edges should overlap the outlines of the pan.

5 Preheat the oven to 325°F. Fill the mini pies three-quarters full with the filling and sauce mixture, and fold the edge of the dough down over the filling. In a small bowl or cup, whisk the egg yolks slightly and brush the dough edges with it. Flour the work surface again and roll out the remaining dough thinly. Using a 3-inch cutter, glass or jar, cut 12 circles out of the dough. Place the dough circles over each portion of filling and press them down slightly to stick the dough edges together. (Optional: With the remaining dough you can cut out decorative strips of dough to adorn the pies. Stick them on with the egg yolk.)

6 Brush the top crusts with the egg yolk. Slip the pies into the oven and in 50 to 60 minutes they'll be nice and crispy. Let the baked pies stand for 10 minutes in the switched-off oven, remove them from the muffin tin using a large spoon, and eat them warm.

Time needed: 2 ¼ hours, 1 ¼ hours active

Flaky Cream Cheese Crescents
For couch potatoes

Makes 18 crescents:

For the pastry:

1 package (17.3 ounces) frozen puff pastry

2 egg yolks

2 tablespoons olive oil

2 teaspoons dried Italian herbs

For the filling:

6 ounces thinly sliced salami

6 ounces thinly sliced Gouda cheese

2 teaspoons poppy seeds

2 teaspoons sesame seeds

1 tablespoon grated Parmesan cheese

1 Take the puff pastry out of the package, spread out the sheets, cover them with a towel, and let them thaw for 15 to 30 minutes.

2 On a floured work surface, roll out one square of the puff pastry to make a 15- by 15-inch square. Cut the pastry into nine 5 inch squares.

3 Preheat the oven to 400°F. Line a baking sheet with parchment paper. Whisk the egg yolks with the oil, brush it on the squares of pastry, and sprinkle them with 1/2 teaspoon of the Italian herbs.

4 For the filling: Divide 1/2 each of the salami and cheese among the squares of pastry, leaving a small border on each side. Sprinkle with another 1/2 teaspoon of the herbs. Roll up the pastry from corner to corner. Bend the rolls slightly to resemble crescents and place them on the baking sheet.

5 Repeat rolling, filling, and shaping (steps 2, 3, and 4) with the remaining puff pastry sheet, salami, cheese, and herbs.

6 Mix the poppy seeds, sesame seeds, and Parmesan cheese into the remaining egg yolk-oil mixture and spread the mixture on the crescents. Bake the crescents for 20 to 25 minutes, until they're golden brown.

Time needed: 55 minutes, including 35 active

Russian Turnovers
These freeze beautifully

Makes 20 turnovers:

1/4 cup (1/2 stick) unsalted butter

1 ²/₃ cups flour

Generous pinch of salt

2 teaspoons rapid-rise yeast

Scant 1/2 cup warm water (about 120°F)

8 ounces green cabbage

8 ounces fresh salmon fillet

1/2 bunch fresh dill

2 teaspoons caraway seeds

1/4 cup crème fraîche or sour cream

1 egg

Salt, black pepper to taste

1 tablespoon unsalted butter

1 Melt the 1/4 cup butter and let it cool slightly. Put the flour and salt in a food processor (metal blade or dough blade) and pulse to combine the ingredients. Add the yeast and pulse until blended. Pour in the water and butter and process until the mixture comes together in a ball. Set the timer for 45 minutes and let the machine run to knead the dough. Transfer the dough to an oiled bowl, cover it with a dishtowel, and let it rise in a warm, draft-free place until it has doubled in size—this should take 1 to 1 ½ hours.

2 Peel the cabbage leaves from the head and wash them. Cut out any thick ribs from the cabbage. Boil the cabbage in salted water for about 5 minutes, then plunge it into cold water. Gently press the water out of the cabbage and finely chop it. Also finely chop the salmon. Wash the dill and mince it. Mix the cabbage, salmon, and dill with the caraway, crème fraîche, and egg, and season with salt, and pepper.

3 Punch down the dough and roll it out on a lightly floured work surface until it is about _ inch thick. Use a large glass to cut out circles measuring about 4 inches in diameter. Divide the filling among the circles, putting it on one-half of the circle. Fold the pasty over the filling to make half-moons, and press the pastry edges together. Line a baking sheet with parchment paper and put the turnovers on it.

4 Preheat the oven to 350°F. Melt the 1 tablespoon butter, brush it on the turnovers, and bake them on the middle oven rack for about 25 minutes, until they are golden brown. These are best when eaten lukewarm.

135

Time needed: 1 ¾ hours, including 1 hour doing something

Focaccia with Rosemary
Our favorite Italian snack

Makes 4 to 6 snack-sized servings:

3 ⅓ cups flour

1 heaping teaspoon salt

2 teaspoons rapid-rise yeast

1/2 cup (8 tablespoons) olive oil

1 cup warm water (about 120°F)

4-5 sprigs fresh rosemary

2-3 cloves garlic

Kosher salt

1 In a food processor (metal blade or dough blade), combine the flour and salt, and pulse to combine the ingredients. Add the yeast and pulse to combine. Mix together 6 tablespoons of the oil and the water. Add the mixture to the food processor and pulse 10 to 20 times, until the dough comes together in a ball. Turn on the food processor and knead the dough for about 45 seconds. Transfer the dough to an oiled bowl. Cover the bowl with a dishtowel and let the dough rise for about 1 to 1 ½ hours in a warm place with no drafts—the dough should about double in size during that time.

2 Set aside 2 sprigs of the rosemary. Wash and dry the rest of it, remove the leaves, and chop them. Remove the skin from the garlic, cut the garlic cloves in half, and cut them into fine slices.

3 Knead the chopped rosemary and garlic into the dough. Brush a baking sheet with oil. Shape the dough into a ball, put it on a lightly floured work surface, and press it until it is somewhat flat. Use a rolling pin to roll it out in all directions, keeping it as round as possible, until it is about 1/4 inch thick. Don't worry if it's not perfect!

4 Put the focaccia on the baking sheet and prick several holes in it with a fork. Cut the remaining rosemary into small pieces and sprinkle it on the dough. Cover the dough again and let it rise for about another 20 to 30 minutes.

5 Preheat the oven to 450°F. Sprinkle the focaccia with kosher salt and drizzle it with the remaining 2 tablespoons of the olive oil. Bake the focaccia on the middle oven rack for about 20 minutes until it has browned nicely. Cool it, break it into pieces, and put them in a basket.

Time needed: 2 hours, but only 20 minutes is active

Chapatis
Indian skillet bread

Makes 8 chapatis:

1/2 cup flour

1 ¼ cups whole-wheat flour

1 teaspoon salt

1 tablespoon unsalted butter, softened

1/2 cup lukewarm water, plus more

as needed

1 Put the two flours and salt in a food processor (metal blade or dough blade) and pulse the machine to blend them. Add the butter in small pieces and process until mixed. While the machine is running, add 1/2 cup water and process until the dough forms a ball. Then, while the machine is still running, gradually drizzle in enough water to make the dough nice and smooth and supple. Process the dough for 60 seconds.

2 Remove the dough from the machine, shape it into a ball, put it in a lightly oiled bowl, and cover it with a damp dishtowel. Let the dough stand for approximately 30 minutes. In the meantime, get the heaviest skillet that you can find out of the cupboard.

3 Divide the dough into 8 equal pieces and shape each one into a ball. Sprinkle flour on the countertop and separately roll out each ball until it is round and thin and as large as the skillet.

4 Put the skillet over medium heat and get it really hot—this will take about 5 minutes. Add one chapati to the skillet, fry it for 2 minutes, turn, and fry for another 2 minutes. Fry all of the chapatis the same way. To keep them warm and moist, put the chapatis in a pan and cover them with a lid. Serve the chapatis warm.

Time needed: 1 ¼ hours, including 45 minutes doing something

Biscuits
Warm and satisfying

Makes 6 to 8 biscuits:

2 cups flour

1 tablespoon baking powder

Pinch of salt

6 tablespoons (3/4 stick) cold unsalted butter

1/2-1 cup milk

1 Preheat the oven to 450°F. Put the flour, baking powder, and salt in a bowl and mix everything well.

2 Cut the butter into small cubes. Put the butter cubes into the flour mixture and, with a fork or your fingers, blend the mixture until it resembles cornmeal.

3 Slowly add the milk, mixing just until the batter is moistened. What you're looking for is a fairly moist mixture with some texture— the more texture, the more nooks and crannies, the more crispiness and crunchiness you'll have. The batter should be able to be "dropped" from a spoon with a little help from your fingers.

4 Line a baking sheet with parchment paper. Spoon large globs of the batter onto the baking sheet—don't worry if the globs are oddly shaped, just make sure they are approximately the same size. Bake the biscuits for about 15 minutes, until they are golden brown and cooked through.

Tip: Savory Biscuits
You can add things to the biscuit batter to get a different flavor. Fresh herbs, such as Italian parsley or chives, are a super addition—use about 1/4 cup, chopped. Green onions, AKA scallions, are also yummy. Or try toasted sunflower seeds or sesame seeds—use about 2 tablespoons.

Pizza Bread
Really very simple

Makes 4 snack-sized servings:

1 ⅔ cups flour

1 teaspoon salt

1 teaspoon rapid-rise yeast

1/2 cup warm water (about 120°F)

1/4 cup olive oil

2 tomatoes

2 cloves garlic

2-3 sprigs fresh rosemary

Salt to taste

Coarsely ground black pepper to taste

1 In a food processor (metal blade or dough blade), combine the flour and salt and pulse to combine the ingredients. Add the yeast and pulse to combine. Mix together the water and 2 tablespoons of the oil and pour it into the food processor. Pulse the mixture

10 to 20 times until the dough comes together in a ball. Turn on the processor and knead the dough for 45 seconds. Transfer the dough to an oiled bowl, cover it with a dishtowel, and put it in a warm, draft-free place for about 1 to 1 ½ hours. It should rise to twice its size.

2 Preheat the oven to 475°F. Brush a baking sheet with oil. Briefly plunge the tomatoes into boiling water, then remove them from the water and slip off the tomato skins with a paring knife. Cut the tomatoes in half and squeeze out most of the seeds. Cut the tomato flesh into small cubes. Peel and mince the garlic. Remove the leaves from the rosemary and mince them. Mix the tomatoes with the garlic, and rosemary, and season with salt and pepper.

3 Thoroughly knead the dough again and roll it out into a circle about 1/4 inch thick; the edges should be a bit thicker than the center. Put the dough on the baking sheet, spread the tomatoes on it, and drizzle with the remaining 2 tablespoons of olive oil. Bake the pizza bread on the middle rack of a hot oven for approximately 12 minutes. Cut the bread into wedges and enjoy!

Time needed: 1 ½ hours, including only about 20 minutes active

Pretzels
Loopy works of art

Makes 12 pretzels:

$3 \frac{1}{3}$ cups flour

Pinch of sugar

1 teaspoon salt

1 tablespoon rapid-rise yeast

1 quart water

$1 \frac{1}{2}$ tablespoons baking soda

Kosher salt or sesame seeds

1 Put the flour, sugar, and salt in a food processor (metal blade or dough blade) and pulse the machine to blend them. Add the yeast and pulse to combine. Heat 1 cup of the water until it reaches 120°F. Pour it into the machine and process until the dough comes together in a ball.

2 Transfer the dough to an oiled bowl, cover it with a dishtowel, and let it rise in a warm, draft-free place for about 1 to $1 \frac{1}{2}$ hours, until it looks about twice its original size.

3 Divide the dough into 12 equal pieces, and knead each one gently on a lightly floured work surface. With both hands, roll each piece of dough into a worm shape, at least 16 inches long. Now close your eyes: Picture a pretzel in your mind. Take one piece of dough and loop the ends up and around the middle to make a pretzel shape. (Hint: Look at the photograph to the right for guidelines on how to prepare.)

4 Preheat the oven to 425°F. Line a baking sheet with parchment paper.

5 Combine the remaining 3 cups water and the baking soda in a saucepan and heat it over high heat. When it is boiling, reduce the heat to low so that the water is simmering. Put the pretzels one at a time into the baking soda bath for 1 minute—don't use your fingers for this; it's best to use a skimmer. Drain the pretzels, then set them next to each other on the baking sheet. Sprinkle them with salt or sesame seeds.

6 Bake the pretzels on the middle oven rack for 20 to 25 minutes. Note: They taste their very best when fresh!

Time needed: almost 2 hours, but only 40 minutes of that is active

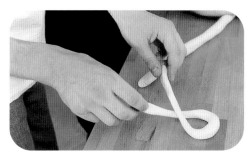

Party Rolls

Make this recipe by hand—the work will be satisfying, and there's too much dough for the food processor.

Makes 20 rolls:

6 ¾ cups flour (try mixing half regular flour with the whole-grain flour of your choice)

Scant 1 tablespoon salt

2 tablespoons rapid-rise yeast

Pinch of honey

1 ½ cups warm water (about 120°F)

1 cup plain yogurt (room temperature if possible)

10 oil-packed sun-dried tomatoes

1 tablespoon capers (drained)

1 tablespoon pine nuts

2-3 sprigs fresh rosemary

2 cloves garlic

2 ounces Parmesan cheese

1 Pour the flour into a large bowl. Add the salt and mix everything with a wooden spoon. Add the yeast, mix it in, then make a well in the center of the bowl. Mix the honey with the water and pour it and the yogurt into the well. Mix everything together with a wooden spoon until you can no longer mix it comfortably. Then, stick your hands in the dough and push and squeeze it until the dough is smooth. Continue to push and squeeze the dough with your hands for about 10 minutes. You may want to pour the dough out onto a floured work surface so you can put your weight into it.

2 Return the dough to the bowl. Cover the bowl with a dishtowel and put it in a warm, draft-free place. Let the dough rise for 1 to 1 1/2 hours, until it has approximately doubled in size.

3 At any point during the rising time, you can keep yourself busy for about 15 minutes assembling the garnishes. Drain the tomatoes, cut them into small pieces, and mix them with the capers and pine nuts. Wash the rosemary and pat it dry. Pull off the rosemary leaves and finely chop them. Peel the garlic and chop it. Grate the cheese. Mix together the rosemary, garlic, and cheese. Line the baking sheet with parchment paper.

4 Cut the dough in half. Place one dough half on a work surface and knead in the tomato-caper mixture. Knead the rosemary-cheese mixture into the other dough half. From each type of dough, form 10 balls of approximately the same size. Assemble the dough balls in any order into a circular arrangement on the baking sheet, letting the sides touch lightly. Cover the rolls with a dishtowel and let them stand for about 20 to 30 minutes.

5 Preheat the oven to 400°F. Brush the rolls with water and bake them on the middle rack of the oven for 25 to 30 minutes, until they have risen nicely and browned. Cool them before eating.

Time needed: 1 ½ hours, including 35 minutes doing something

Olive Rolls
Super with antipasto

Makes 6 large rolls:

4 ½ cups flour

2 teaspoons salt

3 teaspoons rapid-rise yeast

1 cup milk

1 cup water

2 tablespoons olive oil

4 ounces kalamata olives, pitted

1 In a food processor (metal blade or dough blade), mix the flour with the salt and pulse to combine. Add the yeast and pulse again to mix well. Heat the milk and water in a saucepan until they reach 120°F (check it with a thermometer). Add the olive oil. Carefully add the liquid mixture to the machine while pulsing until the dough comes together in a ball—it should take about 25 to 35 pulses. You may not need to add all of the liquid. Turn on the processor and knead the dough for 45 seconds. Transfer the dough to a large oiled bowl. Cover the dough with a clean dishtowel and let it rise in a warm, draft-free place for approximately 1 to 1 1/2 hours. By that time it should have approximately doubled in size.

2 Cut the olives in half, or chop them coarsely, depending on your preference.

3 Transfer the dough to a floured work surface. With floured hands, knead the olives into the dough. Divide the dough into 6 equal pieces and shape each piece into a ball. Line a baking sheet with parchment paper, place the rolls on it, and let them rise for another 15 to 30 minutes.

4 Preheat the oven to 425°F. Dust the rolls with flour and bake them on the middle oven rack for approximately 20 minutes. When done, the rolls will be golden brown and sound hollow when you knock on them.

Time needed: 2 hours, including 30 minutes doing something

Bagels
You won't be able to wait for breakfast

Makes 10 bagels:

4 ⅔ cups flour

2 teaspoons sugar

1 teaspoon salt

1 teaspoon coarsely ground black pepper

1 tablespoons rapid-rise yeast

1 ⅔ cups water

1 tablespoon unsalted butter, softened

2 tablespoons unsalted butter, melted

For boiling:

1 quart water

1/2 cup sugar

1 teaspoon baking soda

For garnishing:

1 egg white

1 teaspoon water

2 tablespoons poppy seeds or sesame seeds

1 In a large bowl, mix the flour, sugar, salt, and pepper with a wooden spoon. Add the yeast and mix it in. Make a well in the center of the bowl. Heat the water to about 120°F (check it on a thermometer), then pour it into the well along with the softened butter. Stir the ingredients together until you can no longer work the dough, then knead it with your hands until it is smooth and elastic (about 5 to 10 minutes).

2 Divide the dough into 10 equal-sized balls. Brush a baking sheet or a large plate with melted butter. Place the balls of dough on it, brush them with the melted butter, and loosely cover them with a dishtowel. Let them stand for about 30 to 45 minutes; by that time they should have approximately doubled in size.

3 Use your finger to poke a hole in the middle of each ball of dough. Shape them into rings of dough. Prepare the boiling liquid: Pour the quart of water into a saucepan and stir in the sugar and baking soda. Bring the liquid to a boil, then reduce the heat so that the liquid just simmers.

4 Preheat the oven to 425°F. Put 2 ovenproof dishes filled with water on the bottom of the oven (or on the lowest oven rack if your oven has coils on the bottom). Line a baking sheet with parchment paper.

5 In batches, lower the bagels into the hot water. Leave them in for 1 minute, then remove them with a skimmer and put them on the baking sheet. Once all of the bagels are on the baking sheet, mix the egg white with the water, brush it on the bagels, and sprinkle them with the poppy or sesame seeds.

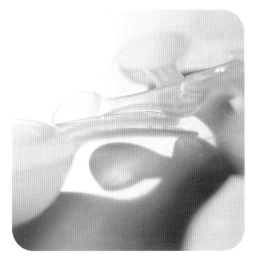

6 Bake the bagels on the middle oven rack for approximately 15 minutes, until they are nice and crisp. Cool slightly before eating.

Time needed: 1 ¼ hours, including 35 minutes active

Old Fashioned Buttermilk Cornbread
Goodness, southern style

Makes 8 servings:

1 ½ cups yellow cornmeal

1 teaspoon salt

1/2 teaspoon baking soda

1/2 teaspoon baking powder

2 eggs

1 ½ cups buttermilk

4 tablespoons bacon grease, melted but not very hot, or melted butter

1 Grease an 8- or 10-inch skillet, preferably cast iron pan. Preheat the oven to 400°F.

2 In a medium bowl, mix the cornmeal, salt, baking soda and baking powder with a wooden spoon. In another bowl, slightly beat the eggs and add them to the cornmeal

mixture along with the buttermilk. Stir until the batter is well blended. Stir in the bacon grease or butter, mix everything well, and pour the batter into the pan.

3 Place the skillet on the stovetop over medium heat for 2 minutes, then transfer it to the oven. Bake for 20 to 25 minutes—the toothpick test works here (see page 38). Cool slightly before cutting.

Herb-Walnut Muffins
We guarantee you can't buy these

Makes 12 muffins:

4 ounces Romano or Parmesan cheese

1/2 bunch mixed fresh herbs (Try: Italian parsley, dill, and chives)

1 ⅔ cups flour

3 teaspoons baking powder

1/4 teaspoon salt

1 egg

1 ¼ cups buttermilk

2 tablespoons vegetable oil

1/2 cup walnut pieces

1 Finely grate the cheese. Wash and dry the herbs. Pull the herbs off their stems and finely chop the leaves.

2 Preheat the oven to 400°F. Grease 12 muffin cups or line them with paper liners.

3 In a medium bowl, mix the flour with the baking powder, salt, cheese, and herbs. In another bowl, blend the egg with the buttermilk. Stir the egg mixture into the flour mixture with a wooden spoon just until moistened. Stir in the oil and walnuts.

4 Spoon the batter into the muffin cups until they are about 2/3 full. Bake the muffins on the middle oven rack for about 20 minutes, until they have all risen and browned. Cool them, take them out of the pan, and eat!

Time needed: 40 minutes, including 20 minutes just watching

Potato Bread
Goodbye, bakery

Makes 1 large loaf (approximately 30 slices of bread):

1 pound potatoes

Scant 1 tablespoon salt

4 cups flour

1 tablespoon rapid-rise yeast

3-4 tablespoons olive oil

1 Peel, wash, and cube the potatoes. Put them in a pot, cover them with water, and sprinkle in half of the salt. Bring the water to a boil, reduce the heat to low, and simmer the potatoes for about 10 minutes, until they are soft.

2 Use a skimmer to fish out the potatoes, and cool them. Don't throw out the potato water; you'll need it later.

3 Once the potatoes are cold, add them to a food processor (metal blade) and pulse briefly just to mash them. Add the flour and remaining salt, and pulse to blend the ingredients. Add the yeast, and pulse to combine.

4 Measure out 1 ½ cups of the potato water (if you don't have enough, fill up the measuring cup with regular warm water). Add the oil to the potato water. Carefully add the liquid mixture to the machine while pulsing until the dough comes together in a ball—it should take about 25 to 35 pulses. You may not need to add all of the liquid. Turn on the processor and knead the dough for 45 seconds. Transfer the dough to a large oiled bowl and let the dough rise in a warm, draft-free place for about 1 to 1 ½ hours—the dough should double in size.

5 Line a baking sheet with parchment paper. Shape the dough into a large, long loaf, put it on the baking sheet, and let it rise for 15 to 30 more minutes.

6 Preheat the oven to 400°F. With a small, sharp knife, score the loaf lengthwise in a couple of places and dust it with flour. Place a couple of baking pans full of water on the bottom of the oven, or on the lowest possible oven rack if your oven's coils are at the bottom. Bake the bread on the middle oven rack for approximately 45 minutes, until it is nice and brown. Pull out the loaf, grab it with a dishtowel, turn it over, and knock on it. If it sounds hollow, it's done. Let it cool before eating.

Time needed: 2 ½ hours, including 30 minutes active

Baguettes
Truly French

Makes 2 baguettes (about 15 slices each):

1/3 cup whole-wheat flour

1/4 cup water

4 cups flour

Scant 1 tablespoon salt

1 tablespoon rapid-rise yeast

2 teaspoons honey

1 ¼ cups warm water (120°F)

1 In a bowl, stir the whole-wheat flour into the water, cover it with plastic wrap, and let it stand for 24 hours at room temperature.

2 The next day, mix the whole wheat mixture with the remaining 4 cups flour and salt in a bowl. Add the yeast and stir it in. Make a well in the center of the flour mixture and pour the honey and water into it. First with a wooden spoon and then with your hands, thoroughly mix everything together. Dump the dough onto a work surface and knead it vigorously—pressing and pushing and pulling it around—for about 10 minutes; it will become more smooth and elastic as you go.

3 Return the dough to a bowl and let it stand in a warm, draft-free place for about 1 to 1 ½ hours, until it has doubled in size. Cut

the dough in half and let it stand for about 15 to 20 more minutes.

4 Roll each piece of dough on a lightly floured work surface into a long cylinder—but be careful not to make them longer than a baking sheet. Make the ends slightly pointy to resemble a baguette you would find at the bakery.

5 Line the baking sheet with parchment paper. Place the baguettes on it and let them rise for about 1 to 1 ½ more hours.

6 Preheat the oven to 425°F. With a small sharp knife, diagonally score the baguettes approximately every 2 inches.

7 Place a couple of baking pans on the bottom of the oven (or the lowest baking rack if your oven's coils are at the bottom) and fill them with an inch or so of water. Slide the baking sheet onto the middle oven rack, immediately close the oven, and bake the baguette in the hot steam for approximately 30 minutes, until it is golden brown. Cool the baguettes slightly before eating. If you believe the French way of thinking, you should never let baguettes get more than a half-day old before eating. But we know even better: After a half-day, heat baguettes briefly at 350°F to revive them. Or, freeze them immediately after cooling; thaw it and reheat at 350° for "fresh" bread anytime.

Time needed: 2 ½ hours,ß (not including 24 hours standing time) only 20 minutes active

Sunflower Bread
Rise and shine

Makes one large loaf (approximately 40 slices of bread):

3/4 cup sunflower kernels

For the starter:

2 cups flour

1 teaspoon honey

1/2 teaspoon rapid-rise yeast

1 ½ cups water

For the dough:

3 ⅓ cups whole-wheat flour

3 ⅓ cups flour

1 teaspoon ground caraway seeds

2 teaspoons ground coriander

1 tablespoon salt

1 tablespoon rapid-rise yeast

2 ½ cups water

1 Put the sunflower kernels in a nonmetallic bowl and cover them with water. Cover the bowl with plastic wrap and let stand at room temperature overnight. With a wooden spoon, vigorously mix the starter ingredients together. Lay one piece of plastic wrap

directly on the surface of the starter. Let the starter stand at warm room temperature for 8 to 12 hours.

2 The next day, make the dough: Mix both types of flour with the caraway, coriander, and salt in a large bowl. Add the yeast, and mix thoroughly. Make a well in the center of the bowl. Heat the water to 120°F, then pour it into the well, and start mixing everything with a wooden spoon. When the dough is starting to come together, add the starter, and mix until the wooden spoon is no longer working.

3 Drain the sunflower kernels and pour them into the bowl. Knead everything with your hands until the whole thing is smooth and stretchy, about 5 to 10 minutes. The dough will be soft.

4 Cover the bowl with a dishtowel and let the dough rise for 1 to 2 hours until it has just about doubled in size. Line a baking sheet with parchment paper.

5 Again briefly knead the dough, shape it into a loaf, and place it on the baking sheet. Let the dough rise for another 30 minutes. Preheat the oven to 400°F. Fill 2 to 3 baking dishes with cold water and place them on the bottom of the oven (or on the lowest oven rack, if the oven's coils are at the bottom).

6 Bake the bread on the middle rack of the oven for approximately 55 minutes. Grab the bread with a dishtowel that has been folded two or three times and use it to turn the loaf over. Knock on it with your knuckles. Bread that is completely done will sound hollow. When it's done, put the loaf on a cooling rack and let it cool.

Time needed: 2-3 hours (not including the overnight standing time), of which about 20 minutes is active

Mouthwa

Meals

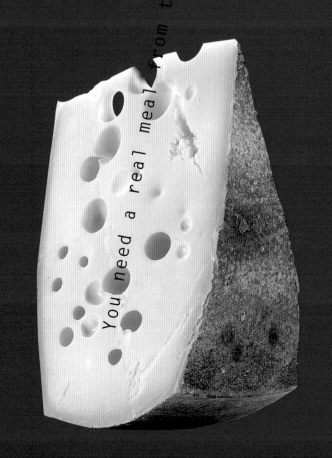

You need a real meal from time to time

tering

Tired of living the sweet life? Need something more satisfying than a snack? You must be the hungry one in the group, the person whose metabolism is always on high gear. On the following pages, you'll find recipes for things more substantial, featuring meats, poultry, vegetables, and cheese. Things that can star at the center of the plate—whether it's at dinner, lunch, or even breakfast and brunch. Think pizzas, savory tarts, and baked French toast. Just add a salad and you've got dinner. After all—you need a real meal from time to time.

Leftover Eggs

Throughout the book, we call for the white of the egg on its own 32 times. That means 32 egg yolks will be left over if you make those recipes. However, since these recipes use the egg yolk 62 times, the yolks will quickly be used up. But then you'd have to bake all of the recipes at once. And you'd still have to separate 30 extra eggs for their yolks, and then there'll be 30 egg whites left over. Too complicated? Here are some alternatives for when you don't want to throw away your extra egg parts:

To use extra egg yolks:
• Beat them slightly and brush them onto pastries before baking. This will lend a nice sheen and encourage things to turn golden brown.
• Make quick French toast: Beat 1 part egg yolk and 1 part milk, dip toast into it, fry it, and eat it with cinnamon sugar, and applesauce.
• Scramble egg yolks with a bit of milk and eat on bread, or cut them into pieces for salad

• Stir egg yolk into cold mashed potatoes, form them into patties, and fry them until they are crisp

To use extra egg whites:
• Make meringue cookies: Beat egg whites until they form very stiff peaks, adding 1/8 teaspoon cream of tartar per egg white and 1/4 cup powdered sugar per egg white. Drop rounded tablespoonfuls of the meringue onto a parchment-lined baking sheet. Before you go to bed, stick the meringue cookies in the oven, which is set to the lowest possible heat setting. In the morning, you'll have beautiful, crisp cookies. You can dip the finished meringues into melted chocolate, and let it dry. You can also mix mini chocolate chips into the batter before baking.
• Use egg white instead of egg yolk to stick puff pastry or pie crust pastry together
• Use egg whites instead of egg yolks for breading fish, or meat
• Make scrambled eggs with extra egg whites

Aunt Betty's Baking Bits

Dear Aunt Betty:
I'm new to baking. I really enjoy most things about it, but I'm really bad with a rolling pin. Do you have any tips for rolling out dough without having a fit?

Frustrated in Fargo

Dear Frustrated:
I feel your pain, dear. More than once I threw in the towel before the dish was completed.

How you handle dough depends on what type it is. Let's start with the most difficult dough, flaky pastry (AKA pie crust). Form the dough into the desired shape immediately after mixing it and press it flat. For example, if the dough is to be rolled out to fit a round pan, it should be formed into a disk. Next, wrap the dough in plastic wrap and put it in the fridge. This chilling will give the moisture in the dough a chance to penetrate the whole thing. It will also give the gluten in the dough a chance to relax again before you work with it, making rolling it easier.

When you get to the rolling part, you can roll out the dough on a lightly floured work surface with a lightly floured rolling pin. This allows you to move the dough around, keeping it even and in the desired shape. Use only enough flour so that it doesn't stick; too much flour will toughen the dough. This is the way to roll out yeast doughs, or relatively lean pastry doughs. For doughs that have a high butter content, a good method is to roll out the dough between two layers of plastic wrap. Use enough plastic wrap so that the dough will still be covered when it's rolled out.

When rolling, start at the middle and roll towards the top of the dough. Then return the rolling pin to the middle and roll once toward the bottom. Repeat with the right and left sides of the dough. Using this method, you'll be more likely to keep the dough at an even thickness. Turn the dough from time to time so that all sides are rolled out evenly; or move to a different spot on your work surface before proceeding.

Five Yummy Ideas for Pizza

Okay, there's frozen pizza, take-out pizza, and pizzas eaten in the pizzeria. If you want one fast, don't even turn on the oven. But if you want to relax and enjoy something special, take a bit of time and make one of these. Use the pizza crust at right.

Bacon & Leek Pizza

Spread the pizza crust with tomato sauce and top it with lightly fried cubes of bacon mixed with sliced leek rings. Mix sour cream and plain yogurt, drizzle it on top, and bake at 450°F for 15 to 20 minutes.

Salmon & Spinach Pizza

Spread the pizza crust with tomato sauce and top with thawed frozen spinach leaves and medium-sized cubes of salmon. Heat 1 to 2 crushed garlic cloves in olive oil until they are aromatic. Discard the garlic cloves and drizzle the oil over the pizza. Bake the pizza at 450°F for 15 to 20 minutes. Drizzle with fresh lemon juice at the table.

Exotic Potato Pizza

Spread the pizza crust with tomato sauce, which has been spiced with curry powder and chopped fresh cilantro. Top with slices of cooked potato, frozen peas, grated mozzarella cheese, and fennel seeds. Drizzle with melted butter and bake at 450°F for 15 to 20 minutes.

Parma Pizza

Spread the pizza crust with tomato sauce, into which you've mixed a little chopped fresh basil. Top it with mushrooms. Spread out some onions that have been slowly softened in butter. Sprinkle the whole thing with grated mozzarella and Parmesan cheeses and a few pine nuts. Bake at 450°F for 15 to 20 minutes. Top the baked pizza with thin slices of prosciutto.

Basic Tip

Pizza Dough

Put 2 cups flour and 1/4 teaspoon salt in a food processor (metal blade) and pulse the machine to blend the ingredients. Add 1½ teaspoons rapid-rise yeast and pulse to blend. Add 1/4 cup olive oil and 1/2 cup very warm water (120°) and process until the dough comes together in a ball. Transfer the dough to a bowl, cover it with a dishtowel, and let it rise in a warm, draft-free place for about 1 to 1½ hours until it has approximately doubled in size. Makes enough for 4 people.

Bacon and Onion Tart
Best eaten with a bunch of friends

Feeds 4 to 5 people:

For the dough:

3 cups flour

Pinch of sugar

1 teaspoon salt

1 tablespoon rapid-rise yeast

1/3 cup sourdough starter (see Tip)

1 cup warm water (120°F)

For the topping:

8 ounces lean smoked bacon

2 onions

2 cups crème fraîche or sour cream

Salt, black pepper to taste

1 Make the dough: Put the flour, sugar, and salt in a food processor (metal blade) and pulse the machine to blend the ingredients. Add the yeast, and pulse to blend. Add the sourdough starter and water and process until the dough comes together in a ball. Transfer the dough to an oiled bowl, cover it with a dishtowel, and let it rise in a warm, draft-free place for about 1 to 1 1/2 hours. By then the dough should have approximately doubled in size.

2 While the dough is rising, make the topping: Cut the bacon into small cubes. Peel the onions, quarter them, and cut them into thin slices.

3 In a large skillet, sauté the bacon over medium heat until the fatty parts are transparent. Add the onions and continue to sauté for another 5 minutes. Remove the skillet from the heat and let the mixture cool slightly.

4 Stir the crème fraîche, or sour cream into the onion mixture and season with salt and pepper (not too much salt, because the bacon is salty already).

5 Preheat the oven to 475°F. Briefly knead the dough with your hands, then cut it in half. Line a baking sheet with parchment paper. Use a floured rolling pin to roll out one dough half right on the baking sheet, until it's thin. Spread half of the bacon mixture on top of the rolled-out dough.

6 Slip the tart into the hot oven on the middle rack and bake for 12 to 15 minutes, until it is crispy. Cut the tart into slices, remove them from the baking sheet, and eat them hot. When the baking sheet cools (or on another baking sheet) you can roll out the second dough half, top it with the bacon mixture, and bake as directed above.

Time needed: 1 ½ hours, but only 1/2 hour active

Variation:

Pissaladière (Savory tart, southern French-style)

Make the dough as described above (step 1). For the topping, peel 10 ounces of onions and 3 cloves of garlic, dice them both, and sauté in 2 tablespoons olive oil over medium heat until soft (this takes about 15 minutes while stirring from time to time). Mix together 3 teaspoons dried herbes de Provence, 1 tablespoon tomato paste, and a little salt and pepper. Spread the mixture on the rolled-out dough, top it with about 10 anchovy fillets and 10 black olives, sprinkle with 4 ounces of grated cheese (Gouda or Emmentaler are good) and bake at 425°F for about 20 minutes.

Improvise your own tart. Consider the following:

- Finely chopped mushrooms
- Chopped fresh herbs
- Small cubes of goat cheese
- A quartet of cheeses: mozzarella, Gruyère, Roquefort, and goat cheese
- Cubes of fresh salmon and chopped fresh dill
- Roasted things: Potatoes, garlic, red peppers

Basic Tip

To make sourdough starter, combine 1½ cups flour, 1 teaspoon yeast, 1 teaspoon honey or sugar, and 1 cup warm water (120°F) in a bowl and stir with a wooden spoon until well blended. Cover the bowl with plastic wrap and let the mixture stand at room temperature overnight. If you don't use it right away, you can refrigerate the starter for a few days before using. After each use, replenish the starter by stirring in 3/4 cup of flour and 1/2 cup of warm water. Cover it, and let it stand at room temperature for a few hours before refrigerating again.

Caraway Tart
Thick, rich and moist

Feeds 8 people:

For the crust:

2 1/3 cups flour

1/2 teaspoon salt

Pinch of sugar

1 tablespoon rapid-rise yeast

About 2/3 cup warm milk (about 120°F)

1/4 cup (1/2 stick) unsalted butter, softened

1 egg (room temperature)

For the topping:

About 2 pounds onions

4 ounces lean smoked bacon

1 tablespoon vegetable oil

1 1/4 cups sour cream

3 eggs

Salt to taste

1 teaspoon caraway seeds

1 Make the dough: Put the flour, salt, and sugar in a food processor (metal blade), and pulse the machine to blend the ingredients. Add the yeast, and pulse to blend. Add the milk, butter, and egg, and process until the dough comes together in a ball. Transfer the dough to an oiled bowl, cover it with a dishtowel, and let it rise in a warm, draft-free place for about 1 to 1 1/2 hours until it has approximately doubled in size.

2 While the dough is rising, make the topping: First go find a ski mask or diving mask. Equipped with this, you can peel and cut tons of onions without later looking like you're having trouble in your love life. Peel the onions and cut them into small cubes. Cut the bacon into small cubes, too.

3 Heat the oil in a large skillet. Sauté the onions and bacon in the oil over medium heat for approximately 10 minutes, stirring from time to time. Now you can take off the diving mask. Slightly cool the onion mixture, mix it with the sour cream and eggs, and season it with salt (just a little—bacon is salty), and the caraway seeds.

4 Preheat the oven to 400°F. Grease a baking sheet. Knead the dough briefly. Using a floured rolling pin, roll out the dough on the baking sheet until it is uniformly thin. Pull up a small crust on the sides. Pour the onion-bacon mixture on the dough and spread it out to the edges.

5 Bake the tart on the middle rack of the oven for approximately 35 minutes, until the crust is golden brown. Eat it slightly cooled.

Time needed: 1 3/4 hours, including approximately 40 minutes with something to do

Savory Potato-Leek Tart
Adapted from a German star-chef's recipe

Feeds 8 to 10 people:

4 medium leeks

2 tablespoons butter

1/2 cup dry white wine

1 3/4 cups whipping cream

Salt, black pepper to taste

Nutmeg to taste (freshly ground if possible)

1 package (17.3 ounces) frozen puff pastry

1 1/4 pounds Yukon gold potatoes

4 ounces Gruyère cheese

2 egg yolks

Salt

1 tablespoon vegetable oil

1 Trim the leeks—cut off the hairy tops and the dark green parts. Cut the leeks in half lengthwise, wash them (being sure to get the grit out between the layers), and cut the leeks into thin strips.

2 Melt the butter over medium heat in a large skillet. Add the leeks and sauté them for about 10 minutes. Add the wine and bring it to a boil. Add the cream, reduce the heat to low, and simmer for 15 to 20 minutes, until they are nice and soft. Season the mixture with salt, pepper, and nutmeg, and cool.

3 Thaw the puff pastry according to package directions.

4 Preheat the oven to 400°F. Rub a baking sheet with butter. With a lightly floured rolling pin, roll out one square of the pastry so that it is slightly larger than the size of the baking sheet. Carefully transfer the pastry to the baking sheet (it helps if you roll it gently around the rolling pin and then move it to the baking sheet). Drape the edges of the pastry over the edges of the pan.

5 Peel the potatoes, cut them into thin slices, and layer half of them on the pastry. Season the potatoes with salt, pepper, and nutmeg. Spread the leek mixture over the

potatoes, and layer the rest of the potatoes on top. Grate the cheese and sprinkle it on top of the potatoes.

6 Roll out the remaining pastry until it is about the size of the baking sheet. Carefully transfer the pastry to the baking sheet and center it over the filling.

7 Mix the egg yolks with a pinch of salt and the oil. Brush the edges of the top pastry with the egg yolk mixture. Fold the extra bottom pastry up and over the top pastry and press the edges together to make a seal. Brush the top of the pastry with the egg yolk mixture—this will help the pastry turn a nice golden brown color while baking. Bake the tart on the lowest oven rack for about 45 minutes, until it's crisp and golden brown. Wait 10 minutes before eating the tart (if you can!).

Time needed: 1 ¾ hours, including 45 minutes waiting

Börek
An easy Turkish treat

Feeds 6 people:

1 pound baby zucchini

4 cloves garlic

2 fresh red chiles

1/2 bunch each fresh dill, Italian parsley, and mint

1 pound feta cheese

1 ½ cups plain yogurt

3 eggs

1/2 cup pine nuts

Salt, black pepper to taste

10 sheets phyllo pastry

3 tablespoons olive oil

1 egg yolk

1 Wash and trim the zucchini. Cut the zucchini in half lengthwise, then cut each half crosswise into thin slices. Peel the garlic and chop it. Wash the chiles and remove the stems. Cut the chiles in half lengthwise, then cut out the seeds and ribs. Cut the chiles into thin strips. Careful: Before proceeding, immediately wash your hands well and take care not to rub your eyes for a couple of hours.

2 Wash the herbs, shake them dry, and finely chop leaves. Coarsely crumble the feta cheese. To a food processor (metal blade), add the feta, yogurt, and eggs, and process until blended. If you don't have a food processor, you can mix the ingredients with a fork. Set aside 1 tablespoon of the pine nuts; stir the rest of them along with the zucchini, garlic, chiles, and herbs into the cheese mixture. Season with salt and pepper.

3 Preheat the oven to 400°F. Lightly grease a large baking dish.

4 Place the phyllo sheets, unfolded, on a work surface and cover them with plastic wrap. Carefully transfer two sheets of the phyllo to the baking dish, covering the remaining phyllo with the plastic wrap to keep it from drying out while you're working. Brush the pastry with olive oil. Spread about 1/4 of the cheese mixture onto it. Again: Carefully transfer two sheets of the phyllo to the baking dish, lining it up with the edges of the pastry below, and covering the remaining phyllo with the plastic wrap. Brush the pastry with olive oil. Spread on another layer of the cheese mixture. Repeat the layering, brushing, and spreading processes until all the ingredients have been used, ending with a layer of phyllo. Mix the egg yolk with the remaining oil, brush it onto the top of the pastry, and sprinkle with the remaining 1 tablespoon of pine nuts.

5 Bake the Börek on the middle rack of the oven for 25 to 30 minutes, until it has browned. Wait 10 minutes before cutting.

Time needed: 25 minutes active, 35 minutes watching

Quiche Pastry
Very versatile

Covers a 10- to 11-inch pan:

1 ⅔ cups flour

Generous pinch of salt

1/2 cup (1 stick) cold unsalted butter

2-4 tablespoons ice water

1 Put the flour and salt in a food processor and pulse to mix the ingredients. Cut the butter into small pieces, add them to the machine, and pulse 25 to 40 times until the mixture is the texture of cornmeal. Add a little cold water and turn the machine on and off several times, until it almost comes together in a ball, adding more water if necessary. Remove the pastry from the machine and press it into a disk. Chill the pastry for about 30 minutes.

2 With a rolling pin, roll the pastry between 2 layers of plastic wrap into a circle that's 1 inch bigger than the diameter of the pan. Carefully transfer the pastry to the pan. Trim the edges with a small knife and patch up any holes in the pastry with the trimmings. Chill the pastry until you're ready to fill it, about 1 hour.

Time needed: 1 ¾ hours, but really only 15 minutes doing something

Mushroom Quiche
Best eaten lukewarm

Feeds 4 to 6 people:

1 medium leek

8 ounces white mushrooms

1 tablespoon butter

1/4 bunch fresh Italian parsley

4 ounces Gruyère or Emmentaller cheese

1 cup sour cream

2 eggs

Salt, black pepper to taste

1 batch Quiche Pastry (recipe at left)

1 Trim and wash the leek (being sure to get the grit out from between the layers), and cut the leek into thin strips. Wipe clean the mushrooms and cut them into thin slices.

2 Preheat the oven to 350°F. In a large skillet, sauté the leek and mushrooms in the butter over high heat for about 5 minutes, then cool the mixture.

3 Wash the parsley, shake it dry, and finely chop it. Grate the cheese. With a whisk, blend the sour cream and eggs, stir in the parsley, cheese, leeks, and mushrooms and season with salt and pepper. Pour the leek mixture into the pastry-lined pan and bake on the middle rack of the oven for about 40 minutes. Cool slightly before eating.
Time needed: 25 minutes for the filling, plus 40 minutes for baking

Red Pepper and Feta Quiche
Spicy and moist

Feeds 4 to 6:

2 medium-sized red bell peppers

1/4 bunch fresh thyme

2 cloves garlic

4 ounces feta cheese

8 ounces cream cheese, softened

3 eggs

Salt to taste

1 batch Quiche Pastry (recipe at left)

Pickled Italian peppers

1 Wash the bell peppers, cut them in half lengthwise, and cut out the seeds and ribs. Cut the peppers into small cubes. Wash the thyme, shake it dry, and remove the leaves from the stems. Peel the garlic and finely chop it.

2 Preheat the oven to 350°F. Crumble the feta cheese. In a bowl, mix the feta, cream cheese, and eggs until well blended and season to taste with a bit of salt.

3 Stir the red pepper cubes, thyme, and garlic into the cheese mixture, pour it into the pastry-lined pan, and top with the drained Italian peppers (if using). Bake the quiche on the middle oven rack for approximately 45 to 50 minutes. Let the quiche cool at least slightly before eating.

Time needed: 30 minutes for the filling, plus 45 minutes for baking

Ham and Cheddar Quiche
Doesn't cost much

Feeds 4 people:

6 ounces ham

1/4 bunch fresh Italian parsley

1 bunch green onions

4 ounces sharp cheddar cheese

1 ¾ cups whipping cream

4 eggs

Salt, black pepper to taste

1 batch Quiche Pastry (recipe at left)

1 Cut the ham into small cubes. Wash the parsley, shake it dry, and finely chop the leaves. Trim and wash the green onions, and cut them into rings.

2 Preheat the oven to 350°F. Grate the cheese. Mix the cheese with the cream, and eggs. Season with salt and pepper.

3 In a bowl, mix the ham with the herbs and green onions, season lightly with salt and pepper, and pour the mixture into the pastry-lined pan. Pour the egg-cream mixture over it and distribute evenly. Bake the quiche on the middle oven rack for approximately 40 minutes. Cool slightly before eating.

Time needed: 30 minutes for the filling, plus 40 minutes for baking

Asparagus Quiche
Deliciously vegetarian

Feeds 4 people:

1 pound asparagus

Salt

3 medium-sized ripe tomatoes

1/2 bunch fresh basil

6 ounces mozzarella cheese

2 ounces Parmesan cheese

8 ounces crème fraîche or sour cream

3 eggs

Black pepper to taste

1 batch Quiche Pastry (recipe at left)

1 Wash the asparagus and cut off the woody ends. Cut the asparagus into pieces about 1 inch long. In a saucepan, bring about 2 cups of salted water to a boil. Add the asparagus and partially cook it for 3 to 4 minutes. Remove the asparagus with tongs, put it into a strainer, and rinse it with cold water. Plunge the tomatoes into the asparagus water for a few seconds to loosen the skins. Peel and dice the tomatoes. Wash, shake dry, and finely chop the basil.

2 Preheat the oven 350°F. Grate the cheeses. In a bowl, mix the asparagus with the tomatoes, basil, mozzarella, Parmesan, crème fraîche or sour cream, and eggs.

Season the mixture with salt and pepper. Pour the asparagus mixture into the pastry-lined pan, smoothing the top evenly. Bake the quiche on the middle rack of the oven for approximately 45 minutes.

Time needed: 30 minutes for the filling, plus 45 minutes for baking

Radicchio and Chèvre Tart
Fancy, but easy

Feeds 4 to 6 people:

1 small head radicchio

2 ounces Parmesan cheese

1 cup ricotta cheese

6 ounces soft goat cheese

3 eggs

1 sheet (1/2 of a 17.3-ounce package) frozen puff pastry

15 green olives (pitted)

1 Wash the radicchio and cut it into quarters. Remove the core and cut the leaves into strips.

2 Preheat the oven to 425°F. Finely grate the Parmesan cheese. In a bowl, stir the ricotta with the goat cheese until smooth. Stir in the Parmesan, eggs, and radicchio strips. On a lightly floured work surface, slightly roll out the pastry. Press the puff pastry into a 10-inch springform pan—you may have to cut pieces from the edges of the squares and fit them into any gaps. Pour in the cheese mixture and press olives into cheese mixture.

3 Bake the tart on the middle oven rack for 30 to 40 minutes, until the filling has set and the pastry is golden brown.

153

Time needed: 55 minutes, including 20 active

Arugula Pizza
Pizza and salad all in one

Feeds 4 people:

1 recipe Pizza Dough (see Tip on page 147)

1 large can peeled tomatoes (28 ounces)

3 cloves garlic

4 tablespoons olive oil

Salt, black pepper to taste

12 ounces fresh mozzarella cheese

2 bunches fresh arugula

1 tablespoon fresh lemon juice

1 Make the dough and set it aside to rise.

2 Drain the tomatoes. Cut the tomatoes into small pieces using kitchen shears or a knife. Peel and mince the garlic and sauté it in a skillet over medium heat until transparent in 1 tablespoon of the oil. Add the tomatoes to the pan and simmer them for approximately 30 minutes. Season with salt and pepper.

3 Cut the mozzarella into slices. Brush a baking sheet with oil. Preheat the oven to 475°F. Knead the dough again, then roll it out on the baking sheet until it is thin. Make the edges a bit thicker than the center. Spread the tomato mixture on it, arrange the mozzarella over the top, and drizzle 1 tablespoon of the olive oil over it. Bake the pizza on the middle

154

oven rack for 13 to 15 minutes, until the crust is crisp and golden brown.

4 Pick over, wash, and shake dry the arugula. Whisk together the remaining 2 tablespoons of olive oil, the lemon juice, and salt and pepper to taste. Spread the arugula on the pizza and drizzle it with the lemon-oil mixture.

Time needed: 1 ½ hours, including 45 minutes active

Fresh Mushroom Pizza
Vegetarian vittles

Feeds 4 people:

1 recipe Pizza Dough (see Tip on page 147)

1 small can peeled tomatoes (14 ounces)

1 teaspoon dried Italian herbs

Salt, black pepper to taste

8 ounces white mushrooms

2 cloves garlic

1/2 bunch fresh Italian parsley

10 ounces mozzarella cheese

2 ounce-chunk Parmesan cheese

1 tablespoon olive oil

1 Make the dough and set it aside to rise.

2 Shortly before the rising time ends, make the topping: Drain the tomatoes and cut them into small pieces. Season the tomatoes with the herbs, salt, and pepper. Clean the mushrooms and cut them into thin slices. Peel the garlic and wash and shake dry the parsley. Finely chop the garlic and parsley leaves, and mix them both with the mushrooms. Season with salt and pepper.

3 Brush a baking sheet with oil. Preheat the oven to 425°F. Knead the dough again and use a rolling pin to roll it out directly on the baking sheet. Make the edges slightly thicker than the center.

4 Spread the tomato mixture on the dough, then spread out the mushrooms on top. Cut the mozzarella into thin slices and arrange it on top of the mushrooms. Bake the pizza on the middle oven rack for about 20 minutes, until the cheese is melted and the crust is crisp and brown.

5 Use a vegetable peeler to cut strips of Parmesan cheese, put them on the pizza, and drizzle the whole thing with the olive oil.

Time needed: 1 ¼ hours, including 30 minutes active

Potato Pizza
From Southern Italy

Feeds 3 to 4 people:

1 recipe Pizza Dough (see Tip on page 147)

1 ¼ pounds Yukon gold potatoes

2-3 sprigs fresh rosemary

4 ounces fresh mozzarella (comes packed in liquid)

2-3 tablespoons readymade pesto or olive paste

Salt, black pepper to taste

3 tablespoons olive oil

1 Make the dough and set it aside to rise.

2 A few minutes before the rising time ends, make the topping: Peel and wash the potatoes and cut them into very thin slices. Cook them for 4 minutes in boiling water, plunge them into cold water, and drain them well. Wash and shake dry the rosemary. Remove the rosemary leaves from the branches. Drain the mozzarella and cut it into small cubes.

3 Brush a baking sheet with oil. Preheat the oven to 425°F. Knead the dough again and use a rolling pin to roll it out on the baking sheet. Make the edges slightly thicker than the center.

4 Spread the pesto or olive paste on top of the dough. Lay the potatoes on top like shingles on a roof. Sprinkle on the rosemary and the mozzarella. Season with salt and pepper. Drizzle the olive oil over the top. Bake the pizza on the middle oven rack for 20 to 25 minutes, until the potatoes are soft, the cheese is melted, and the crust is crisp.

Time needed: 1 ½ hours, at least half of which is active

Turkish Pizza
Nice and spicy

Feeds 4 people:

1 recipe Pizza Dough (see Tip on page 147)

For the cucumber sauce:

1/2 cucumber

1 teaspoon salt (or more if necessary)

2 cloves garlic

1/4-1/2 bunch fresh dill

1 ¾ cups plain yogurt

1 teaspoon fresh lemon juice

1 tablespoon olive oil

Black pepper to taste

For the topping:

1 bunch green onions

2 cloves garlic

1/2 bunch fresh Italian parsley

1/2 teaspoons ground cumin

Pinch of chili powder

2-3 tablespoons plain yogurt

1 tablespoon tomato paste

1 pound ground beef or turkey

Salt to taste

1 Make the dough and set it aside to rise.

2 Make the sauce: Peel the half cucumber and cut it in half lengthwise. Use a spoon to remove the seeds. Coarsely grate the cucumber, mix it with the salt, and let stand for about 10 minutes. Drain the cucumber in a colander, pressing it with your hands to push out as much of the liquid as possible. Peel the garlic, mince it, and add it to the bowl with the cucumber. Wash and shake dry the dill, remove the leaves from the stems, chop the leaves finely, and add them to the bowl with the cucumber. Stir in the yogurt, lemon juice, and olive oil. Taste the sauce and season if necessary with more salt and pepper. Refrigerate until ready to use.

3 Make the topping: Trim and wash the green onions, and cut them into rings. Peel the garlic and finely chop it. Wash, shake dry, and finely chop the parsley. Mix those three ingredients with the cumin, chili powder, yogurt, and tomato paste. Put the ground meat in a large bowl, add the yogurt mixture and salt, and mix everything well.

4 Brush the baking sheets with oil. Preheat the oven to 475°F. Divide the dough in half. Roll out each dough half on a lightly floured work surface into an oval-shaped flatbread and put each of them on a baking sheet. Spread the ground meat mixture on the dough pieces, dividing it evenly. Bake the pizzas one after the other on the middle oven rack for approximately 12 minutes, until they have browned. Serve the cucumber sauce on top or on the side.

Time needed: about 1 ½ hours

155

Calzones
Pocketsful of pleasure

Feeds 4 people:

For the dough:

2 ²/₃ cups flour

Generous pinch of salt

1 ½ teaspoons rapid-rise yeast

1/4 cup olive oil

1 cup warm water (120°F)

For the filling:

About 1 pound onions

1 tablespoon olive oil

1 jar black olives (6 ounces; buy them pitted if you're lazy)

2 tablespoons capers

6 anchovy fillets (optional)

1 small can peeled tomatoes (14 ounces)

1/2 bunch fresh basil

4 ounces mozzarella cheese (Fresh mozzarella, packed in brine, is delicious, but drain it first)

4 ounces Romano or Parmesan cheese

Salt, black pepper to taste

1 Make the dough: Put the flour and salt in a food processor (metal blade) and pulse the machine to blend the ingredients. Add the yeast and pulse to blend. Add the olive oil and water and process until the dough comes together in a ball. Transfer the dough to a bowl, cover it with a dishtowel, and let it rise in a warm, draft-free place for about 1 to 1 1/2 hours. By then the dough should have approximately doubled in size.

2 While the dough is rising, make the filling: Peel the onions and finely chop them. Heat the oil in a large skillet and pour in the onions. Sauté them lightly over medium heat for 10 minutes, stirring frequently. Cool them in a large bowl.

3 Cut the olives from their pits, and chop the olives. Also chop the capers and drained anchovies (if using). Drain the tomatoes and finely chop them. Wash and dry the basil and cut the leaves into strips. Cut the mozzarella into little cubes. Grate the Romano or Parmesan. Add the olives, capers, anchovies, tomatoes, mozzarella cubes, and grated cheese to the bowl with the onions. Mix everything well and season with salt and pepper.

4 Preheat the oven to 475°F. Brush a baking sheet with oil.

5 Lightly sprinkle a work surface with flour. Divide the dough in half and roll each half out into a thin circle. Move the circles to the baking sheet, spread the filling over half of each dough circle, and fold the other halves over the filling. Carefully press the dough edges together. Brush olive oil on the tops of the calzones. Let the calzones stand for about 10 minutes, then bake them on the middle oven rack for approximately 25 minutes, until they are nice and brown.

Time needed: 1 hour 40 minutes, including 1 1/4 hours with something to do

Tuna Pockets
Taste great hot, room temp, or cold

Feeds 4 people:

For the filling:

1 red and 1 yellow bell pepper

1 tomato

1 bunch fresh arugula

1 red onion

2 cloves garlic

2 cans water-packed tuna (6 ounces each)

1 tablespoon capers

8 ounces fresh mozzarella (the stuff that's packed in brine)

1 egg

Salt, cayenne pepper to taste

For the dough:

6 ounces cream cheese, softened

6 tablespoons vegetable oil

1 egg

1/2 teaspoon salt

2 cups flour

3 teaspoons baking powder

1 Make the filling: Trim and wash the peppers. Cut them in half lengthwise and remove the seeds and ribs. Cut the peppers into small squares. Wash and dice the tomato. Wash, shake dry, and chop the arugula. Peel the onion and the garlic, and finely chop both of them.

2 Drain the tuna and break it into pieces with a fork. Drain and coarsely chop the capers. Drain the mozzarella, then cut it into small cubes. In a bowl, combine the tuna, capers, mozzarella, and egg and mix well. Season generously with salt and cayenne.

3 Now for the dough: Thoroughly mix the cream cheese, oil, egg, and salt using a food processor (metal blade). In a bowl, mix together the flour, and baking powder. Add half of it to the food processor and pulse to combine. Add the rest and process until the dough comes together.

4 Preheat the oven to 350°F. Line two baking sheets with parchment paper.

5 Lightly sprinkle a work surface with flour. Divide the dough into quarters and roll each of them out to a thin rectangle. Place 2 rectangles on each baking sheet. Spread 1/4 of the tuna filling on one half of each rectangle, but not all the way to the edge. Fold the other half of the dough over the filling and press the edges together well. Bake the pockets one sheet at a time on the middle oven rack for approximately 30 minutes, until they are golden brown.

Time needed: 1 ½ hours, including 1 hour active

Another filling:
Prosciutto-Mozzarella
Cut 4 ounces of prosciutto into small cubes and put them in a bowl. Add one 6-ounce can of artichoke hearts, cut into eighths, 6 to 8 oil-packed sun-dried tomatoes, cut into strips, 8 ounces of drained fresh mozzarella, cut into cubes, and 1 egg. Mix everything well and season the mixture to taste with salt, pepper, and dried Italian herbs. Make the dough and fill and bake the turnovers as directed above (steps 3, 4, and 5).

Endive-Roquefort Tartlets
Elegant as an hors d'oeuvre

Feeds 2 as an entrée and 4 as an appetizer:

For the pastry:

1 cup flour

Pinch of salt

6 tablespoons (3/4 stick) cold unsalted butter

2-4 tablespoons ice water

For the filling:

1 head Belgian endive (about 5 ounces)

1/4 bunch fresh Italian parsley

4 ounces Roquefort cheese

1 egg

1 tablespoon crème fraîche or sour cream

Black pepper to taste

1 Make the pastry: Put the flour and salt in a food processor and pulse to mix the ingredients. Cut the butter into small pieces, add them to the machine, and pulse 25 to 40 times until the mixture is the texture of cornmeal. Add a little of the water and turn the machine on and off several times until it almost comes together in a ball, adding more water if necessary. Divide the dough into

quarters, shape each quarter into a ball, and press each one into an ungreased 4-inch tartlet pan. Chill the pastry in the pans for 1 hour.

2 After about 15 minutes, you can make the filling: Wash the endive and cut it into strips about 1/2 inch wide, discarding the core. Bring about 2 inches of water to a boil in a saucepan, throw in the endive, and boil for barely 1 minute. Pour the endive into a strainer, rinse it with cold water, and drain it well.

3 Preheat the oven to 400°F. Wash and shake dry the parsley. Remove the parsley leaves and chop them finely. Crumble the Roquefort with your fingers.

4 In a bowl, mix the endive, parsley, Roquefort, egg, and crème fraîche, and season with pepper. You won't need any salt because there is plenty in the cheese. Pour the mixture into the pastry-lined pans, pop them into the oven, and leave them there for approximately 25 minutes, until the filling is nice and brown. Use a small knife to loosen the tartlets from the sides of the pans, then transfer them to a cooling rack. Serve the tartlets at room temperature.

Time needed: 1 ¾ hours, including approximately 35 minutes active

Waffles—Savory and Sweet
This could turn into a party

Choose one or more: Plain, bacon, blueberry, or chocolate.

For 12 waffles each
Plain Waffles:

2 eggs

1 ⅓ cups flour

3 tablespoons sugar

2 teaspoons ground cinnamon (optional)

Large pinch of salt

1 ½ cups buttermilk or milk

1/2 teaspoon vanilla extract

For serving:

Butter, maple syrup, fresh fruit, and/or

fruit compote

Bacon Waffles:

4 ounces lean smoked bacon

2 eggs

1 ⅓ cups flour

1 teaspoon sugar

1 teaspoon caraway seeds (optional)

1 cup milk or buttermilk

1/2 cup light-colored beer

For serving:

Butter and maple syrup

Blueberry Waffles:

2 eggs

1 ⅓ cups flour

2 tablespoons sugar

Large pinch of salt

1 teaspoon grated lemon zest

1 ½ cups milk or buttermilk

1/2 teaspoon almond extract (optional)

8 ounces fresh or frozen, thawed blueberries

For serving:

Butter, maple syrup, sweetened

whipped cream

Chocolate Waffles:

2 eggs

1 cup flour

1/4 cup sugar

2 teaspoons ground cinnamon (optional)

Large pinch of salt

1 cup milk

1/2 teaspoon vanilla extract

1/3 cup cocoa powder

1/2 cup whipping cream

For serving:

Sliced fresh strawberries and/or

sweetened whipped cream

For the Plain Waffles:

1 Separate the eggs. In a clean, grease-free bowl, beat the egg whites with a mixer or hand whisk until they stand in stiff peaks. In another bowl, mix together the flour, sugar, cinnamon (if using), and salt. In another bowl, lightly beat the egg yolks. Add the milk and vanilla extract and mix well.

2 Pour the egg-milk mixture into the bowl with the flour mixture and stir just until the ingredients are mixed. With a rubber spatula, carefully fold the beaten egg whites into the batter.

3 Follow the manufacturers' instructions for preheating the waffle iron and baking the waffles. Serve the baked waffles with butter and melted syrup, sliced fresh fruit, or fruit compote.

For the Bacon Waffles

1 Fry the bacon in a skillet until it is very crisp. Drain the bacon on paper towels, set it aside to cool, and then crumble it into small pieces.

2 Separate the eggs. In a clean, grease-free bowl, beat the egg whites with a mixer or hand whisk until they stand in stiff peaks. In another bowl, mix together the flour, sugar, and caraway seeds (if using). In another bowl, lightly beat the egg yolks. Add the milk and beer and mix well.

3 Pour the egg-milk-beer mixture into the bowl with the flour mixture and stir just until the ingredients are mixed. With a rubber spatula, carefully fold the beaten egg whites into the batter.

4 Follow the manufacturers' instructions for preheating the waffle iron and baking the waffles. Serve the baked waffles with butter and maple syrup.

For the Blueberry Waffles:

1 Separate the eggs. In a clean, grease-free bowl, beat the egg whites with a mixer or hand whisk until they stand in stiff peaks. In another bowl, mix together the flour, sugar, salt, and lemon zest. In another bowl, lightly beat the egg yolks. Add the milk, and almond extract (if using) and mix well.

2 Pour the egg-milk mixture into the bowl with the flour mixture and stir just until the ingredients are mixed. With a rubber spatula, carefully fold the beaten egg whites into the batter. Carefully stir in the blueberries.

3 Follow the manufacturers' instructions for preheating the waffle iron and baking the waffles. Serve the baked waffles with butter, maple syrup, and/or whipped cream.

For the Chocolate Waffles:

1 Separate the eggs. In a clean, grease-free bowl, beat the egg whites with a mixer or hand whisk until they stand in stiff peaks. In another bowl, mix together the flour, sugar, cinnamon (if using), and salt. In another bowl, lightly beat the egg yolks. Add the milk and vanilla extract and mix well. In a small bowl or cup, stir together the cocoa powder and the cream until the mixture is smooth. Stir the cocoa mixture into the egg-milk mixture until everything is blended.

2 Pour the egg-milk mixture into the bowl with the flour mixture and stir just until the ingredients are mixed. With a rubber spatula, carefully fold the beaten egg whites into the batter.

3 Follow the manufacturers' instructions for preheating the waffle iron and baking the waffles. Serve the baked waffles with strawberries and whipped cream.

Time needed: About 45 minutes

Baked French Toast with Dried Cherries
Don't throw away the leftover bread

Feeds 4 to 8 people:

3 cups milk

Grated zest of 1 lemon

5 eggs

1 teaspoon vanilla extract

1/2 cup sugar

1 package dried cherries (6 ounces)

2 small day-old baguettes

2 tablespoons unsalted butter

Powdered sugar

1 In a bowl, thoroughly mix the milk, lemon zest, eggs, vanilla extract, sugar, and cherries. Set the mixture aside. Cut the bread into thin slices.

2 Preheat the oven to 400°F. Butter a long, shallow baking dish.

3 Layer the bread in the casserole, spooning on the soaked cherries (you can fish them out of the egg-milk mixture with a slotted spoon). Pour the egg-milk mixture over the top and let the bread soak for 10 minutes.

Cut the butter into cubes and distribute it over the top of the bread. Bake the French toast on the middle oven rack for approximately 30 minutes, until it is brown. Let it stand briefly, sprinkle it with powdered sugar, and eat it soon!

Time needed: 1 hour 10 minutes, including 25 minutes doing something

Apple Crumble
Quickly satisfies a sweet tooth

Feeds 4 to 8 people:

For the topping:

1/2 cup (1 stick) cold unsalted butter

1 ¼ cups flour

5 tablespoons sugar

1/2 teaspoon ground cinnamon

For the filling:

2/3 cup raisins

3 medium-sized tart apples

5 tablespoons brown sugar

Juice from 1/2 lemon

1/2 teaspoon ground cinnamon

For serving:

Vanilla ice cream or whipping cream

1 Make the topping: Cut the butter into small cubes. Put the flour, sugar, and cinnamon in a bowl. Add the butter and, with a fork or your hands, work the ingredients until they are well mixed and crumbly. Refrigerate the mixture until you need it.

2 Preheat the oven to 400°F. Rinse the raisins in hot water and drain them well. Peel, quarter, and core the apples. Cut them into thin slices and mix them in a bowl with the sugar, lemon juice, cinnamon, and the raisins.

3 Butter an 8-inch square baking dish and pour in the apple mixture. Spread the topping over the top and press it down a little. Bake the apple crumble on the middle oven rack for 25 to 30 minutes, until the apples are soft. Eat it warm with vanilla ice cream, or unwhipped cream.

Time needed: 50 minutes, including 25 minutes in action

Baked French Toast with Apricot Sauce
A new twist on brunch

Feeds 4 people:

For the apricot sauce:

12 ounces dried apricots (preferably unsulfered)

5 tablespoons sugar

Juice of 1/2 lemon

2 cups water (plus more if needed)

For the French toast:

5 large or 8 small day-old butter croissants

1/2 cup milk

3 tablespoons rum

4 eggs

6 tablespoons (3/4 stick) unsalted butter, softened

3 tablespoons sugar

Grated zest of 1/2 lemon

1 Make the sauce: Combine the apricots, sugar, lemon juice, and water in a saucepan and bring the mixture to a boil. Reduce the heat to low and simmer for about 30 minutes. Carefully transfer the mixture to a food processor and process until smooth.

You may want to thin the sauce with a little water to get the right consistency. Chill until ready to serve.

2 Preheat the oven to 400°F. Make the French toast: Cut the croissants into 1/2inch slices. In a large bowl, mix the milk with the rum and 2 of the eggs. Add the croissants and mix well. In another bowl, blend the butter, sugar, lemon zest, and the remaining 2 eggs. Mix the butter mixture into the croissant mixture.

3 Butter a long, shallow baking dish. Pour the croissant mixture into the dish. Bake the French toast on the middle oven rack for 30 to 40 minutes, until golden brown. Serve the cold sauce with the hot French toast.

Time needed: 55 minutes, including 25 minutes doing something

Jen's Mom's Oven Pancake
Perfect for breakfast in bed

This recipe doesn't double well. Instead, make separate batches and use separate skillets. Remember: Be sure that your skillet can withstand high oven heats. In other words, the skillet you choose should not have a plastic handle! If you don't have a good skillet, use a cake pan or pie pan. Jen grew up eating this with apples sautéed in butter. You can also enjoy it with other fresh fruits, such as strawberries, raspberries, or peaches.

Serves 2 to 4:

2 eggs

1/2 cup milk

1/2 cup flour

1/8 teaspoon ground nutmeg (preferably freshly ground!)

Generous pinch of salt

1/4 cup (1/2 stick) unsalted butter

1/2 lemon

1 tablespoon powdered sugar

For serving:

Fresh fruit

Sour cream (optional)

1 Preheat the oven to 350°F. In a bowl, beat the eggs and milk together with a whisk. Add the flour, nutmeg, and salt, and whisk until the batter is smooth.

2 Melt the butter in an 8-inch ovenproof skillet. When the butter is completely melted and bubbling well, pour the batter into the pan. Return the pan to the oven and set the timer for 20 minutes.

3 The oven pancake will be very puffy when it's ready. Remove the pan from the oven and squeeze the juice of the half-lemon all over the surface of the pancake—it will sizzle and deflate. Sprinkle it with the powdered sugar and return it to the oven for 5 minutes.

4 Remove the pan from the oven and cut the pancake into quarters. Divide the pancakes among warm serving plates and top with the fruit and sour cream (if desired).

The Basics—
Glossary—
Unlike any you've ever seen

Don't see any words like "fondant" or "frangipane" in this book? That's because, like in this book's predecessor, Basic cooking, we wanted our readers to understand everything we talk about. No fancy culinary terms, no intimidating instructions, just good, solid, Basic baking recipes.

We know that many of you out there are terrified at the idea of working with yeast or using anything more complicated than a pastry blender to make your pie crust. The recipes and instructions should be pretty clear throughout the book, but just in case you need a little more to go on, the following information will supplement your Basic knowledge.

Bakery
A place for inspiration and emergencies (see "Leftovers" and "Black").

Black
If you see this color when baking, it can be very bad. If there's only a bit of charred material on the outside of the cake, it can probably be scraped off the top, and the lower part bandaged with powdered sugar or frosting. More blackness will require an operation—scalpel, please. But often the burnt taste is so deep that the only place to go is to the trash can and then to your favorite bakery. Baking things until they turn black can be prevented by putting aluminum foil on top, slipping a baking sheet underneath, setting the timer for a little less than the directed time, and checking the oven heat with an oven thermometer (available in kitchenware stores). It's a good idea to write down whether the oven runs cooler or hotter than the dial indicates, and whether the recipe bakes faster than it says in the book. This way you will have a better chance next time at success.

Burns
Very bad. If you very briefly burn your fingertips, quickly touching your earlobes will cool them. If things stay hot for a bit longer, hold your hand under cold water for a long time. If a burn is terribly painful or if a blister immediately forms, go straight to the doctor. But don't forget the cake in the oven!

Calories
A unit measuring the amount of energy in food. But when it comes to baking, we think, calories don't count. Or else you shouldn't count them.

Filberts
Another word for hazelnuts. When shopping for these, you may find them labeled under either name.

Génoise
You'll see this term in a lot of fancy baking books, but we find it rather pretentious. For Basic purposes, we'll just call it sponge cake, génoise's close cousin.

Leftovers
Leftovers happen. Question: The dinner party's over, but there's still some buttercream torte left. What do you do? Answer: It depends. If a group of 20 people ate only 2 slices, there's only one thing you can do—throw it away and keep practicing (or have your next party in a restaurant!). If just a few pieces are left, store the leftovers. It's a good idea to keep the cake cold, well protected so that nothing tastes like the refrigerator. A cake cover is a good idea. But if you're not a domestic goddess, or didn't register for the crystal cake pedestal with matching dome at your wedding, try an upturned mixing bowl or punchbowl. Doesn't fit? Surround the torte with tall glasses and cover the whole thing with plastic wrap—that way the wrap won't stick to the whipped cream. Or, punctuate the cake on the top and sides with toothpicks before wrapping it well with plastic wrap (this also keeps the wrap from sticking to the topping). And have some more people over for coffee and cake the next day.

Liqueur
It's very chic to pour small glasses of liqueur, or sweet wine to serve with cake. Try sweet Italian wine (Vin Santo or Marsala) with crispy little cookies. Port goes well with anything chocolate. Sip orange liqueur with almond cake, or almond liqueur with orange cake. Use your imagination!

Neatness

It's tough, we know. But baking is even more difficult without it, particularly for beginners. So first clear a bit of workspace and put away the rest of your last meal. Take out whatever you need (mixer, flour, baking book, etc.) and, if possible, measure the ingredients before you start. As you are working, put away what you no longer need and clean up what you'll need again. And always keep your hands clean!

Proofing

Mixing yeast with warm liquid and something sweet in order to activate it before mixing into yeast dough. We get to skip this step in Basic baking by using rapid-rise yeast, which can be mixed right into the dry ingredients.

Short Pastry

Also known as pâte brisée. Or pie dough. For our book, we just say flaky pastry. It's as simple as that.

Temper

What pastry chefs do to chocolate to keep it smooth and glossy. We don't need to worry about it here.

Worry

What a lot of people do when they are faced with the prospect of baking. We hope that, after you read this book, you'll realize that there's no need to stress.

Basic Index A-Z

Credits

The Authors:

Sebastian Dickhaut, author, journalist, and cook, currently lives in Australia, where more oatmeal cookies and chocolate eggs are eaten per capita than anywhere else in the world. Born in Frankfurt, he grew up in Vienna and traveled back and forth to Munich while working on this book. He's still pondering whether Streusel Cake, Sachertorte, or deep-fried Austrian pastries are the best things in the world.

Jennifer Newens, writer and cook, lives in San Francisco where the sourdough bread is the best in the world. There are some pretty good patisseries and chocolatiers, there too. Her favorite desserts are things with apples, caramel, and almond paste.

Cornelia Schinharl, author and journalist, lives in southern Germany, where things are pretty sweet anyway. With a clear preference for the even deeper south, her list of favorites includes anything crispy and fruity along with Lemon Tart and Chocolate Cake.

Photography
Germany:
Food photographs: Barbara Bonisolli
People, action, and still life photographs: Alexander Walter
Recipe stylist: Hans Gerlach
Models: Christian Finger, Markus Röleke, Janna Sälzer, Gabie Schnitzlein

U.S.:
Photographs: Lisa Keenan
Recipe stylist: Shanti Nelson
Models: Patrick Foster, Joy Jones, Anita Luu, Brian Rivera
Props courtesy of: Lois & Curt Nelson, Dan Wooddell Glass

Photo Credits:
StockFood/ Molly Hunter: Egg on cover and throughout
Barbara Bonisolli: all recipe photos except where noted below
Alexander Walter: All people photos except where noted below
Lisa Keenan: 2, 3, 4, 6, 7, page 16-17: extracts, fresh fruit, sprinkles, page 25: measuring spoons, 32, 33, 37, 45, 46, 48, 49, 59, 61, 62, 67, 68, 72, people photo: 84, 87, 89, 97, 100, 106, 113, 128, 131, 137, 141, 157, 163, Jennifer Newens photo: 168

Stock Photos:
S & P Eising: Plum page 54, cheese, page 144
Rosenfeld/Maximilian: Chocolate, page 85
Marimilian Stock: page 30: egg , page 128: tomato, page 129: baguettes
Private: pages 84, 168

German Team:
Editor: Sabine Sälzer
Editorial department: Katharina Lisson, Cornelia Schinharl
Design and layout: Sybille Engels and Thomas Jankocvic
Production: Susanne Mühldorfer
Set: Filmset Schröter
Repro: Fotolito Longo
Printing and binding: Druckhaus Kaufmann

Thank you to Christa Schmedes, Sigrid Burghard and Annika Möller, Erdmute and Klaus for the apartment, Nicola Härms

U.S. Team:

Project editor: Lisa M. Tooker
Art director: Shanti Nelson
Translator: Kate Walker
Additional recipes: Janis Judd, CCP, Lemon Bars, page 46, Banana Bread, page 48, Streusel Coffee Cake, page 49, Strawberry Tart, page 67, Cornbread, page 141Oven Pancake, page 161

A special thank you to Carrie Donner, Melissa Gauthier, Larry Kennan, Judie Nelson—and to Lois and Curt Nelson for sharing their beautiful kitchen

Published originally under the title
BASIC BAKING:
Alles, was man braucht, um schnell gut zu kochen

© 2000 Gräfe und Unzer Verlag GmbH, Munich

English translation copyright:
© 2001, Silverback Books, Inc.

ISBN: 1-930603-01-0

Printed in Hong Kong through Global Interprint, Santa Rosa, California.